Not by Faith Alone

Not by Faith Alone

Social Services, Social Justice, and Faith-Based Organizations in the United States

Edited by Julie Adkins, Laurie Occhipinti,
and Tara Hefferan

LEXINGTON BOOKS
A division of
ROWMAN & LITTLEFIELD PUBLISHERS, INC.
Lanham • Boulder • New York • Toronto • Plymouth, UK

Published by Lexington Books
A division of Rowman & Littlefield Publishers, Inc.
A wholly owned subsidiary of The Rowman & Littlefield Publishing Group, Inc.
4501 Forbes Boulevard, Suite 200, Lanham, Maryland 20706
http://www.lexingtonbooks.com

Estover Road, Plymouth PL6 7PY, United Kingdom

British Library Cataloguing in Publication Information Available

Library of Congress Cataloging-in-Publication Data

Not by faith alone : social services, social justice, and faith-based organizations in the United States / edited by Julie Adkins, Laurie Occhipinti, and Tara Hefferan.
    p. cm.
Includes bibliographical references and index.
ISBN 978-0-7391-4658-3 (cloth : alk. paper)
1. Social service--United States. 2. Social justice--United States. 3. Religious institutions--United States. I. Adkins, Julie, 1960- II. Occhipinti, Laurie A., 1968- III. Hefferan, Tara, 1972-
HV91.N68 2010
361.7'50973--dc22   2010019169

♾™ The paper used in this publication meets the minimum requirements of American National Standard for Information Sciences—Permanence of Paper for Printed Library Materials, ANSI/NISO Z39.48-1992.

Printed in the United States of America

For Thurman and Sue. –*J.A.*

For Joe and Paul. –*L.O.*

For Jerry and our daughters: Quinn, Connelly, and Landry. –*T.H.*

Contents

Tables and Figures

Chapter 1
Social Services, Social Justice, and Faith-Based Organizations in the United States: An Introduction

Julie Adkins, Laurie Occhipinti, and Tara Hefferan

As neoliberal philosophies and economic models continue their spread across the globe, faith-based non-governmental ("third sector") organizations have proliferated. They increasingly fill the gaps born of state neglect and retraction, standing in for the state by designing and delivering social services and development programming. This volume shines a much needed critical light onto these organizations and their role in the United States by exploring the varied ways that faith-based organizations attempt to mend the fissures and mitigate the effects of neoliberal capitalism, poverty, and the social service sector on the poor and powerless. In so doing, the volume generates provocative and sophisticated analyses—grounded in empirical case studies—of such topics as the meaning of "faith-based" in the identity of these organizations, the nature of faith-based versus secular approaches, the influence of faith-orientation on program formulation and delivery, and examinations of faith-based organizations' impacts on structural inequality and poverty alleviation.

Taken together, the chapters in this volume demonstrate the vital importance of ethnography for understanding the particular role of faith-based agencies across the spectrum of social service provision in the United States. The contributors argue for an understanding of FBOs that moves beyond either dismissing or uncritically supporting faith-based initiatives. Instead, contributors demonstrate the importance of grounded analysis of the specific discourses, practices, and beliefs that imbue faith-based organizations and programs with such power. Richly describing the philosophies and work of faith-based organizations, the chapters reveal both the promise and the limitations of this particular vehicle of service delivery.

In this introduction, we consider what is meant by the term "faith-based" organization, recognizing that the term describes a heterogeneous collection of

1

organizations, employing a wide range of theories, ideologies, practices, and strategies. We begin by reviewing the history of the work that religious organizations have done in offering charity and social services; for hundreds of years, religious organizations have "bridged the gap" by providing much-needed services for the poor. We then offer a number of different frameworks that have been proposed by theorists to understand the role of FBOs today, and synthesize the critical elements of these typologies. Then, the chapter moves to contextualize research on FBOs in the United States: first, through an examination of the work that anthropologists have done on NGOs and FBOs in the developing world, and second, through a review of the research and commentary on FBOs by religious practitioners and scholars, and by social scientists in other disciplines. The chapter concludes by describing key themes and frameworks that are interrogated by the chapters in the volume.

A Brief History of Faithful Service

In the U.S. context, and particularly in light of the effort in recent years to privilege faith-based organizations in the provision of social care, the question is often framed as "Should faith-based organizations (be asked to) take on tasks that are properly the role of the nation-state?" But to pose the question in this manner reveals a certain historical amnesia—often on the part of both FBOs and the state—that needs to be unmasked. Religious organizations have been feeding the hungry, clothing the naked, visiting the sick and those in prison (cf. Matthew 25) for centuries, long before the rise of the modern nation-state. In medieval Europe, it was the monasteries and convents of the Roman Catholic Church that built orphanages and hospitals, leprosariums and universities. The institutional church provided the necessary physical facilities and staffed them with hundreds if not thousands of nuns and monks who taught both children and adults, nursed the sick, fed and sheltered orphaned children, and tended the needs of the poor. To be sure, the Church had the accumulated wealth to do so; it has been estimated that at the end of the thirteenth century the Church owned fully one-third of the land in Europe (International World History Project 1992). Popes and kings sent armies against one another over the question of whether the Church would pay taxes to monarchs, taxes which assuredly were *not* for the purpose of providing social services and amelioration of poverty for the peasantry.

One of the unintended consequences of the Protestant Reformation was that not only did the Catholic Church lose its monopoly on religious power in Europe, it also lost immense wealth and vast tracts of property. As a result, it was less able to provide social goods than it had previously been. For whatever reason, the gaps were not subsequently filled by either the new Protestant churches or by the rulers who had confiscated the Church's wealth and property. Thus, at a time when many of the rich were getting richer—a king could assure himself of the nobility's loyalty by bestowing upon them lands and treasures confiscated from the monasteries—the poor lost a significant safety net and institutional advocate at the very time that broader social forces were beginning to move in a direction that would leave many in far worse poverty than before.

This is not to suggest that religious institutions since that time have abdicated their role in charitable care and service provision, but rather to note that historically there has been debate and sometimes confusion over the roles and spheres of church, state, and society. Within the U.S. context, with its constitutional "separation of church and state," there are consistent attempts to delineate, define, and delimit the separate roles of religious institutions and political/governmental institutions. Yet the history of congregational and religious involvement in social ills in the United States begins long before a Constitution existed to separate institutional domains from one another.[1] As long as the prevailing ethos held that the aim of charity was either to support the few who could not fend for themselves (the biblical "widows and orphans") or to reform those particular persons whose problems kept them from providing for themselves (gamblers, alcoholics), there was no real conflict. Such efforts tacitly supported eighteenth- and nineteenth-century beliefs in individualism, progress, and growth by implying that those who were left out were either exceptional (the few "truly needy") and thus worthy of outside support, or pathological. Winter (2002) notes as an example that the YMCA, as it came to America in the 1850s and 1860s, focused its programs on individuals in need and, when it did address social unrest, it did so by encouraging working-class men to exhibit Christian piety and manliness rather than to engage in radical politics and/or labor movements.

During the nineteenth century there were a few faith-based groups speaking out to challenge the prevailing social order—one notable example being the Society of Friends (Quakers) with their commitment to abolitionism and to helping freed slaves escape. But for the most part poverty and social misery, particularly among the urban poor and immigrant classes, were understood not as problems inherent in industrial society but as individual and family pathologies.

The Social Gospel movement emerged at the end of the nineteenth century as a challenge to such notions. Finding its most eloquent prophet in New York pastor and professor Walter Rauschenbusch (1991 [1907]; 1997 [1917]), the movement asserted that poverty and inequality were the result of societal forces, not individuals' shortcomings, and that Christians had a responsibility to work for the transformation of the social order. Rauschenbusch's words sound as though they could have been written today rather than one hundred years earlier:

> We are assured that the poor are poor through their own fault; that rent and profits are the just due of foresight and ability; that immigrants are the cause of corruption in our city politics; that we cannot compete with foreign countries unless our working class will descend to the wages paid abroad. These are all very plausible assertions, but they are lies dressed up in truth (Rauschenbusch 1991 [1907], 350).

While the Social Gospel movement was influential among many mainline Protestant denominations, there also arose during this period many "parachurch" organizations—what today might well be called FBOs—to address the needs of the urban poor. These organizations, such as the Salvation Army, Hull House in Chicago, and other urban settlement houses and missions, focused mostly on offering humanitarian aid such as emergency food and social services like employment bureaus and health clinics. Although these organizations generally did not choose to raise questions of societal injustice, they largely moved away from an understanding of poverty that blamed its victims.

With increasing religious diversity in the United States—beginning with the explosive growth of the Catholic Church as a result of immigration and continuing through the increasing presence of non-Christian religions—has also come increasing diversity of opinion about the role of religious organizations and institutions vis-à-vis the state. It is important to note, however, that these divisions are far more likely to be found *within* the different religious traditions than *between* them. That is, one finds politically progressive Protestants, Catholics, Jews, Muslims, and others making common cause to transform the social order on the grounds of their faith traditions; while one finds more politically conservative adherents of the same traditions also claiming their faith stance as the basis for transforming society in opposite directions. Faith-based organizations support everything from ending abortion to a woman's right to choose; from criminalizing homosexual acts to celebrating gay marriage; from school vouchers to education for undocumented immigrants; from active community organizing in the manner of Saul Alinsky and his "radicals" (1946; 1971) to praying for community change.

For as long as government funding has been made available for charitable and social-service purposes, faith-based organizations have been able to apply and compete for funds, so long as the "faith" aspect was carefully kept separate. One of the most common methods for doing this was for congregations to form 501(c)(3) nonprofit corporations, separate from the congregation and its religious functions, to address social needs and concerns. By keeping separate governance and financial functions from those of the religious congregation—even if many of the same people were involved—many churches, synagogues, temples, and mosques were able to access federal funds to serve their communities. Such 501(c)(3) organizations blossomed in the aftermath of President Clinton's efforts at welfare reform and the accompanying "Charitable Choice" provision.

Questions about FBOs seem to have exploded in the more recent context of the Bush White House's initiatives, beginning in 2001, which permitted congregations to apply directly for funds without going through the bureaucratic red tape of creating a separate nonprofit. (See Fitzgerald, this volume, for an excellent discussion and outline of the Bush initiatives and their results.) While there are still rules designed to keep inappropriate[2] expressions of faith out of the provision of charity and social services, a larger concern has arisen: by providing funds to congregations directly, eliminating the "middleman" of the separate nonprofit, is the federal government now subsidizing religion? Should taxpayer funds *ever* be given to a religious congregation, no matter what their purpose? What is the impact of government funding on the religious organizations themselves? Does the acceptance of federal funds require a religious organization to change the ways in which it provides services? The chapters in this volume address a wide range of FBO involvement with federal dollars—ranging from small congregations receiving such monies to large organizations that receive none, and everything in between.

Defining and Delimiting Faith-Based Organizations

In the midst of the ongoing debate about the proper role of FBOs, it is worth taking a step back to consider a prior question: just what *is* a "faith-based organization"? In the context of charitable aid, disaster relief, and social services, particularly in the U.S. setting, we often presume that an FBO is a nonprofit organization of some type, perhaps incorporated as a 501(c)(3) for tax purposes. Gerard Clarke reminds us, however, that this is only one possibility. He suggests five primary types, realizing, of course, that many organizations will blend elements of the five in some proportion or another:

1.   *faith-based representative organizations or apex bodies* which rule on doctrinal matters, govern the faithful and represent them through engagement with the state and other actors;
2.   *faith-based charitable or development organizations* which mobilize the faithful in support of the poor and other social groups, and which fund or manage programmes which tackle poverty and social exclusion;
3.   *faith-based socio-political organisations* [sic] which interpret and deploy faith as a political construct, organizing and mobilizing social groups on the basis of faith identities but in pursuit of broader political objectives, or, alternatively, promote faith as a socio-cultural construct, as a means of uniting disparate social groups on the basis of faith-based cultural identities;
4.   *faith-based missionary organizations* which spread key faith messages beyond the faithful, by actively promoting the faith and seeking converts to it, or by supporting and engaging with other faith communities on the basis of key faith principles; and
5.   *faith-based radical, illegal or terrorist organizations* which promote radical or militant forms of faith identity, engage in illegal practices on the basis of faith beliefs or engage in armed struggle or violent acts justified on the grounds of faith (Clarke 2008, 25).

Ascribing such categories may be complex in practice, however. Just to give one example: a Palestinian group (Hamas) that the United States labels as a terrorist organization (category 5) perceives itself largely as a political entity (category 3), and is lauded by many of its adherents as a dependable provider of social goods to a people deprived of their land and, in many cases, their means of livelihood (category 2).

Clarke's broad typology includes caveats for those who argue both for and against the usefulness of FBOs in meeting human needs. For those who uncritically affirm that faith-based programming is the answer to all social ills, Clarke reminds us that "faith" may lead its proponents in all sorts of directions. Al-Qaeda, for example, is unequivocally a faith-based organization, as are most of the militant white supremacist groups in the United States (type 5). On the other hand, for those who harbor suspicion about the "true" motives of FBOs that offer charitable assistance, the typology requires that we recognize that many FBOs that engage people from outside their own faith tradition have no intention of trying to convert them to a different set of beliefs. Several of the chapters in this volume emphasize this trait in the organizations they describe.

Robert V. Kemper and Julie Adkins (2005) remind us that FBOs need to be situated and examined in the context of and in comparison with other kinds of organizations that engage with communities. Their framework suggests a two-dimensional grid: a "faith" dimension and an "engagement" dimension, in which "engagement" reflects an organization's level of involvement with its community and/or the world outside itself (Table 1.1).

Table 1.1 - A framework for contextualizing FBOs

Engagement Dimension	**Positive Engagement/ Negative to Neutral Faith** Example: Government-Based Community Development Agencies	**Positive Engagement/ Positive Faith** Example: Faith-Based Community Development Organizations
	Negative to Neutral Engagement/ Negative to Neutral Faith Example: Natural Resources-Extracting Corporations	**Negative to Neutral Engagement/ Positive Faith** Example: Separatist Religious Cults
	Faith Dimension	

Source: Kemper and Adkins (2005, 75)

Whereas typologies like that of Clarke (above) and Sider and Unruh (2004; 2005) presume a "positive" faith dimension, Kemper and Adkins remind us that FBOs are situated among organizations that are "neutral" or even "negative" on the faith dimension. For example, international development organizations after World War II were grounded in modernization theory, which generally assumed that religion, along with other "traditional" institutions, necessarily stood in the way of progress (e.g., Rostow 1959). They therefore saw religion as an obstacle to be overcome and were negatively oriented toward it. Many relief organizations are faith-"neutral"; that is, they neither embrace a faith stance nor oppose it. NGOs such as CARE and Doctors Without Borders would fit into such a category, as would most programs of the United Nations. Similarly, Kemper and Adkins ask us to examine whether an FBO's engagement with its community is positive, neutral, or negative; and to what extent. They suggest a separatist cult as perhaps "neutral" in terms of engagement; one might consider a terrorist cell as "negative." Providing charity would be a "low positive" form of engagement with the community—providing for immediate needs but without necessarily engaging community members in dialogue or sharing life experiences—whereas community organizing or community development would be viewed as a "high positive" on the engagement dimension. We will return to this continuum from charity to social justice in a subsequent section.

In a previous volume (Hefferan, Adkins, and Occhipinti 2009), we have suggested a typology for understanding FBOs that we have found to be useful in a number of settings: in the United States as well as internationally, and for FBOs based in a number of different religious traditions (Table 1.2, pages 8-13). Based on prior work by Sider and Unruh (2004; 2005) and the Working Group on Human Needs and Faith-Based and Community Initiatives (2002), this typology seeks to describe FBOs' engagement with their communities along a spectrum that ranges from "faith-permeated" (an organization in which the faith component, often including conversion, remains an important part of their agenda in the provision of care) to "secular" (the negative-to-neutral side of Kemper and Adkins's "faith" dimension).

Most of the FBOs highlighted in this volume have a "faith background" or "faith-affiliated" orientation to their work and their community. This is perhaps not surprising: such organizations are somewhat more likely than the "faith-permeated" to seek outside funding and help to support their work; they are thus likely to be larger organizations and more likely to attract attention. In addition, it must be said that most social scientists have a far higher comfort level dealing with organizations that are not "in your face" about faith in every conversation. Some of the FBOs described here are clearly engaged in faith-secular partnerships, such as the refugee resettlement agencies analyzed by Bauer and Chivakos, and the medical clinics whose history is traced by Laird and Cadge. Interestingly, both of these case studies involve Muslim FBOs. At the opposite end of the spectrum, Rodriguez immerses us in the worldview of drug rehabilitation programs that are (faith-)permeated with a particular perspective on what it means to be human, and, thus, what they believe it takes to overcome addiction.

Table 1.2 – FBO Typology

	Faith-Permeated	*Faith-Centered*
Self-description	Includes explicit references to faith	Includes explicit references to faith
Founded / Organized	By faith group and/or for faith purpose	By faith group and/or for faith purpose
Management / Leaders	Faith or ecclesiastical commitment an explicit prerequisite	Faith commitment understood to be a prerequisite (may be implicit or explicit)
Staff / Volunteers	Faith commitment is important; most or all share organization's faith orientation; faith an explicit factor in hiring/recruitment decisions	Faith commitment may be an explicit selection factor for tasks involving religion, but may be less important in other positions
Financial and other support	Garners support from faith community	Garners support from faith community

Faith-Affiliated	Faith Background	Faith-Secular Partnership	Secular
Faith references may be either explicit or implicit	May have implicit references to faith (e.g., references to values)	No reference to faith in mission of the partnership or of the secular partner	No faith content, but references to values are often present
By faith group and/or for faith purpose	May have historic tie to a faith group or purpose, but that connection is no longer strong	Faith partners founded by faith group or for faith purpose; no reference to faith identity of founders of the secular partner; founders of the partnership may or may not be religious	No reference to faith identity or spiritual views (if any) of founders(s)/ organizer(s)
Normally share the organization's faith orientation, but explicit faith criteria are considered irrelevant or improper	Faith criteria considered irrelevant or improper	Required to respect but not necessarily share faith of the faith partners	Faith criteria considered improper
Staff/volunteers are expected to respect but not necessarily share the faith orientation of the organization; faith beliefs motivate self-selection of some staff/volunteers	Little to no consideration of faith commitment; faith beliefs may motivate self-selection of some staff/volunteers	Staff/volunteers expected to respect faith of the faith partner(s); program relies significantly on volunteers from faith partners	Faith criteria for any staff/volunteer considered improper
Able to garner some support from faith community	Able to garner some support from faith community	Able to garner some support from faith community	Little to no ability to garner support from faith community

Table 1.2 continued

	Faith-Permeated	Faith-Centered
Organized faith practices of personnel/ volunteers (prayer, devotions, etc.)	Faith practices play a significant role in the functioning of the organization; personnel/volunteers expected or required to participate	Faith practices often play a significant role in the organization; personnel/volunteers may be expected to participate
Faith content of program	In addition to acts of compassion and care, also includes explicit and mandatory faith content integrated into the program; beneficiaries are expected to participate in faith activities and discussions of faith	In addition to acts of compassion and care, also includes explicit faith content that may be segregated from provision of care; beneficiaries have the option not to participate in faith program components; beneficiaries may also be invited to faith activities outside the program parameters
Main form of integrating faith content with other program variables	Integrated/ Mandatory (engagement with explicit faith content is required of all beneficiaries)	Integrated/Optional or Invitational (engagement of beneficiaries with explicit faith content is optional or takes place in activities outside program parameters)

Faith-Affiliated	Faith Background	Faith-Secular Partnership	Secular
Faith practices are optional and not extensive	Faith practices are rare and peripheral to the organization	Faith partners may sponsor voluntary faith practices; secular partners do not	No organized faith practices
The faith component is primarily in acts of compassion and care; program includes little (and entirely optional) or no explicit faith content; staff may invite beneficiaries to faith activities outside program parameters or hold informal faith conversations with beneficiaries	No explicit faith content in the program; faith materials or resources may be available to beneficiaries who seek them out; the faith component is seen primarily in the motivation of individual staff members and/or volunteers	No explicit faith content in program activities designed by secular partners; faith partners sometimes supplement with optional faith resources and activities	No faith content
Invitational, Relational, or Implicit (engagement of participants with explicit faith content takes place in optional activities outside the program parameters or in informal relationships with staff and/or volunteers)	Implicit (beneficiaries only encounter faith content if they seek it out)	Implicit, Invitational, or Relational, depending on staff/ volunteers of the faith partner	None

Table 1.2 continued

	Faith-Permeated	*Faith-Centered*
Expected connection between faith content and outcome	Expectation of explicit faith experience or change, and belief that this is essential or significant to desired outcome	Strong hope for explicit faith experience or change, and belief that this contributes significantly to desired outcome
Faith symbols present	Usually	Usually

Source: Hefferan, Adkins, and Occhipinti (2009, 20-25)

International Perspectives

Anthropologists who work with issues of poverty and development most often discuss cases in "underdeveloped" regions of the world. These researchers have examined development discourse and practice and suggested that often the work of developers and social services deliverers serves to depoliticize the problems faced by the poor and marginalized (Ferguson 1994). Such work serves to pacify and redirect the energies of those who are being oppressed and exploited in ways that replicate rather than challenge the status quo.

We noted above that during the late 1990s and early 2000s, the government in the United States began to shift social service funding to FBOs. While this can accurately be understood as reflecting both changing trends within the United States as a whole and the priorities of the Bush administration in particular,it also reflects a process that we can trace internationally. As states in economically underdeveloped regions shifted toward policies of neoliberalism that

Faith-Affiliated	Faith Background	Faith-Secular Partnership	Secular
Little expectation that faith change or activity is necessary for desired outcome, though it may be valued for its own sake; some believe that acts of compassion and care alone have an implicit spiritual impact that contributes to outcome	No expectation that faith experience or change is necessary for desired outcome	No expectation that faith experience or change is necessary for desired outcome, but the faith of volunteers from faith partners is expected to add value to the program	No expectation of faith change or experience
Often	Sometimes	Sometimes (program's administration usually located in a secular environment; program activities may be located in a faith environment)	No

encouraged the reduction of state spending, non-governmental organizations, or NGOs, moved to fill the gaps left by the retreating state (Hefferan, Adkins, and Occhipinti 2009; Igoe and Kelsall 2005). Neoliberal reforms created conditions that favored NGOs internationally during the 1980s, as development aid shifted from the public to the private sector. Thus, the shift to privatize social services in the United States to a perhaps unprecedented degree, and with more explicit government support, reflects this global movement.

NGOs include an amazingly heterogeneous collection of organizations, with a correspondingly wide range of theories, ideologies, practices, and strategies aimed at mitigating conditions of poverty. While the development studies literature, in general, has engaged in a number of lively debates about NGOs—e.g., the relative strengths of NGOs vis-à-vis state-led development (Edwards and Hulme 1996; Riddell and Robinson 1995; Zaidi 1999); the degree to which NGOs are particularly efficient, participatory, or "local" purveyors of development (Lister 2000; Lorgen 1998; Unnithan and Srivastava 1997); and the extent to which NGOs might operate outside development's conventional and bureaucratic spheres of power, politics, and discourses (Farrington and Bebbington

1993; Gardner and Lewis 1996; Grillo 1997)—there has been much less consideration of the religiously-driven or "faith-based" NGO.

Historically, there has often been tension between the secular world of economic development and the faith-based organizations that have a long-standing role in the provision of services internationally (Clarke 2008). A number of works have taken an applied focus to promote "dialogue" between the worlds of faith and development (Belshaw, Calderisi, and Sugden 2001; Tyndale 2006; Hoksbergen and Ewert 2002). Frequently underlying these recent works is an assumption about and endorsement of the power and promise of faith-based organizations to make international development more efficient, effective, and relevant than it is currently.

Ethnographers interested in NGOs and development have only recently begun to examine the specific dynamics of faith-based organizations (Occhipinti 2005; Hefferan 2007; Bornstein 2005; Hefferan, Adkins, and Occhipinti 2009). Some of this work has suggested that faith-based organizations might constitute alternatives *to* development, representing a qualitatively different approach to questions of wealth and power (Hefferan 2007). Gerard Clarke and Michael Jennings note that the values of some FBOs, embedded in a moral and religious framework, "create in the FBO an institution that (in the best of examples) directly addresses poverty and the marginalization of the poor" (Clarke and Jennings 2008, 15).

As noted above, religious institutions have always filled a critical role in caring for the poor and will no doubt continue to do so. It is legitimate to interrogate and to negotiate the relative roles and responsibilities of "church" and state in caring for those within a society who have needs greater than they themselves can address. Neoliberal philosophies of governance assume that such is not the role of the state. And given that state provision of public welfare is a relatively recent development in the history of human social organization, we suggest that there is a need to interrogate the frequent assumption, particularly among progressive social scientists, that it is the "government's" job to ameliorate social ills. It is not difficult to argue that, when poverty is the inevitable consequence of the economic system and climate within a particular nation-state, the governing authorities do indeed bear responsibility for those who have suffered the consequences of their choices. But this is an argument that must be made and supported; one cannot presume the answer without making the case.

While studies of neoliberalism's effects on the global south have proliferated over the past few decades, scholars have only recently begun to contextualize their work on community development in the United States as informed, constrained, and resulting from a neoliberal global economy (e.g., Collins, di Leonardo, and Williams 2008). While faith-based organizations have been given a privileged status in U.S. anti-poverty and social service funding over the last decade, they have only recently been examined by scholars, many of whom are interested in religious organizations as an element of civil society (e.g., Schreck 1994; Perry 2004). The observation made by Hefferan, Adkins and Occhipinti (2009) that faith-based organizations "bridge the gap" left by state withdrawal from social services in a neoliberal context is not only relevant to research on international development, but also can shed light on the role of FBOs in the United States.

Who Else Is Interested in FBOs?

While anthropologists have been slow to begin critical examination of faith-based NGOs in general (see discussion above and in Hefferan, Adkins, and Occhipinti 2009), and especially in the United States (but for exceptions, see Bartkowski and Regis [2003]; Elisha [2004]; Adkins and Kemper [2006]; Kemper [2006]; Goode [2006]; Woodrick [2006]), other disciplines have shown no such reticence. In view of the history noted above, it is hardly surprising to find that religious practitioners and scholars have been interested in describing the charitable and community engagement of groups and organizations. A second body of literature that focuses on FBOs has arisen in the realm of social sciences other than anthropology: sociology, in particular the sociology of religion; social work, which has been especially concerned with the effectiveness (or lack of it) of the programs and interventions offered by FBOs; and political science, particularly around church-state questions and concerns, and the role of religious sensibilities in shaping public policy. Here, we draw out multidisciplinary themes relevant to the chapters in this volume and of interest to anthropologists.

Voices from the World of Faith

As noted in the introduction to a recent special issue of the *NAPA Bulletin* (Hefferan and Fogarty 2010), academic scholars cannot hope to understand FBOs without understanding the theological ground on which they base their actions and interventions. We note that the vast majority of the literature on FBOs among religious scholars and practitioners in the United States focuses solely on Christian organizations and Christian theology. Since Christianity remains the majority religion—although its status is clearly on a decline—most of the work done thus far by scholars in other disciplines (see sections below) is also focused on Christian organizations. This is partially explained by the fact that there are many more Christian FBOs in the United States than FBOs related to other religious traditions. We also believe, however, that it may reflect concern among social scientists about the possible privileging of specifically Christian FBOs since 2001.

The majority of this literature is either richly descriptive of particular efforts (Green 1996; Polis Center 1998; Delloff 2002; Sider and Unruh 2007) or helpfully pragmatic in the "how-to" genre (Dudley 1991; 1996; 2002; Skjegstad 2002; 2007; Sider, Olson, and Unruh 2002); little of it is deeply analytical or critical. It is, however, useful as illustration and background in laying out the incredible variety of grassroots faith-based engagement.

One of the most consistent forums within the faith community for the discussion of FBOs has been the journal *Sojourners,* which blends an evangelical to moderate theological stance with progressive politics. Editor-in-chief Jim Wallis addressed FBOs directly or indirectly in half of his columns in 2001 (Wallis 2001a; 2001b; 2001c); the magazine has also published two lengthy interviews with John DiIulio, Jr. (1997; 2001), who headed up George W. Bush's White House Office for Faith-Based and Community Initiatives. To accompany an article entitled "Compassion is good, but justice is better" (Dionne 2001), the magazine's center spread portrayed a game it called "FBO LAND," modeled on the children's game Candy Land, which included such pathways and hazards as "The Church-State Morass" and "Our Lady of the 501(c)(3)" on the way to the goal, the "Land O' Milk and Honey"—and included instructions such as: "The pastor of your church-run shelter requires a Christian commitment from each person before they are allowed a bed. Go back 6 spaces" (Berger and Shank 2001).

Justice versus Charity

Questions of poverty and injustice are one area in which scholars from a range of divergent faith backgrounds often unite to make common cause.[3] Writing from within the evangelical Protestant tradition, Sider (2007) offers specific policy proposals for ending poverty in the United States. Previously, he notes, he had argued in a more traditional evangelical line of reasoning that prayer and charity alone were sufficient; he no longer believes this to be the case. Perkins (1993), speaking from within an evangelical African American tradition, argues that biblical justice requires that affluent white Christians live in solidarity, not charity, with their impoverished inner city neighbors. To this end, he not only lays out a plan for inner-city community development on a Christian basis, but insists that those who have fled the poverty and violence of the inner city must return and make their lives among the poor. At the other end of the spectrum— steeped in the language and praxis of liberation theology—Myers (1994) argues similarly that charity and social-service provision allow the "givers" to maintain distance from "receivers" and control over them, thus promoting paternalism. He argues instead for solidarity with the poor as they seek justice.

Nile Harper, a sociologist and Presbyterian minister who directs Urban Church Research in Minneapolis, suggests that it is useful to frame the question of charity, social service, and social justice as a continuum (Harper 1999; see also the discussion of Farmer [2003] in Brashler [this volume]). While he acknowledges his own bias toward justice, he acknowledges the need for all three. Harper's descriptive typology outlines commonalities and differences among the three orientations (Table 1.3). We have modified it only to remove a row that he entitles "biblical model," because we believe the typology is applicable to FBOs arising out of a variety of faith traditions.

Table 1.3 – Continuum from Charity through Justice

	CHARITY	SERVICE	JUSTICE
REALM	Private; personal acts of compassion; individual deeds of assistance; voluntary aid organizations	Private and public; organized delivery of assistance to families, individuals, and groups	Public; public policy-making based upon equity; fairness, shareholding, community
TIME	Quick response to urgent, emergency needs; can meet immediate needs	Intermediate timeliness: can be fast response, but tends to be more deliberate, slow paced	Long term: does not produce a quick fix; does not serve urgent, immediate needs
WHO BENEFITS	Direct help to individuals, families, small groups, neighborhood communities	Direct help to individuals, families, small groups, and can provide long-term aid to large, diverse populations	Can bring long-term improvement to large sectors of society; challenges oppressed to change basic conditions
RESPONDS TO	The secondary effects of injustice, social crisis, people in pain and need—food, shelter, clothing.	The secondary consequences of unjust conditions, social upheaval, groups in pain, and emergency disaster situations.	Basic causes of injustice, the roots of injustice, socioeconomic and political sources of suffering, group oppression.
PATTERN	Requires repeated responses to meet individual needs after repeated requests	Can deliver dependable, stable, continuous supply of goods and services efficiently	Changes basic public policy and priorities; changes structures and institutions
CURRENT MODEL	Soup kitchen feeds hungry people; Salvation Army sells used clothes to individuals; shelters give overnight housing; donor gives aid to the homeless.	Government welfare program gives aid to unemployed person; aid to dependent children; food stamps for family living in poverty; public housing; emergency health care. Can be a base for recovery.	Community Development organizes people to create affordable housing, develop jobs, train workers, develop community health care, advocate legislative change.

Table 1.3 continued

	CHARITY	SERVICE	JUSTICE
STRENGTH	Personal, simple, quick, deals with immediate need; involves volunteers; promotes giving; provides tax deductions.	Organized, prepared in advance, provides accountability; public tax supported, provides social safety net; serves large number of people. Can promote new beginnings.	Engages people in self-development; empowers people to meet their needs, take charge of their lives, form partnerships, take political action.
LIMITS	Does not deal with the basic causes of human problems; is reactive, sporadic; promotes one-way giving; may inhibit responsibility.	May create dependency, apathy; does not deal with basic causes; often expensive/wasteful, and can be dehumanizing.	Requires time, risk-taking, hard work, compromise, financial resources; can cause conflict; may fail; no guarantee of success.

SOURCE: Harper 1999, 302-3 (amended)

FBOs and Their Relationship with the State

Political scientists, together with scholars of law and public policy, have analyzed at length the nuances of relationship between the state and religious organizations. Monsma (1996) argues for a stance of "positive neutrality" on the part of the state toward religious nonprofits, which he defines as

> . . . the principle that public money could go to fund the programs and activities of religiously based nonprofits that are of a temporal, this-world benefit to society, as long as public funds are supporting similar or parallel programs of all religious traditions without favoritism and of similar or parallel programs of a secular nature, whether sponsored by secularly based nonprofits or by government itself (1996, 178).

While Monsma's work arose in light of the Charitable Choice provisions of welfare reform under the Clinton administration, a near explosion of interest has resulted from the subsequent Bush administration's privileging of FBOs. Daly (2009), Owens (2007), Solomon (2003), and Ryden and Polet (2005), while cautiously optimistic about religion's role in solving social ills, also raise concerns not only about whether the state has gone or will go too far in transferring social services to religious organizations, but also about the effect of such policy shifts on the religious institutions themselves.

Robert Wuthnow (2004), the sociologist most associated with study of the relationship between faith or religion and public life in the United States, presents the results of several long-term studies on FBOs. In considering the neoliberal trend toward transfer of social service provision to religious organizations, in particular the Bush administration's willingness to fund congregations directly, Wuthnow notes that his findings

> do underscore the gap that often exists between political rhetoric and local realities. The faith-based organizations that politicians often point to as reasons for expanding government support are often the exception rather than the rule. What congregations do best generally cannot be replaced by or even reinforced through government support. Yet there is considerable evidence to suggest that specialized faith-based service agencies function *just as well* as nonsectarian agencies and, for this reason, should not be discriminated against in receiving government support (Wuthnow 2004, xvii; emphasis in original).

Ram Cnaan has examined in great detail the shift of social service provision from the public to the nonprofit sector (Cnaan 1999; 2002; Boddie and Cnaan 2006). Based on a three-year study of congregations in six U.S. cities, he reaches the conclusion that "congregational involvement [in service provision] is an American norm, rather than the outcome of specific preconditions" such as theological stance. Cnaan continues:

> The norm of congregational involvement in social provision did not develop in a vacuum. Such a norm develops only when a government neglects responsibility for the social needs of its citizens. This has been the case in the United States, the modern society in which public authorities are least concerned for the welfare and the rights of the poor. When the public sector fails to assume responsibility for the care of the indigent, then the responsibility falls on others. In the case of the United States, this responsibility has been taken on by the nation's congregations and religious organizations. When no single social entity takes responsibility for helping the disadvantaged, those whose faith calls for compassion and caring for the needy stranger find meaningful ways to put their faith into practice (Cnaan 2002, 295-6).

Despite appreciation for the work done by congregations and faith-based nonprofits, Cnaan and his colleagues are quick to note that little work has actually been done to study the effectiveness of their social ministries (Boddie and Cnaan 2006); rather, it has been assumed.

Based on more than twenty years studying social service delivery systems, Wineburg (2007) sounds this warning about the program implemented by the Bush administration:

> *The "faith" in the president's "faith-based initiative" may be defined as a marriage between the government and a group of Christians who believe effective social services can be delivered only if one accepts Jesus as his or her Personal Savior. . . .* President Bush's faith-based initiative has been a top-down, inside-

the-Beltway effort that has promoted more competition for fewer dollars because the effort is not really geared to enhance effective service delivery but rather to promote right-wing evangelical Protestant social services while starving equivalent government programs (Wineburg 2007, xi; emphasis in original).

More general work on the relationship between religion and politics also provides useful framing for the work of FBOs, such as Swarts (2008) on secular and faith-based progressive movements; Gutterman (2005) on Christian social movements and democracy, DiIulio (2007) on "America's faith-based future"; and Wilburn (2002) and Griffith and McAlister (2008), both edited volumes of reflection and analysis on faith/religion and policy/politics.

FBOs and Social Capital

Sociologists of religion have contributed much to the discussion of the service work of religious institutions. Robert Wuthnow noted in the early 1990s the "American paradox" of individualism coupled with a high degree of participation in "caring" activities that range from neighbors helping neighbors through working for the transformation of society (Wuthnow 1991). An edited volume a decade later examines the public role and activism of mainline Protestant denominations in the United States (Wuthnow and Evans 2002).

Cnaan (2006) takes as his unit of analysis the city of Philadelphia, reporting on a study of over 1,000 congregations which found that nearly all of them provide some kind of help and service to their communities, even if it is modest in scope. Farnsley (2003) conducted similar research on a smaller scale among urban congregations in Indianapolis, examining some of the assumptions that have been voiced about the value of religious-based services (e.g., how well *do* congregations actually know their neighbors?).

Nancy Ammerman (1997; 2005), whose books are widely referenced in mainline Protestant seminaries, writes rich ethnographic descriptions of congregations' engagement with their communities and considers how both congregation and community benefit from such engagement. She and colleagues also provide tools to assist congregations in visioning and planning how they will learn about community needs and craft appropriate responses (Ammerman, Carroll, Dudley, and McKinney 1998: Dudley and Ammerman 2002). There is a particularly rich body of literature on African American congregations and their community activities, ranging from charitable provision through community organizing and social reform (cf. Billingsley 1999; Wood 2002; McRoberts 2003). Similar to Perkins (1993) above, a number of these authors consider whether living in the neighborhoods whose needs congregants hope to address makes a difference in the style or the success of their interventions.

In addition to engaging the topic of FBOs directly, political scientists have contributed useful discussions of religion in general as social capital (cf. Smidt 2003), a concept also elaborated by anthropologist Jo Anne Schneider (2006) in examining FBOs' response to welfare reform initiatives. Wuthnow also suggests that further attention needs to be paid to whether FBOs are able to create bridging social capital between the privileged and the disadvantaged segments of society (2004, xviii). If so, then their contribution to civil society is far greater than just the provision of charity and social service.

In This Volume

The chapters of this volume examine FBOs at a number of different scales, beginning with analyses of single, locally based organizations and ranging up through studies of communities and large multi-sited organizations. This diversity reflects the diversity of FBOs themselves, and allows us to capture a sense of the heterogeneity of faith-based efforts across the United States.

Leah Mundell's study of a partnership between an FBO called Bainbridge House and a local elementary school in Philadelphia offers an example of an FBO working at an intensely—and intentionally—local scale. Mundell's analysis problematizes the very notion of "community," while simultaneously demonstrating the importance of the FBO as a "local" actor. In this case study, a small group of "outsiders," religiously motivated activists, established a long-term relationship with a poor urban community. Using a model that Mundell calls "a theology of presence," the activists, much like ethnographers, integrate themselves into the community through establishing an ongoing presence. Rather than imposing their own political, social, or aid agenda, the FBO instead steps in to fill a need that emerges in the community when the school is threatened with closure.

Ethan Sharp's chapter examines a different kind of FBO: one which exists within, and is comprised of, members of a local community. In this case study, a small, local Pentecostal church is able to access federal funds to support various programs, in collaboration with a university-based initiative. He compares this to an FBO in the same community that has a more traditional social service model. Sharp's analysis critically examines the ways in which funding agencies and congregations may employ fundamentally different discourses and practices, as congregations redirect resources to place more, not less, attention on the explicitly religious dimensions of their work, a process that Sharp calls a "transvaluation of faith." His analysis suggests that as researchers, we must be cautious in our categorization of "faith" versus "secular" spheres, as these distinctions may be analytically useful but fundamentally misrepresentative of the lived reality of faith communities.

The chapter by Katherine Lambert-Pennington and Julie Pfromm also explores the relationship between the discourses of faith and approaches to community development. In this study, a larger congregation perhaps more successfully employs the strategies of community development funding agencies in order to effect change in its South Memphis neighborhood. Drawing on a membership that comes mostly from "outside" the poor urban neighborhood where the church is actually situated, the congregation serves as a conduit of resources. Lambert-Pennington and Pfromm explore the ways in which this has led to an unequal relationship of dependence as well as the potential for transformative community development.

Julie Adkins's chapter examines the history of efforts in Dallas to address the needs of the homeless solely through the work of faith-based organizations. The city is an object lesson in the variety of FBOs at different places on the "faith" typology and the fragmentation of services for the homeless. Ultimately, she concludes that while there are some things that FBOs do extraordinarily well, the one thing they have not succeeded in doing is reducing the number of homeless in the city. If faith-based solutions alone cannot solve the problem in a solidly Bible-belt location, she argues, we cannot hope that they will do so alone on a larger scale.

The expression of religious values and narratives in the work of FBOs is explored further in the chapter by Lance Laird and Wendy Cadge. In this case study of Muslim FBOs in California, the religious motivations of founders and volunteers drive the work of the organizations; a religious mandate to serve the community and care for others is a familiar theme in the work of most FBOs. For these organizations, however, their position as representatives of a minority faith is keenly felt in their internal discourse, and their work is seen as an opportunity to demonstrate the positive contributions of the Muslim community.

Janet Brashler explores the intersection of culture, faith, and development in her chapter on the FBO Tree of Life on the Rosebud Sioux reservation in South Dakota. Using Farmer's (2003) framework that situates the work of NGOs on a continuum from charity to development to social justice, Brashler contextualizes the relationships between volunteers, professional staff, and the Sicangu Lakota in terms of the long and often turbulent history of white-Native relations in the region. Like Lambert-Pennington and Pfromm, she finds that the relationship in this case is more one of dependence and "doing for" than one of transformation and "doing with." Despite the good intentions of short-term volunteers to engage with the Lakota community, the FBO most often acts as a conduit of resources rather than a cultural bridge.

Yet, in a case study of a wide range of FBOs working to resettle refugees in the Greater Hartford area, Janet Bauer and Andrea Chivakos suggest that the experience of working in FBOs does have transformative potential for individuals. In this case, FBO workers often make a personal transition from an approach characterized by charity to one which is grounded in a larger language of human rights and social justice. Here, FBOs build on a religious discourse of morality to construct a more ecumenical and universalizing approach to providing social services to clients from a wide range of faith traditions.

The chapter by Joanne Schneider, Laura Polk, and Isaac Morrison also compares the approaches of FBOs across a range of faith traditions, in this case in the Philadelphia and Washington, D.C. metro areas. They find that while religious traditions and theology are reflected in the work of each FBO, organizations from a wide range of religious communities work within a shared institutional structure that also shapes their work as providers of social services. The authors argue that an ethnographic approach is vital in understanding the practices of FBOs in the United States, in order to best understand the complexities of these organizations and their sociopolitical context.

Scott Fitzgerald also finds that the work of FBOs is constrained by federal funding and collaborative work with government agencies at different levels. He focuses on faith-based community development organizations (FBCDOs), which have responded to the increased reliance of the U.S. government on FBOs and other nonprofits to provide social services and community development, to explore the mechanisms that serve to maintain religious identity within this institutional framework. He argues that even as religious congregations create legally distinct FBCDOs, these service organizations do reflect the religious expressions and priorities of the congregation and its religious tradition.

The chapter by Timoteo Rodriguez argues that FBOs in urban California, established as treatment options for drug users, deploy a religious discourse of morality and strength as the means to rehabilitate not just the body, but the soul; and, as a result, to improve society as a whole. Rodriguez's chapter examines how these religious organizations collaborate with the state in court mandated rehabilitation to exercise power over individuals and populations.

The final chapter in the volume, by William Garriott, examines how Christian traditions broadly shape programmatic responses to drug addiction in Appalachia. While most of our volume contributors focus on how religion and religious organizations have created and maintained institutions, Garriott demonstrates that religious conceptions of addiction and morality have inhibited a response to drug addiction as a matter of public health. Like Rodriguez, Garriott finds that by positing drug use as a moral failing, FBOs reframe the issue of drug use from one of the body to one of the soul.

Connections and Directions

A variety of themes connect many of the chapters in this volume. We suggest that all are topics that bear further exploration, not only in the work of the authors represented here but among social scientists in general and anthropologists in particular.

Faith-fulness

This theme addresses the issues raised by the Hefferan, Adkins, and Occhipinti (2009) typology to consider to what extent "faith" content is a critical piece of the programming, self-presentation, and intent of the organizations represented here. At one end of the spectrum we find Sharp's "faith-permeated" Pentecostals in south Texas, carefully balancing their fervent belief in the need for conversion with caution for the appropriate use of federal grant monies. We can make a useful comparison to the AME congregation in Memphis described by Lambert-Pennington and Pfromm: The Saint, a much larger congregation, is also active in its community but far less concerned about whether those who benefit from its programs and handouts are in some sense "converted." Its outreach ministries might better be construed as "faith-affiliated." Mundell offers us yet a third congregation engaged in a "faith-secular partnership" to preserve a neighborhood school. Faith motivates the participants in Bainbridge House to be a "presence" in their neighborhood, but they have no expectation that the neighbors with whom they worked to save Stanton Elementary should share their beliefs in any way, nor did these beliefs enter into their engagement with school district and city personnel over the school.

The chapters by Rodriguez and Garriott frame the question in larger terms, as both examine the role of "faith" in treatment of addictions. Rodriguez posits the model of "bio-pistis" to suggest that faith-based treatment programs present what attempts to be an integrated notion of body, faith, and society. Garriott is less sanguine about the faith-based realm, and fears that the generalized faith-imbued ethos of the language commonly used about addiction is actually detrimental to those seeking treatment and healing. Faith language about "demon drugs" also becomes a substitute for the professional mental health care that is largely absent in the rural United States.

Fitzgerald notes differences among three FBOs that can be traced to the organizational identity of their founding denominations, and notes that such origins must be taken into account when investigating an FBO's own presentation of its faith stance. Schneider, Polk, and Morrison note the ways in which a founding faith organization's own structure and hierarchy, as well as its theology, shape the FBOs which it births. Such differences bear further investigation, as, indeed, Schneider's ongoing research is working to accomplish. (See the Faith and Organizations project website at http://www.faithandorganizations.umd.edu/.)

Additional study might prove interesting on the topic of differing emphases *within* organizations such as all of these. What happens if paid staff and volunteers disagree about the importance of faith content? What happens when a founder's vision differs from that of the folks involved on a day-to-day basis? Or when donors insist on more faith content than aid recipients are willing to tolerate? How do organizations work out differing visions within their own faith traditions and communities?

Motivation

Another theme that recurs in several chapters is that of an FBO's motivation in providing service(s). Obviously, one aspect of this is the question of providing faith content and seeking conversion: for some organizations, their primary motivation is "to seek and to save the lost" (Luke 19:10). However, there exist many faith-based organizations (at least, as these are framed by Clarke) that exist for this purpose alone and do not seek to offer charity or strive for social change. Such organizations, though numerous in the United States, are not considered in this volume.

For many FBOs, the motivation is simply obedience to the command of a religion's founder and/or sacred texts. Followers become aware of needs in the world around them; they recall commandments that urge feeding the hungry, or leaving the gleanings for the widow and orphan, or giving away a percentage of income; and they respond. Though the theological rationales differ, all of the major world religions challenge followers to care for the unfortunate in their midst. For some FBOs, this is motivation enough.

Other organizations express additional reasons for engaging in service, many of these grounded in their faith. Brashler describes United Methodist work among the Lakota Sioux as serving, in part, to atone for past wrongs done to Native Americans. In providing "mission trip" experiences for adults and youth from the majority U.S. society, the FBO that she describes, Tree of Life, seeks to educate white Americans about their own history as it relates to the native peoples who preceded them—a reversal of the oft-held assumption that it is the *recipients* of services who need to be educated.

Laird and Cadge outline yet another possible motivation for some faith-based groups. The Muslim health clinics they have studied see their purpose as being not only to serve the needy, but also to define and claim their own identity. On the one hand, the clinics are clearly Muslim in origin, and thus make a statement to their surrounding communities about Muslim care and concern for neighbors. On the other hand, those involved see this outreach as a form of claiming their identity as Americans as well: they are providing service to members of their community regardless of the recipients' religious background. By providing a service to neighbors, they claim their common citizenship.

Who Owns the Lake?

"Give a person a fish, and you feed her for a day. Teach a person to fish, and you feed her for a lifetime." We suspect that there is no one who works on a regular basis with NGOs who has not heard this statement in some form or another. Helping organizations use this metaphor to reassure themselves and their supporters that they are not simply placing a band-aid on social problems, but are actively working to help people solve their own problems. As such, it draws a distinction between what is often glossed as *charity*, or a "handout," and *social services*, or a "hand up." It marks the difference between handing out a bowl of soup, and teaching the recipient a job skill so he can afford to purchase his own soup; between providing a shelter bed for a few nights, and matching the sleeper's skills with an employer so she can find her own place to live.

Both charity and social services ministries clearly have an important place; without them, social suffering would be far worse than it is. But frequently, FBOs provide only short term assistance that rarely challenges the forces that create poverty. An anthropological perspective encourages the questioning of the assumptions that drive the answers FBOs often provide. Why are so many people who "know how to fish" still unemployed? Why do some people "catch fish" day after day after day but still cannot feed their families? Why do some get to fish in the lake, and others only in the drainage ditches? Obviously, one can stretch a metaphor to its breaking point—but one key theme that runs through many of the chapters here is the question of social justice: Who owns the lake? And how do FBOs challenge or perpetuate the status quo?

We suggest that addressing this issue is a necessary consideration for the social-scientific study of FBOs, not only in the United States but around the world. While it would require three-dimensional paper to draw it, perhaps a mental map is sufficient. Organizations which occupy similar spaces on the "faith" continuum (Hefferan, Adkins, and Occhipinti 2009) may find themselves far separated on the charity/justice continuum (Harper 1999), and vice versa. Thus, a faith-affiliated FBO may do no more than feed the homeless men in a city park; or it may, like Bread for the World, focus its entire attention on legislation and policy-making with no direct provision of services at all.

The (Un)Importance of Effectiveness

Political scientists and scholars of social work have been interested in the question of whether FBOs are, as the rhetoric suggests, somehow more effective deliverers of social services than is the public sector (see, for example, an entire double issue of the *Journal of Religion and Spirituality in Social Work*, 25[3/4]). However, this comparison is often of little interest to FBOs themselves, and we find it raised only rarely in the chapters that follow. For one thing, FBOs believe that the work they do extends far beyond the mere provision of goods and services, whether their goal is understood as sharing a faith message or creating relationships of support, and such goals are not easily quantifiable.

Furthermore, in some situations such comparisons are difficult if not impossible to make. Adkins's chapter notes her surprise at finding *only* faith-based emergency shelters for the homeless of Dallas; there was no "public option" with which to compare. Bauer and Chivakos describe questions raised in Hartford about whether new immigrant refugees are "better" settled by co-religionists than by FBOs representing a different faith tradition—but here, too, there is no public option for comparison, only different FBOs engaging in similar work. We believe that this is an area where anthropologists have critical skills to bring to the table: How do we *qualitatively* assess interventions, changes, or outreach by organizations seeking to offer help? Our fellow social scientists may be too concerned with quantitative data in this realm. Boddie and Cnaan (2006) are undoubtedly correct that not enough work has been done to assess the effectiveness of FBO service providers—even so, the methods and skills employed by anthropologists seem uniquely suited to the kinds of work that needs to be done.

Moving Forward

As becomes clear in the detailed ethnographic studies in the following chapters, organizations which have similar qualities on paper may behave very differently in practice. An ethnographic perspective allows us to represent the incredible diversity of FBOs along a number of dimensions, and such case studies allow meaningful comparisons and generalizations to be made.

Ethnographic studies of FBOs throw into sharp relief the inextricable linkages between culture, religion, economics, and politics. FBOs themselves encourage us to understand poverty as a moral question and "helping" as a moral choice. At the same time, as the shifting relationship between "private" and "public" services and benefits has become increasingly blurred, these case studies explore the meaning of this dynamic and cast a new light on the work of FBOs as central actors in social service provision in the United States.

Notes

1. Readers interested in a more detailed history of FBO engagement in American society may wish to consult Kemper and Adkins (2005), particularly the section entitled "Historical Background" on pages 76-88, from which we draw in this section.

2. "Inappropriate" is, of course, largely in the eye of the beholder.

3. For those unfamiliar with the names of various writers and scholars across the theological spectrum, one needs only to discover who published their work to know immediately their preferred stance: Baker Books (which publishes Sider and Perkins) is a well known evangelical publishing house; Orbis (publisher of Myers) is a Catholic-related press that has published many of the key works in liberation theology.

Works Cited

Adkins, Julie, and Robert V. Kemper. 2006. Oasis Housing Corporation: From solutions to dissolution in a faith-based organization. *Urban Anthropology* 35(2-3):237-64.

Alinsky, Saul David. 1946. *Reveille for radicals*. Chicago: University of Chicago Press.

———. 1971. *Rules for radicals: A practical primer for realistic radicals*. New York: Vintage Books.

Ammerman, Nancy Tatom. 1997. *Congregation and community*. New Brunswick, NJ: Rutgers University Press.

———. 2005. *Pillars of faith: American congregations and their partners*. Berkeley: University of California Press.

Ammerman, Nancy T., Jackson W. Carroll, Carl S. Dudley, and William McKinney. 1998. *Studying congregations: A new handbook*. Nashville: Abingdon Press.

Bartkowski, John P., and Helen A. Regis. 2003. *Charitable choices: Religion, race, and poverty in the post-welfare era*. New York: New York University Press.

Belshaw, Deryke, Robert Calderisi, and Chris Sugden, eds. 2001. *Faith in development: Partnership between the World Bank and the churches of Africa*. Oxford: Regnum Book International.

Berger, Rose Marie, and Duane Shank. 2001. FBO Land: A game of faith-based organizations. *Sojourners*, May-June:34-35.

Billingsley, Andrew. 1999. *Mighty like a river: The black church and social reform*. New York: Oxford University Press.

Boddie, Stephanie, and Ram A. Cnaan. 2006. *Faith-based social services: Measures, Assessments, and Effectiveness*. Binghamton, NY: The Haworth Pastoral Press. Published simultaneously as *Journal of Religion and Spirituality in Social Work* 25(3/4).

Bornstein, Erica. 2005. *The spirit of development: Protestant NGOs, morality, and economics in Zimbabwe*. Stanford, CA: Stanford University Press.

Clarke, Gerard. 2008. Faith-based organizations and international development: An overview. In *Development, civil society and faith-based organizations: Bridging the sacred and the secular*, ed. Gerard Clarke and Michael Jennings, 17-45. New York: Palgrave Macmillan.

Clarke, Gerard, and Michael Jennings, eds. 2008. *Development, civil society and faith-based organizations: Bridging the sacred and the secular*, London: Palgrave Macmillan.

Cnaan, Ram A. 1999. *The newer deal: Social work and religion in partnership*. New York: Columbia University Press.

———. 2002. *The invisible caring hand: American congregations and the provision of welfare*. New York: New York University Press.

———. 2006. *The other Philadelphia story: How local congregations support quality of life in urban America*. Philadelphia: University of Pennsylania Press.

Collins, Jane L., Micaela di Leonardo, and Brett Williams, eds. 2008. *New landscapes of inequality: Neoliberalism and the erosion of democracy in America*. Santa Fe, NM: SAR Press.

Daly, Lew. 2009. *God's economy: Faith-based initiatives and the caring state*. Chicago: University of Chicago Press.

Delloff, Linda-Marie. 2002. *Public offerings: Stories from the front lines of community ministry*. Bethesda, MD: The Alban Institute.

Dilulio, John J., Jr. 1997. With unconditional love: Criminologist John Dilulio explains why a God-centered and problem-focused approach is needed to save our youth (Interview). *Sojourners*, September-October:16-22.

———. 2001. Acting in good faith: An interview with John Dilulio, point man for the White House's controversial new "faith-based" initiative. *Sojourners*, May-June: 26-30.

———. 2007. *Godly republic: A centrist blueprint for America's faith-based future.* Berkeley: University of California Press.

Dionne, E. J., Jr. 2001. Compassion is good, but justice is better. *Sojourners*, May-June: 31-33.

Dudley, Carl S. 1991. *Basic steps toward community ministry.* New York: The Alban Institute.

———. 1996. *Next steps in community ministry: Hands-on leadership.* Washington, DC: The Alban Institute.

———. *Community ministry: New challenges, proven steps to faith-based initiatives.* Bethesda, MD: The Alban Institute.

Dudley, Carl S., and Nancy T. Ammerman. 2002. *Congregations in transition: A guide for analyzing, assessing, and adapting in changing communities.* San Francisco: Jossey-Bass.

Edwards, Michael, and David Hulme, eds. 1996. *Beyond the magic bullet: NGO performance and accountability in the post-Cold War world.* West Hartford, CT: Kumarian Press.

Elisha, Omri. 2004. Sins of our soccer moms: Servant evangelism and the spiritual injuries of class. In *Local actions: Cultural activism, power, and public life in America,* ed. Melissa Checker and Maggie Fishman, 136-58.

Farmer, Paul. 2003. *Pathologies of power: Health, human rights and the new war on the poor.* Berkeley: University of California Press.

Farnsley, Arthur E., II. 2003. *Rising expectations: Urban congregations, welfare reform, and civil life.* Bloomington, IN: Indiana University Press.

Farrington, John, and Anthony J. Bebbington. 1993. *Reluctant partners? Nongovernmental organizations, the state and sustainable agricultural development.* London: Routledge.

Ferguson, James. 1994. *The anti-politics machine: "Development," depoliticization, and bureaucratic power in Lesotho.* Minneapolis: University of Minnesota Press.

Gardner, Katy, and David Lewis. 1996. *Anthropology, development, and the post-modern challenge.* Chicago: Pluto Press.

Goode, Judith. 2006. Faith-based organizations in Philadelphia: Neoliberal ideology and the decline of political activism. *Urban Anthropology* 35(2-3):203-36.

Green, Clifford J., ed. 1996. *Churches, cities, and human community: Urban ministry in the United States, 1945-1985.* Grand Rapids, MI: Eerdmans.

Griffith, R. Marie, and Melani McAlister, eds. 2008. *Religion and politics in the contemporary United States.* Baltimore: Johns Hopkins University Press.

Grillo, R. D. 1997. Discourses of development: The view from anthropology. In *Discourses of development: Anthropological perspectives,* ed. R. D. Grillo and R. L. Stirrat, 1-33. Oxford: Berg.

Gutterman, David S. 2005. *Prophetic politics: Christian social movements and American democracy.* Ithaca, NY: Cornell University Press.

Harper, Nile. 1999. *Urban churches, vital signs: Beyond charity toward justice.* Grand Rapids, MI: Eerdmans.

Hefferan, Tara. 2007. *Twinning faith and development: Catholic parish partnering in the US and Haiti.* Bloomfield, CT: Kumarian Press.

Hefferan, Tara, Julie Adkins, and Laurie Occhipinti. 2009. *Bridging the gaps: Faith-based organizations, neoliberalism, and development in Latin America and the Caribbean.* Lanham, MD: Lexington Books.

Hefferan, Tara, and Tim Fogarty. 2010. The anthropology of faith and development: An introduction. *NAPA Bulletin* 32.

Hoksbergen, Roland, and Lowell Ewert, eds. 2002. *Local ownership, global change: Will civil society change the world?* Monrovia, CA: World Vision International.

Igoe, Jim, and Tim Kelsall. 2005. Introduction: Between a rock and a hard place. In *Between a Rock and a hard place: African NGOs, donors, and the state,* ed. Jim Igoe and Tim Kelsall, 1-34. Durham, NC: Carolina Academic Press.

International World History Project. 1992. The church in the high middle ages. Available online at history-world.org/midchurchhigh.htm (last accessed March 7, 2010).

Kemper, Robert V. 2006. Anthropological perspectives on faith-based organizations. *Urban Anthropology* 35(2-3):141-53.

Kemper, Robert V., and Julie Adkins. 2005. The world as it should be: Faith-based community development in America. In *Community building in the twenty-first century,* ed. Stanley E. Hyland, 71-100. Albuquerque, NM: SAR Press.

Lister, Sara. 2000. Power in partnership? An analysis of an NGO's relationship with its partners. *Journal of International Development* 12(2):227-39.

Lorgen, Christy Cannon. 1998. Dancing with the state: The role of NGOs in health care and health policy. *Journal of International Development* 10(3):323-39.

McRoberts, Omar M. 2003. *Streets of glory: Church and community in a black urban neighborhood.* Chicago: University of Chicago Press.

Monsma, Stephen V. 1996. *When sacred and secular mix: Religious nonprofit organizations and public money.* Lanham, MD: Rowman and Littlefield.

Myers, Ched. 1994. *Who will roll away the stone? Discipleship queries for first world Christians.* Maryknoll, NY: Orbis Books.

Owens, Michael Leo. 2007. *God and government in the ghetto: The politics of church-state collaboration in Black America.* Chicago: University of Chicago Press.

Perkins, John M. 1993. *Beyond charity: The call to Christian community develoment.* Grand Rapids, MI: Baker Books.

Perry, James L. 2004. Civic service in North America. *Nonprofit and Voluntary Sector Quarterly* Supplement 33(4):167s-83s.

(The) Polis Center. 1998. *Voice of faith: Making a difference in urban neighborhoods.* Indianapolis: The Polis Center.

Rauschenbusch, Walter. 1991 [1907]. *Christianity and the social crisis.* Louisville, KY: Westminster/John Knox Press.

———. 1997 [1917]. *A theology for the social gospel.* Louisville, KY: Westminster/John Knox Press.

Riddell, Roger C., and Mark Robinson. 1995. *Non-governmental organizations and rural poverty alleviation.* Oxford: Oxford University Press.

Rostow, W. W. 1959. The stages of economic growth. *The Economic History Review* 12(1):1-16.

Ryden, David K., and Jeffrey Polet, eds. 2005. *Sanctioning religion? Politics, law, and faith-based public services.* Boulder, CO: Lynne Rienner.

Schneider, Jo Anne. 2006. *Social capital and welfare reform: Organizations, congregations, and communities.* New York: Columbia University Press.

Schreck, Harley. 1994. The church at work in creating community: Strengthening support networks for the homebound elderly. *City and Society* 7(1):163-73.

Sider, Ronald J. 2007. *Just generosity: A new vision for overcoming poverty in America.* Second Edition. Grand Rapids, MI: Baker Books.

Sider, Ronald J., Philip N. Olson, and Heidi Rolland Unruh. 2002. *Churches that make a difference: Reaching your community with good news and good works.* Grand Rapids, MI: Baker Books.

Sider, Ronald J., and Heidi Rolland Unruh. 2004. Typology of religious characteristics of social service and educational organizations and programs. *Nonprofit and Voluntary Sector Quarterly* 33(1):109-34.

———. 2005. *Saving souls, serving society: Understanding the faith factor in church-based social ministry.* New York: Oxford University Press.

———. 2007. *Hope for children in poverty: Profiles and possibilities.* Valley Forge, PA: Judson Press.

Skjegstad, Joy. 2002. *Starting a nonprofit at your church.* Bethesda, MD: The Alban Institute.

———. 2007. *Winning grants to strengthen your ministry.* Herndon, VA: The Alban Institute.

Smidt, Corwin. 2003. *Religion as social capital: Producing the common good.* Waco, TX: Baylor University Press.

Solomon, Lewis D. 2003. *In God we trust? Faith-based organizations and the quest to solve America's social ills.* Lanham, MD: Lexington Books.

Swarts, Heidi J. 2008. *Organizing urban America: Secular and faith-based progressive movements.* Minneapolis: University of Minnesota Press.

Tyndale, Wendy. 2006. *Visions of development: Faith-based initiatives.* London: Ashgate.

Unnithan, Maya, and Kavita Srivastava. 1997. Gender politics, development, and women's agency in Rajasthan. In *Discourses of development: Anthropological perspectives,* ed. R. D. Grillo and R. L. Stirrat, 157-81. Oxford: Berg.

Wallis, Jim. 2001a. The conscience of the state. *Sojourners* March-April:7-8.

———. 2001b. Eyes on the prize. *Sojourners,* May-June:7-8.

———. 2001c. Terms of engagement. *Sojourners,* July-August:7-8.

Wilburn, James R., ed. 2002. *Faith and public policy.* Lanham, MD: Lexington Books.

Wineburg, Bob. 2007. *Faith-based inefficiency: The follies of Bush's Initiatives.* Westport, CT: Praeger.

Winter, Thomas. 2002. *Making men, making class: The YMCA and workingmen, 1877-1920.* Chicago: University of Chicago Press.

Wood, Richard L. 2002. *Faith in action: Religion, race, and democratic organizing in America.* Chicago: University of Chicago Press.

Woodrick, Anne C. 2006. Preparing the way: Hispanic ministry and community transformation in Marshalltown, Iowa. *Urban Anthropology* 35(2-3):265-94.

Working Group on Human Needs and Faith-Based and Community Initiatives. 2002. Finding common ground: 29 recommendations of the Working Group on Human Needs and Faith-Based and Community Initiatives. Available online at www.sfcg.org/programmes/us/report.pdf (last accessed February 24, 2010).

Wuthnow, Robert. 1991. *Acts of compassion: Caring for others and helping ourselves.* Princeton, NJ: Princeton University Press.

———. 2004. *Saving America? Faith-based service and the future of civil society.* Princeton, NJ: Princeton University Press.

Wuthnow, Robert J., and John H. Evans, eds. 2002. *The quiet hand of God: Faith-based activism and the public role of mainline Protestantism.* Berkeley: University of California Press.
Zaidi, S. Akbar. 1999. NGO failure and the need to bring back the state. *Journal of International Development* 11(2):259-71.

Chapter 2
A Theology of Presence:
Faith Partnerships with U.S. Public Schools
Leah Mundell

Philadelphians, like residents of so many other American urban centers, have struggled for decades against the deterioration of their public school system. In the face of inadequate state funding, teacher shortages, neighborhood flight, and poverty, this massive school district has tried ongoing experiments in community partnership, state management, and privatization to turn itself around. Here, I focus on an initiative introduced by the district in 1999, one that fit seamlessly into an emerging national policy emphasis on faith-based service provision. The initiative required that each public school in the city develop a relationship with a "faith partner," a religious organization that would provide the school with human, financial, and other resources.

Faith partnerships took many forms and varied widely in their effectiveness; here I analyze just one such partnership, a mentoring program at Stanton School, a small elementary school in South Philadelphia, where I did ethnographic fieldwork from 2000-2003. When I completed my initial fieldwork, I was ready to conclude that this mentoring program, by privileging the volunteer efforts of white middle-class adults from outside the neighborhood, disenfranchised local African American parents and perpetuated the dominance of white teachers and administrators at the school. But in 2003, the district's decision to close the school revealed this program to be something quite different, a catalyst for community mobilization. That ability to transform from volunteer program to activist organization is not, I would argue, a general characteristic of faith-based organizations, but rather a potential of this particular "faith-partner," a local Christian prayer group called Bainbridge House. Why did this school, unlike so many other public schools, become a locus of neighborhood activism, and how did Bainbridge House gain the legitimacy to help lead that effort? In following the Bainbridge House mentoring program through a school crisis, I observed both the possibilities and the limitations for neighborhood activism built on a fragile identity as both insider and outsider.

A Theology of Presence

Bainbridge House members practice what I call a theology of presence. They are currently a group of eight white, middle-class Protestants and Catholics who gather daily for morning prayer at one member's home in a largely African American and low-income neighborhood. The group has evolved from a residential community to a community of daily prayer, but their presence in this neighborhood remains integral to their identity. The simple ritual of morning prayer is the thread that holds Bainbridge House together; out of that experience of prayer comes the ability to act—or the wisdom to know when not to act—in the neighborhood. When Bainbridge House members speak about prayer, they rarely refer to God. Rather, it is the experience of daily prayer itself that creates the conditions by which they can act with discernment in the world.

According to Vicki Ellis, who lives in Bainbridge House, the house began in about 1984, when the priest of a local Episcopal Church "wondered . . . What would it be like for lay people who have jobs and professions and relationships and families to live in the city in a particular place, to share in the worship life of a particular community of faith, and to be continually present in that place, both in the life of the parish and in the life of that neighborhood?" Vicki was intrigued from the beginning and, with a small initial group, founded this experiment. Today, Vicki is the only one who still lives in the neighborhood. The group continues to meet every weekday for morning prayer, once a week for a meal and discussion of spiritual development, and yearly for a retreat. Their presence in the neighborhood is very conscious; Vicki says that it is a spiritual discipline, paying attention to their environment, listening to the neighborhood.

In many ways, Bainbridge House echoes the approach of traditional community organizers, who see their role—at least initially—as listeners and learners in the neighborhood where they work. But the members of Bainbridge House are, in many ways, more like ethnographers. They are outsiders to this community who have become insiders by virtue of long-term commitment and interest. Their legitimacy in the neighborhood, like the experiential authority sought through classic participant-observation, is based, as Jim Clifford describes it, on "a 'feel' for the foreign context, a kind of accumulated savvy and a sense of the style of a people or place" (Clifford 1988, 35). And like interpretive ethnographers, they understand their presence "not as the experience and interpretation of a circumscribed 'other' reality, but rather as a constructive negotiation involving at least two, and usually more, conscious, politically significant subjects" (Clifford 1988, 41).

Eight years ago the group paid one member, Sue Kettell, to be, in effect, a full-time ethnographer one day a week, spending that day intentionally getting to know the neighborhood and building relationships. Sue developed contacts with the local elementary school, and the principal asked whether Bainbridge House would organize a mentoring program at the school. The Bainbridge House members agreed and began to reach out to their wider circles of friends, church networks, and neighborhood institutions to recruit mentors. Drawing volunteers from churches in the neighborhood and around Center City, the mentoring program brings adults to Stanton School for an hour a week to meet individually with students and offer academic and social support. There are no strict rules or guidelines for the interaction; the main purpose is for the adult to be a "wise and trusted friend" for a student with whom he or she develops a potentially long-term relationship.

For Vicki, the genesis of the mentoring program fit her unspecified but general hope that Bainbridge House could be a vital part of the community without judgment or imposition. As she told the mentors, "That actually in many ways is a good example of, again, how we at Bainbridge House feel called to be present in the neighborhood, not with an agenda, not with big program ideas, but present in a way where we're intentionally listening, intentionally being neighbors, understanding in some ways that we're neighbors but we're newer neighbors and that it's very important for us to listen." This notion of being new neighbors is at the core of what Sue called a "theology of being," a constant reciprocity of living as "both guest and host" while being present in the neighborhood.

Presence and Place-Making

The heavy emphasis that Sue and Vicki put on "presence" and neighborliness draws attention to the importance of a sense of place for Bainbridge House. The name itself confuses things; when the prayer group left St. Mary's Church on Bainbridge Street and eventually settled into a new space a few blocks away at Vicki's home on Christian Street, they retained their original, place-based name: Bainbridge House. Though it no longer refers to their actual location, the group felt strongly about keeping the name. As Vicki told me, "We're not the House of Joy or something. We reference a place."

Anthropological theories of place have blossomed over the past decade, demonstrating the innumerable ways that places are produced through cultural and political practices and the ways that affective connection to place can lead to (and reveal preexisting) cultural contestation. Yet few of these ethnographic accounts describe connections to place that are so deliberately constructed as is Bainbridge House's dedication to this neighborhood. As Keith Basso reminds us, "Sense of place . . . is neither biological imperative, aid to emotional stability, nor means to group cohesiveness. What it is, as N. Scott Momaday (1976) has suggested, is a kind of imaginative experience . . . a way of *appropriating* portions of the earth" (Basso 1996, 143; emphasis in original). In Basso's work on Apache place names, this appropriation is of an emotional and not a political nature. But for members of Bainbridge House, appropriation is understood as a *danger* that accompanies developing that sense of place, the danger of making the kinds of judgments and impositions that they worked so hard to avoid.

Bainbridge House is today composed of white, middle-class, Christian professionals who have intentionally developed an attachment to a place that is primarily black, mixed-income, and with a growing Muslim presence. Their sense of place is not "fueled by sentiments of inclusion, belonging, and connectedness to the past" (Basso 1996, 145-6) but rather by a firm commitment to build connection with a place to which they do not fully belong. When Sue described to me why they chose to commit themselves to this neighborhood, she echoed the often unstated goals of ethnographic inquiry:

> We wanted to be committed to *this* neighborhood because it is integrated and really feel like it's so easy just to really lose touch with—being a white middle class person—with what it's like to be a minority and also poor, although in this neighborhood there is great riches, and you wouldn't know that if you weren't here living it. And I mean, it's one thing to go visit a place and then leave, but to be committed to this space every day—the good, the bad, and the indifferent—it really does give you a sense. And the biggest gift that comes with that, I think, is that you really realize how rich every neighborhood is. I kind of always felt that. Just because you see abandoned houses, it does not mean that there is not great riches here. And that, I think, is kind of the basis of my faith, is kind of the hope.

In Sue's statement, there is a romantic appreciation of the richness of close community life—a nostalgia repeated by several of the Stanton School mentors who were amazed by the dense relationships in the neighborhood. But more powerful is her recognition that "presence" in this neighborhood does not mean merely physical, geographic location but rather inserting oneself in the web of human relationships that make up that place.

Bainbridge House as Cultural Mediator

During the 2001-02 school year, forty-four adults volunteered for the Bainbridge House mentoring program. Most were middle- or upper-middle-class and learned about mentoring through their church affiliations. Many lived fairly close by, in the affluent neighborhood of Society Hill and other parts of Center City, although a few commuted from the near suburbs. Approximately two-thirds of mentors were white and one-third were African American. A handful of mentors lived in the neighborhood, including several older, retired, African American volunteers who had lived near Stanton School most of their lives. For each volunteer, the cultural lines he or she crossed by mentoring were different. For some, the lines were geographic, pushing them into a part of the city they had passed by but never before known. For others, the lines were generational, highlighting the differences between their own childhoods and the lives of the children they mentored. Some noticed linguistic difference, while others focused on the enormous and obvious inequities in income, education, and privilege that separated their own families from the families of their mentees.

I argue here that Bainbridge House members acted as cultural mediators between mostly white, middle-class volunteers and African American, low-income students and families, interpolating mentors into the House's theology of "presence." Meanwhile, the mentoring program facilitated the construction of a far-reaching and often invisible network of relationships, inflected by the hierarchies of race, class, and neighborhood. When a crisis arose, it was Bainbridge House's liminal position as insider/outsider that imbued it with the legitimacy to represent the local while making important use of larger, citywide network links. Ultimately, this case demonstrates the importance of not just the existence but also the content of social networks in building social capital: in this case, the specifics of Bainbridge House's enactment of "presence."

Research on mentoring programs in the United States has focused primarily on the outcomes of mentoring relationships for the children or mentees involved. These studies are often evaluations of the stated goals of such programs—providing support for at-risk youth—and give little attention to the wider social and cultural implications of mentoring (Herrera 1999; Johnson 1998; Jucovy 2002; Tierney and Grossman 1995). Even studies that address the complexities of cross-race matching focus exclusively on effects on the *youth* involved in such a match (Jucovy 2002). The assumptions underlying the mentoring movement might be traced to two influential analyses of inequality: William Julius Wilson's discussion of the increasing isolation of the urban poor as a result of economic restructuring and black middle class flight, and James Coleman's assertion of the importance of "social capital" in educational attainment (Coleman 1990; Wilson 1987).[1] The two are linked in mentoring programs that seek to counter this increasing isolation of the urban poor by making available to students the social networks and educational values that a middle-class mentor can offer.

This research tends to focus on the flow of knowledge and experience from mentor to child. In fact, mentors themselves are also often profoundly affected by the relationships they forge. The mentors I observed struggle to make sense of the inequity they witness, to develop "natural" relationships across class and/or racial lines, and to apply their newfound knowledge. As individuals, they may use that knowledge either to develop a deeper commitment to social equity or to distance themselves further from the community they have entered as volunteers, to build cross-cultural identification or to deepen negative stereotypes and exotic fascination. Bainbridge House plays an important informal role in guiding mentors through this interpretive experience. Despite the desire of some mentors to transcend the boundaries of a volunteering relationship, their experiences are, nonetheless, mediated by Bainbridge House and its theology of pres-

ence. The cultural knowledge that mentors gain and the relationships they establish also serve to bolster Bainbridge House's presence in this neighborhood. The
mentoring program, which attracts adults from all over the city to this school of
primarily low-income African American children and middle-class, primarily
white teachers, is its own kind of cultural borderland. And the members of
Bainbridge House—themselves firmly situated as white, middle-class liberals—
often serve as either cultural intermediaries or border police in these encounters
among mentors, school staff, and members of the various communities making
up this small corner of South Philadelphia.

Bainbridge House generally operated as a fairly hands-off manager of the
mentoring program; once mentors were matched with students, they were given
great freedom in their activities and agendas. But the orientations and regular
training workshops organized by the program coordinator did allow Bainbridge
House to infuse the mentoring program with its approach to neighborhood presence. At these workshops and celebratory gatherings during the year, volunteers
had the opportunity to share their mentoring experiences and perspectives with
one another. And at these gatherings, members of Bainbridge House quietly
challenged volunteers who persisted in focusing on family deficits and need in
the neighborhood.

At a mentoring workshop focusing on writing strategies, held in January
2001, one participant described her mentoring experience in terms that set her
firmly apart from her mentee. She lamented the child's poor verbal skills, explaining that it was particularly difficult to teach him grammar, because her cor-
rections didn't *sound* right to him. Since the way "they" speak is grammatically
incorrect, correct grammar is just a bunch of rules to them, she said. Later, during a discussion of creative writing activities, one of the writers leading the
workshop told about his experience with a child who was writing a story about a
superhero. The child couldn't decide how to continue, and the teacher asked him
what happened next: does he run into a bank robber? The child said, "My superhero doesn't stop bank robbers. He stops men who beat women." The boy's response disrupted the traditional narrative of the superhero villain and suggested
the child's experience with a world of domestic violence. The group sighed
sadly at this evidence of the probable violence in this little boy's daily life.

Despite the generally sympathetic tone of these mentors' reflections, they
did not sit well with Vicki and with Sue, who had stopped in during a free class
period to join the group. In response to the writer's story about the child's superhero, Vicki tried to turn the conversation away from an emphasis on difference—the ostensible difference between middle class fantasies and the realities
of poverty. "There is the truth of the children's lives and alongside that there is
the resiliency inside the child and inside the family, right alongside those trage-
dies," she said, adding, "More than likely, there is somebody within that kid's
family or extended family who is there for them." Sue nodded and agreed with
Vicki. Her next comments seemed directed at the woman who struggled with

teaching standard English grammar to her student: "Sometimes in our speaking, we refer to the kids as 'these children' rather than 'the children' or 'our children,' and that can separate us, make the kids into the other," she said. In responding to the mentor's concerns about teaching "correct" language, Sue turned the tables and questioned the "correctness" of the mentor's own language use, in terms of its othering effects.

Much of the language of "faith partnerships" proposed by the school district—as well as the language of mentoring workshops and literature—emphasizes the benefits that accrue to children and to schools when outside institutions and individuals develop relationships with schoolchildren. They generally do not address either the motivations and circumstances of volunteer involvement or the experience of cultural learning that is inherent in these relationships. While Bainbridge House members rarely addressed these issues explicitly, events such as the mentoring workshops provided opportunities for them subtly to challenge the motivations of participating mentors and to offer their own vision for "volunteering": their theology of presence. Vicki's comments highlighting the resiliency of poor families seemed designed to discourage the notion that a mentor's role is to fill a deficit in the lives of poor children.[2] Instead, she suggested that mentors see their role as learners, to supplement their own deficient understanding of the lives of poor, African American families. At this mentoring workshop, which had consisted primarily of open-ended discussion among the mentors, Vicki and Sue, as the two participants most invested in the neighborhood and the school, had the last words. And it was their longstanding commitment to forging a reciprocal relationship with the neighborhood that allowed Bainbridge House to help catalyze a new kind of neighborhood activism.

Saving Stanton School

When I conducted my initial fieldwork at E.M. Stanton School, from January 2001 to June 2002, there was no effort to organize parents or to welcome parents into school governance. At the time, I concluded that because the Bainbridge House mentoring program was undertaken without a parallel effort to organize parents, the result was that white adults from outside the community became invested in the school—though without real decision-making power—in ways that most local African American parents were not. The circumstances seemed to support Susan Brin Hyatt's thesis that America's post-welfare state has championed the volunteer efforts of the middle class while limiting the possibilities for such civic engagement on the part of the poor and working class (Hyatt 2001).

During the winter of 2002-03, however, the circumstances at Stanton changed. In December 2002, a crisis at the school led to the formation of an unusual coalition of parents, teachers, volunteers, and community members that had the potential to engage disenfranchised parents in the daily life of Stanton School. When the school district announced that Stanton was slated to close at the end of the 2002-03 school year, Stanton's "faith partner," Bainbridge House, expanded from being the administrative center of the mentoring program to also serving as the home base for the Coalition to Save Stanton School. The shift from service to activism was fairly seamless, and the Bainbridge House community easily widened to include the parents and grandparents who took charge of organizing a strategic plan to reverse the district's decision to close the school.

How might we understand the appearance of this new voluntary organization at Stanton School? The formation of the Coalition to Save Stanton School revealed that the Bainbridge House mentoring program not only facilitated relationships between mentors and students but also provided the scaffolding for a broad network of students, teachers, administrators, parents, neighbors, mentors, and church leaders (from inside and outside the neighborhood). Here I draw on Epstein's classic discussion of "effective networks," which contain strong connections between links, and "extended networks," which are loosely connected and often cross-cut social categories (Epstein 1969). I suggest that the mentoring program, while somewhat successful at fostering small effective networks around the relationships between mentors and students, was also successful at creating a broad and loose extended network that was largely invisible until a moment of crisis. At that moment, when the district proposed the closure of Stanton School, this subterranean network could be activated for a phenomenally powerful organizing effort.[3]

The work of J. Clyde Mitchell and his colleagues on social networks in the urban centers of central Africa still stands as a model for network analysis and anticipates much of the current debate over the meaning and importance of social capital. Mitchell (1969) showed that networks have both morphological characteristics, describing the way the links relate to one another (e.g., their density and range), and interactional characteristics, describing the nature of the links themselves (e.g., their "content," durability, and intensity). Mitchell emphasized the importance of these interactional characteristics, particularly the *content* of network links: "the meanings which the persons in the network attribute to their relationships" (1969, 20). In much the same way, scholars of social capital today critique the notion that the density of social ties necessarily leads to increased social capital. Foley, Edwards, and Diani call for a return to Bourdieu's understanding of social capital as *resources* linked to networks (Bourdieu 1986). They argue, " . . . social infrastructures such as networks and associations cannot be understood as social capital by themselves. Social relations may or may not facilitate individual and collective action—and therefore operate as social capital—depending on the contexts in which they are generated" (Foley, Edwards, and Diani 2001, 266-7).

The context in which the Coalition to Save Stanton School formed was shaped by two very different factors: the theology of presence through which Bainbridge House operated in the neighborhood, and the sense of crisis around Philadelphia public schools that came to a head with the proposal to close Stanton. Bainbridge House's longstanding presence in the neighborhood gave it the legitimacy to serve as the center for the organizing effort, and the sense of educational crisis provided the motivation for the members of their extended network to step forward and participate in the ways described below. In the process, Bainbridge House itself was transformed as well. At a moment of crisis, that deepened commitment and legitimacy established through the mentoring program allowed Bainbridge House to transition from listening *to* the neighborhood to speaking *with* the neighborhood. These events also reveal the ways that the school district's perception of communities as "local" conflicts with the realities of the cross-sectoral, cross-geographic nature of school partnerships.

The Emergence of Parent Leadership

On the morning of December 20, 2002, the *Philadelphia Inquirer* reported that Stanton was one of four elementary schools slated to close at the end of the school year as part of the district's far-reaching capital construction plan (Dean 2002). The closures were portrayed as a cost-cutting measure targeting under-enrolled schools with outdated facilities. That morning, an awards ceremony was scheduled at Stanton. At the end of the program, the principal asked the students to return to their classes, then closed the auditorium doors and turned to the 35-40 parents and several mentors left in the room. With tears leaking down her cheeks, she told us that the district had decided to close Stanton in June.

Parents gasped in surprise. The principal apologized that this news had to come just before Christmas, but she explained that she had only heard of the decision the day before. Thanking her staff and lauding the many accomplishments of the school, she handed out the letter given to her by the school district, announcing the closure. She told parents that she didn't know where their children would be sent in the fall; all she knew was that the district would be holding a meeting early in January to discuss the decision. A parent asked whether this was the final decision; the principal said that she only knew what she had been told.

Now the tone of the discussion turned from surprise and sadness to anger and resolve. One of the first to respond was a grandmother who said that, as a taxpayer, she was not going to just give up. Explaining that she chose to send her grandchildren to Stanton because of the success her other grandchildren had experienced there, she said she would organize to oppose the closure. "This is about education, this is about freedom. This is our neighborhood . . ." she said with conviction. A parent, perhaps twenty years younger, reminded the group that the closure was not inevitable, that the district had tried to shut Stanton down before and failed. When she was a student at Stanton in the 1980s, she said, the parents marched downtown and convinced the district to keep the school open. "So, don't give up now," she urged. "I heard everyone yelling and clapping for their baby today. Let's go yell and clap for them tomorrow, downtown!"

These two women, Stepheni Trott-Batipps and Verna Rae Miller, went on to become leaders in what became known as the Coalition to Save Stanton School. At the beginning of January, this small group of parents, teachers, community members, and mentors met at Bainbridge House to plan their strategy for keeping Stanton open and successful. They compiled a list of Stanton's strengths, including its small size and small classes, its mentoring program, and its cultural arts curriculum. They discussed the proposed boundary changes and the fact that two of the four schools slated for closure were located in their neighborhood. They speculated about whether this was an attempt to drive African-Americans out of this gentrifying neighborhood. And informally, they re-established connections built through the school. At the end of the evening, they resolved to continue meeting every week until Stanton was saved.

The following week, a meeting at Stanton called by the School Reform Commission to explain the proposed closure revealed the breadth of the network that would be mobilized to save the school. About 120 people, perhaps a quarter of them parents, climbed the stairs to Stanton's third floor auditorium space, stopping at the registration table to pick up two packets of information. The first contained materials provided by the district about transferring to other schools. The second packet of information, slipped onto the registration table by Vicki Ellis, had a cover page that demanded, "Keep Stanton School a School." This packet included a description of Stanton's strengths and contact information for the members of the School Reform Commission, so that parents could write to protest the closure.

Inside, Sue was leading the audience in a song that—at her insistence—would become the anthem for the Coalition to Save Stanton School: "Freedom is Coming." At her side, a group of students ably accompanied her on drums from around the world. The meeting was called to order so that a lineup of district officials could explain the under-enrollment pattern that had led them to recommend Stanton for closure. They pointed out the deficiencies of the building—including the makeshift double-classroom auditorium in which we were seated—and told parents that they would have first choice of other schools to which they could transfer their children. Then, the moderator began to call up speakers in the order they had signed up at the door. The list was lengthy and surprisingly diverse. Parents spoke about the small classes and caring teachers at Stanton; community members spoke about Stanton's historical importance in the neighborhood and the recent improvements at the school; a minister from St. Peter's Episcopal Church in Society Hill spoke about her congregants' work as

Stanton mentors as a model of school-community partnerships; mentors decried the negative message that closing the school would send to children; and Sue Kettell described the new spirit in place at Stanton with the arrival of the new principal. Representing the faculty, a teacher presented three proposals for keeping Stanton open, including bringing back the Head Start program that had only recently been moved out of the building. Two members of the local neighborhood association spoke, one of them a young, white man, who had moved to the neighborhood with his wife only six months previously, and who argued that the many young couples now moving to the neighborhood would someday want to send their children to neighborhood schools. The last speaker was City Council President Anna Verna, who reinforced this testimony to neighborhood growth and development and asked the district point-blank when it would be meeting with the community again.

Over the course of January, February, and March, the Coalition meeting at Bainbridge House gathered data on the design of the school building, the potential for overcrowding in neighboring schools if Stanton were to close, the community partnerships in place at Stanton, and the district's recent investment in the Stanton facilities. With the help of school staff, they developed several proposals for increasing enrollment at Stanton. They developed a partnership with the president of the neighborhood association, who provided crucial information about the rapid pace of neighborhood development and growing pool of school-aged children. Vicki's district connections helped them gather school data, and Sue's husband, an architect, drew a blueprint for a possible school expansion. The Coalition also forged a bond with the local Democratic ward leader, who helped guide them through the process of gaining support from elected officials at the city and state levels. The media responded with considerable attention, reporting on public meetings and sometimes highlighting the role of mentors in the effort (Dean 2003; Snyder 2003; Tuleya 2003; Woodall 2003).

For Bainbridge House, this was the beginning of a new kind of presence in the neighborhood. More than just serving as host to the group, Vicki in particular became one of its most active leaders. The house became coalition headquarters, its large picture window plastered with signs on bright construction paper: "Keep Stanton School a School" and "I am a Mentor at Stanton School." The members of Bainbridge House never formally decided to take on this more active, politicized role, but the moment felt right to everyone. Just as Bainbridge House's original conception of the mentoring program had sprung from a long process of "being" in the neighborhood, this new role emerged as a result of nine years of slowly expanding relationships with teachers, students, and parents at the school.

The Coalition was, in many ways, a perfect enactment of Bainbridge House's model of neighborhood presence. They had listened to their neighbors, heard the call to action that Stepheni and Verna Rae had made at the school assembly, and opened their home to serve as host for the months-long political

battle. As Vicki cooked chili for lunch after a cold morning of circulating petitions, or poured us tea when meetings dragged on into the night, her pleasure at
these developments was visible. Stepheni's rapidly expanding leadership of the
Coalition also fit easily into Bainbridge House's vision of its position as "new
neighbors" in this place. Though members of the house did do much of the work
of planning meetings, conducting research, and organizing crowds of supporters
for public events, they were happy to relinquish leadership to an African American woman who, though she now lived a bus ride away, had a long history in the
neighborhood. In fact, I would argue that it was this circumstance, in which
Bainbridge House could serve as support and host to a campaign led by "legitimate" community members, that made it possible for Bainbridge House to move
so easily from presence to action.

The Power and Promise of the Local

By the end of March, after two months of meeting with city and school district
officials, it appeared that the battle was nearly won. At the school district's
budget hearing before the city council, when the coalition made a lengthy presentation appealing for the council's support, district CEO Paul Vallas admitted
that he was reconsidering his recommendation to close Stanton. At that hearing,
the president of the city council, Anna Verna, offered a standing ovation to the
Coalition to Save Stanton School, saying, "In all of my years in the community,
I have never seen the community rally on one issue as they have on the Stanton
School issue." Vallas himself responded enthusiastically to the councilwoman's
support, showering praises on the Coalition for its civility and lack of hostility as
well as the "multiculturalism" and "socioeconomic diversity" of the group.

   From the first announcement of the school's potential closing, members of
Bainbridge House mourned the possibility that their multiple and extended relationships with the school would be lost. At the public meetings when the district
presented its case for closure, officials insisted that the programs in place at
Stanton would move with the students to their new schools nearby. But to
Stanton's partners, these arguments only revealed more clearly that the district,
in Vicki's words, "didn't get it"; they didn't understand that the mentoring program was not just a social service program but an offshoot of Bainbridge
House's rootedness in their small piece of the neighborhood. Once the Coalition
to Save Stanton School formed and began to build power, Vallas glimpsed in the
group not only an unusually diverse local association but also a potential ally in
his attempts to gain the support of a wide range of constituencies throughout the
city. From the start, he attempted to recruit the group's leaders as district employees, a tactic that the Coalition members agreed was a ploy to co-opt them.
Later, Vallas began to consider how, if Stanton remained open, he might use
these leaders and this model to build support for public schools in the rest of

South Philadelphia. At the city council budget hearing, Vallas explained why he was reconsidering the recommendation to close Stanton:

> There are other circumstances to consider. There's also the circumstance of a community coming together. There's something to be said for the community coming together, whatever the catalyst is, whether it's a good catalyst or a bad catalyst. And I need this community not only for Stanton. I need this community to come together for Arthur, for Peirce. I need the community to come together for Audenried. I need this community to come together for *all* the schools in that cluster, because all the schools need this kind of community effort and this outreach and these partnerships. So, there is this factor to consider too, not just for Stanton but for all the schools in the community. (From field notes.)

This coalition, like the mentoring program out of which it grew and Bainbridge House itself, represents a particular kind of "local" activism. The district's faith partnership initiative assumed that proximity of religious institutions and schools implied a shared experience of the local neighborhood; in reality, most church members (and even clergy), teachers, and some students commute to those institutions from very different homes and life circumstances. Similarly, the Coalition to Save Stanton School, which Vallas identified as the "community" for South Philadelphia schools, was both much broader and much narrower than he seemed able to imagine. At public hearings and open meetings on the school closure issue, when supporters of the school packed the Stanton auditorium and the city council chambers, the majority of those participants were not residents of the Stanton area. Many of the vocal activists were neighborhood parents, alumni, staff, and other residents, but many were also mentors and teachers who developed a longstanding commitment to Stanton despite the varied distances they traveled to get there from their homes in other parts of the city and suburbs. In this way, the coalition was much broader than the Stanton neighborhood.

At the same time, this broad-based partnership was extraordinarily local, dependent on long-standing and deep relationships established through Bainbridge House, the mentoring program, and attachments to this particular elementary school. Although some of the most vocal and active members of the coalition were parents who had newly become acquainted with Bainbridge House, the House's theology of presence permeated the group. This was a presence rooted in face-to-face relationships, in walks around the neighborhood and shared meals. This commitment to the local could not easily be either expanded or abandoned in order for the coalition to become advocates for all of South Philadelphia, as Vallas suggested. If, as Vallas hoped, the members of the Coalition were to expand their advocacy efforts to other schools in the South Philadelphia cluster without the relational base that sustained their work thus far, they would be unlikely to be received as legitimate representatives of "the community."

Nonetheless, this model of a "faith partnership" leading to coordinated activism on behalf of schools should not be ignored. It is a testament to the force and potential of Bainbridge House's theology of presence and its members' commitment to guide mentors toward reciprocal relationships with the community. After completing my primary fieldwork, I concluded that Bainbridge House was a faith partnership that supported schools not by bolstering local institutions or empowering parents, but by garnering the human resources of middle class neighborhoods and the suburbs. I critiqued the circumstances under which such faith partnerships operate, in which the volunteer service of the middle class is privileged over the participation of the poor and working class parents in the school their own children attend. But the events of 2003 showed that, at a moment of crisis, those dynamics of inequality within the school could be reconfigured, transformed into a collaborative power-building effort. The mentoring program's broad social network linked the school to citywide power structures and resources, while the program's deep relationships rooted it firmly in a community of accountability. Parents whose children participated in the mentoring program trusted Bainbridge House to host meetings of the Coalition to Save Stanton School. Mentors wrote letters to elected officials and school district administrators with whom they had relationships. Members of Bainbridge House used their longstanding experience in the neighborhood to reach out to community leaders and neighborhood associations. And Bainbridge House itself, through its members' nine-year experience of listening and learning from Stanton School, activated its notion of "presence," stepping into the heart of a political battle that not only prevented Stanton's closure but invigorated the community to ensure its long-term success.

Notes

I am most grateful to the members of Bainbridge House and the Stanton School community, who welcomed me to morning prayer and the mentoring program. They also provided valuable feedback on the written work. I am particularly grateful to members Vicki Ellis, Sue Kettell, Joe Bradley, and Pat Hogan for their friendship and their thoughtful reflections on Bainbridge House, mentoring, and the Coalition to Save Stanton School. Thanks to the many mentors, teachers, and parents who granted interviews and talked with me in the halls. I deeply respect the important work that they do.

This chapter has benefited from the comments of many close readers. I am particularly grateful for the comments of Maia Cucchiara on this chapter and for the comments of Sasha Welland and Shiho Satsuka on the dissertation from which this chapter was drawn. Thanks also go to Sukey Blanc, Jolley Christman, and Eva Gold for their input on ideas presented here, and to Susan Harding, Dan Linger, Don Brenneis, and Mary Beth Pudup for their guidance in conducting this research.

This research was supported by a Graduate Student Research Fellowship from the National Science Foundation and a dissertation fellowship from the Indiana University Center on Philanthropy.

1. Marc Freedman traces the contemporary ideology of mentoring to the 1983 annual report of the Commonwealth Fund, in which the Fund's president "argues that young people have lost 'natural proximity to caring, maturing adults,' leaving their 'basic need for constructive guidance' unfulfilled" (Freedman 1993, 3; Mahoney 1983, 4).

2. For an overview of the education literature discussing the dangers of deficit thinking among teachers and policy-makers, see Valencia (1997).

3. J. Clyde Mitchell, an originator of network theory, describes this activated network as an action-set: "An action-set may be looked upon as an aspect of a personal network isolated in terms of a specific short-term instrumentally-defined interactional content: the personal network itself is more extensive and more durable" (Mitchell 1969, 40).

Works Cited

Basso, Keith H. 1996. *Wisdom sits in places: Landscape and language among the Western Apache.* Albuquerque: University of New Mexico Press.

Bourdieu, Pierre. 1986. The forms of capital. In *Handbook of theory and research for the sociology of education,* ed. John G. Richardson, 241-58. New York: Greenwood Press.

Clifford, James. 1988. *The predicament of culture: Twentieth-century ethnography, literature, and art.* Cambridge, MA: Harvard University Press.

Coleman, James. 1990. *Foundations of social theory.* Cambridge, MA: Harvard University Press.

Dean, Mensah M. 2002. Building bonanza is set. *Philadelphia Daily News,* December 20.

————. 2003. Supporters: Why close Stanton? *Philadelphia Daily News,* January 14.

Epstein, A. L. 1969. The network and urban social organisation. In *Social networks in urban situations: Analyses of personal relationships in Central African towns,* ed. J. Clyde Mitchell, 77-116. Manchester, U.K.: University of Manchester Press.

Foley, Michael W., Bob Edwards, and Mario Diani. 2001. Social capital reconsidered. In *Beyond Tocqueville: Civil society and the social capital debate in comparative perspective,* ed. Bob Edwards, Michael W. Foley, and Mario Diani, 266-80. Hanover, NH: Tufts University Press.

Freedman, Marc. 1993. *The kindness of strangers: Adult mentors, urban youth, and the new voluntarism.* Cambridge: Cambridge University Press.

Herrera, Carla. 1999. *School based mentoring: A first look into its potential.* Philadelphia: Public/Private Ventures.

Hyatt, Susan Brin. 2001. From citizen to volunteer: Neoliberal governance and the erasure of poverty. In *The new poverty studies: The ethnography of power, politics, and impoverished people in the United States,* ed. Judith Goode and Jeff Maskovsky, 201-35. New York: New York University Press.

Johnson, Amy W. 1998. *An evaluation of the long-term impacts of the Sponsor-a-Scholar program on student performance: Final report to the Commonwealth Fund.* Princeton, NJ: Mathematica Policy Research.

Jucovy, Linda. 2002. *Same-race and cross-race matching.* Portland, OR: Northwest Regional Educational Laboratory.

Mahoney, Margaret. 1983. *Annual report.* New York: Commonwealth Fund.

Mitchell, J. Clyde. 1969. The concept and use of social networks. In *Social networks in urban situations: Analyses of personal relationships in Central African towns,* ed. J. Clyde Mitchell, 1-50. Manchester, U.K.: University of Manchester Press.

Momaday, N. Scott. 1976. *The names.* Tucson: University of Arizona Press.

Snyder, Susan. 2003. 100 rally to save Philadelphia school. *Philadelphia Inquirer,* January 14.

Tierney, Joseph P., and Jean B. Grossman. 1995. *Making a difference: An impact study of Big Brothers/Big Sisters.* Philadelphia: Public/Private Ventures.

Tuleya, R. Jonathan. 2003. A lesson in survival. *South Philly Review,* April 24.

Valencia, Richard R. 1997. *The evolution of deficit thinking: Educational thought and practice.* Stanford Series on Education and Public Policy. Washington, DC: Falmer Press.

Wilson, William Julius. 1987. *The truly disadvantaged: The inner city, the underclass, and public policy.* Chicago: University of Chicago Press.

Woodall, Martha. 2003. Supporters continue quest to save Stanton Elementary. *Philadelphia Inquirer*, March 25.

Chapter 3
On the Border: Faith-Based Initiatives and Pentecostal Praxis in Brownsville, Texas
Ethan P. Sharp

In recent years, a short walk away from one of the main bridges that connects Mexico with the United States, in the troubled yet historic Buena Vida neighborhood of Brownsville, Texas, a group of mothers and grandmothers has gathered weekly to participate in a quilting club in the Good Neighbor Settlement House. Established in 1953, the settlement house has grown into a small compound of simple concrete block buildings, some of which bear inspirational murals on their outside walls. In addition to providing a meeting place for the club, Good Neighbor gives out food, clothing, and other types of assistance to thousands of people each year. As the women stitch their quilts, they often listen to someone read passages from the Bible, and sing songs like "Un día a la vez" and "Cristo vive." Good Neighbor long ago evolved into a nonsectarian service agency which has counted on grants from the city and federal governments, yet the songs of the quilting club have reminded people who pass through the settlement house that it originated as a ministry of the Methodist church and continues to provide spaces where people can express their faith.

Across the street from Good Neighbor, adolescent girls have met on Tuesday evenings for another kind of club in a small classroom behind the red brick, two-story church building where La Iglesia del Pueblo Pentecostal, a Pentecostal congregation of Mexican immigrants and Mexican Americans, meets. On Tuesday evenings, the grounds of the church are often peaceful compared with Sunday mornings, when dozens of cars can be found parked along the street and well dressed families gather in the sanctuary to sing along with a skilled praise and worship band and to listen to energetic sermons. In their meetings, the girls—including a few from a nearby housing project—have listened to a series of lessons in a mix of Spanish and English by the young mothers who lead the club. Topics in the series have included "Personal Appearance," "Managing Stress," and "Friendship." Even though the congregation continues to believe

51

that its fundamental purpose is to offer a path to salvation by faithfully communicating the gospel, the girls' club is evidence that the congregation has been engaged in providing services that can reinforce programs offered by schools and other civic institutions.

By revisiting the quilting club and the girls' club, this chapter offers insights into the separations and the cyclical interplay of spiritual and mundane pursuits in Brownsville. Although the clubs involve relatively small numbers of people, they have been highly prized within their respective organizations, revealing important aspects of each. The quilting club is a testament to the deepest aspirations of the settlement house, a project that at its origins combined Christianization, Americanization, and support for women in their domestic roles.[1] The girls' club, based on a curriculum developed by professional educators in the national offices of the Assemblies of God, offers assurance that the congregation has been pursuing direct and measured responses to the cultural challenges that most affect its members, especially changes in gender orders. Furthermore, a comparison of the clubs suggests why Good Neighbor has recently faced severe cuts in its city and federal support even while the church has for the first time received invitations from civic activists to expand its services to the neighborhood and to apply for small sub-awards from federal grants. Apparently, the relationship between faith and civic life in the settlement house has become outmoded, whereas the spiritual fortification offered by the church is ideally suited to current political-economic conditions.

Maintaining the sense of paradox that marks the divergent development of Good Neighbor and La Iglesia del Pueblo Pentecostal, this chapter turns to an assessment of the origins, nature, and outcome of the partnerships that the church has pursued with civic activists in conjunction with initiatives by the federal government to engage congregations within distressed neighborhoods in civic projects. I use the term *faith-based initiatives* to refer to this set of initiatives at the federal level, although I recognize that the term has taken on a broader set of referents. My assessment offers critical perspectives on federal policymaking regarding churches and faith-based organizations, the prospects for civic renewal in the South Texas borderlands, and the capacity of small Pentecostal churches to play a role in such a renewal. First, the chapter reviews the public discourse that has generated and guided faith-based initiatives in the 1990s and 2000s. Then, by drawing on periodic observations and interviews that I have conducted in and around the church since 2005, I illuminate the possibilities and challenges of adapting these initiatives to Brownsville. Last, the chapter addresses how the leaders of La Iglesia del Pueblo Pentecostal have responded to and reshaped the discourse of faith-based initiatives, and points out the ways in which the congregation has come to share the spatial sensibilities of policymakers and civic activists and incorporated these sensibilities into their religious praxis. In conclusion, I reassess the relationship between the consolidation of neoliberal regimes and evangelical faiths, and suggest that many of the faith-based initiatives that originated in the 2000s have been caught in a web of contradictions that complicates their ability to fulfill a civic mission while gradually rendering them obsolete.

Many studies of faith-based initiatives have tended to focus on arguments about the degree to which they are or can be effective for meeting specific goals in the civic realm (see, for example, Cnaan 1999). These studies have largely adopted the confusing terms used in public discourse, and have taken for granted the ability of congregations to attain fluency in the use of these terms. This taken-for-grantedness is rooted in constitutional language and practices in the United States, cultural forms that require further anthropological analysis (cf. Urban 2008).[2] The analyses that I pursue in this chapter are intended to open a space for postcolonial and poststructural critiques of faith-based initiatives by exploring the circulations and disjunctions of discourse that give meaning to faith and secularism. A point of departure for these critiques is that "faith-based"ness is an exotic construction that privileges the perspectives of academic and political elites in the United States, who have attempted to reestablish distinctions between faith and civic life and to regulate movements between these spheres of action. The concept attained popular appeal through the discourse of federal policymakers at a specific historical moment, a fact that suggests it was at first a political tool for inviting certain kinds of congregations and church leaders, especially evangelical Protestants, to exercise influence in and receive benefits from the federal government.[3]

The Transvaluation of Faith

For more than four centuries, Protestants in the Americas have formed and re-formed congregations that correspond to their varying interpretations of Christian faith, creating and maintaining spaces for spiritual pursuits that are separate from larger social fields. As they have drawn lines of division between their church bodies and the societies around them, however, many congregants have also sought to exercise their faith in settings outside of their houses of worship, and have contributed to and re-established a "secular civil society" by promoting health, literacy, morality, and productive citizenship (Hall 2005, 57). In this way, the involvement of congregations in secular projects—while a vital source of civic renewal in the United States—has been an ambivalent process. It has involved first establishing the boundaries that distinguish them from other groups of people and then traversing these boundaries. As a result, it has generated ongoing gradual shifts in the missions and meanings that hold church bodies together. Faith-based initiatives have become the most recent and notable iterations of this process. Such initiatives have effectively drawn into the secular realm some churches that had once remained largely opposed to secular entanglements.

In the 1990s, politicians first began to reach a consensus that the government should pursue partnerships with congregations in distressed neighborhoods. In 1996 Henry Cisneros, the Secretary of Housing and Urban Development during President Bill Clinton's first term and a former mayor of San Antonio, Texas, provided a basis for this consensus by publishing a widely referenced essay in which he argued that congregations could play a critical role in restoring a sense of community in the inner city. He explained that the potential of congregations, or "faith communities," to exercise such a role was tied to four key aspects of their institutional life: congregations remained rooted in urban districts, built community through acts of charity, offered unique resources such as pools of ready volunteers, and touched "the soul" by nurturing people at all stages of life and offering them a moral structure (Cisneros 1996; see also Farnsley 2003, 2-11). Three years later, George W. Bush, then governor of Texas, reaffirmed the ability of churches to be partners of the government in a speech that helped to set in motion his presidential campaign. In that speech, he noted, "I visit churches and charities serving their neighbors nearly everywhere I go in this country . . . Wherever we can, we must expand their role and reach, without changing them or corrupting them. It is the next, bold step of welfare reform."[4] Some social scientists helped to formulate and to promote the proposals that politicians like Cisneros and Bush offered. They documented, for example, the deterioration of "mediating institutions" and "social capital" in the United States, and suggested that churches and related organizations could counteract such losses (Farnsley 2007).

In 2001, after assuming the presidency, Bush established the Office of Faith-Based and Community Initiatives (OFBCI) within the White House and appointed John DiIulio, a prominent political scientist, to act as its first director. DiIulio determined that the OFBCI was poised to increase access to federal funding for "community-serving religious nonprofit organizations" (DiIulio 2007, 20). According to him, the organizations that would be and should remain a priority were small missions that fulfilled a "civic purpose" in urban districts, and had previously been unable to compete with prominent secular and religious nonprofits for grants (DiIulio 2007, 228-30). Although the OFBCI faced challenges in its attempts to alter the distribution of federal resources in favor of such organizations, it accomplished some of the changes that it sought.[5] In 2002 it helped to establish the Compassion Capital Fund in the Department of Health and Human Services. The fund was intended for collaborations among government agencies, nonprofits, and small religious organizations that could enhance the capacity of the religious organizations to provide services to their communities.

The OFBCI and the accomplishments that became associated with it constitute the most significant series of innovations in social advocacy and policy at the federal level in the 2000s, and will likely endure.[6] One close observer claims that the ongoing commitment to faith-based initiatives at the federal level could fuel the rise of a Christian democracy like those that prevailed in some European countries, which allowed churches to assume important social responsibilities in conjunction with the welfare state (Daly 2009, 180). Nevertheless, it must be noted that the OFBCI emerged amid diminishing opportunities for the federal government to reinforce and to expand social programs because of the ascendancy of neoliberalism. Furthermore, the connections between the interest in congregations that prominent politicians promoted in the 1990s and the changes that the OFBCI helped to generate in the 2000s have not been at all clear. For example, DiIulio's effort to identify the faith-based organizations that most deserve the support of the government obscures whether or not congregations always qualify, and, if not, what kinds of congregations must be excluded.[7]

The social scientists who contributed to the implementation of faith-based initiatives, by virtue of their success, stimulated debate and increasing numbers of studies about faith-based organizations. Some studies, like those that appear in this book, have employed ethnographic methods in ways that have yielded insights into the diversity of faith-based organizations that originated before the era of the OFBCI and the negative effects that the promotion of faith-based initiatives at the federal level had on these organizations (see, for example, Adkins and Kemper 2006; Goode 2006). These studies have confirmed, for example, that support for faith-based initiatives has participated in the ongoing erosion of the social citizenship of the poor (Morgen and Maskovsky 2003), but there remains a need for a more thorough analysis of the rationale that has insisted on the capacity of congregations to bring their faith to bear on civic projects.[8] In order to frame such an analysis, I contend that the construction of faith-based initiatives by policymakers in the 1990s and 2000s has been similar to the production of cultural heritage, which, according to folklorist Barbara Kirshenblatt-Gimblett, involves a "collaborative hallucination in an equivocal relationship with actualities" (Kirshenblatt-Gimblett 1998, 167). In this sense, faith-based initiatives have relied on the objectification of faith, by which an evangelical faith can be detached from the strict spatial oppositions in which it was first formulated, removed to a more complex and heterogeneous civic sphere than it was originally intended for, and ascribed a neutral value for civic purposes. Borrowing a term from Kirshenblatt-Gimblett, I call this process the transvaluation of faith. Congregations that participate in such a process run the risk of diminishing the strength of the spiritual supports that they can offer in exclusivist gatherings, one of the reasons they first attracted the attention of politicians and some social scientists.

Encounters on the Border

In the 1840s, Brownsville became the southernmost outpost of the United States on the Rio Grande, and, unlike many U.S. cities where Protestantism played an important role in the formation of urban civil society, Protestant congregations have held a precarious position amid Brownsville's civic structures. Protestant institutions were virtually absent in the city until the early twentieth century, when Methodists, Baptists, and other Protestants began to open competing churches for the influx of people who moved from other states to participate in the agricultural boom in the surrounding region.[9] These Protestants attained some influence in the city, but their influence weakened considerably in the 1950s as their churches began to lose members. Since the 1950s, Pentecostal and evangelical congregations in Brownsville have grown and multiplied, but Protestants of Mexican descent have continued to wrestle with racism in national denominational structures, as well as isolation from the larger numbers of Mexican and Mexican American Catholics (see Vila 2005, chapter 2). Catholicism has effectively retained its dominance among most of the city's inhabitants and has become one of the most important forces in the civil society of south Texas. Some important activist and social service organizations formed in Brownsville as a result of Catholic engagements in struggles for social justice in the 1970s and 1980s, including Valley Interfaith and the Ozanam Center, but the city has not afforded any models for the formation of faith-based initiatives of the kind that could find favor in the Bush administration.

In the latter half of the twentieth century, Brownsville evolved into a jumble of barriers and crossings that has sustained stark disparities between the United States and Mexico.[10] The promise of better-paying jobs and other benefits not available in Mexico has drawn increasing numbers of Mexican immigrants to and through Brownsville, resulting in population and economic growth for the city. By 2006, the city's inhabitants surpassed 170,000 (McKenzie 2007). In comparison with other U.S. cities, however, Brownsville and nearby settlements have remained less connected with major industrial and financial centers in the United States and more reliant on flows of capital and people from Mexico. As a result, jobs in the city and surrounding region are harder to find and pay less than the jobs that immigrants can find elsewhere in the United States. According to the Census Bureau, the county where Brownsville is located has one of the lowest median incomes, the highest rates of poverty, and the highest percentage of people who did not complete high school of all U.S. counties with a population of more than 250,000 (Hirschberg 2004).

In the context of the city's striking growth and impoverishment, some activists have sought opportunities to cultivate civic projects that might receive support from the federal government, including the possibility of forming faith-based initiatives. Inevitably, they have faced challenges in adapting the logic of federal programs to Brownsville. One of the most important projects, spear-headed by a university in south Texas, focused on the Buena Vida neighbor-hood. In 2003, a study of the neighborhood—situated between the downtown district and an interstate highway that leads to expanding residential and com-mercial zones on the north side of the city—concluded that the neighborhood was the most "disadvantaged" urban district in the most "distressed" region in the United States (Arispe y Acevedo, Rodríguez, and de los Reyes 2003, viii). It noted, for example, that the neighborhood had a median household income that ranked below the median household income in Matamoros, Mexico, a more populous city than Brownsville, on the opposite side of the Rio Grande. The statistics proved useful for a variety of purposes, although the study of Buena Vida makes clear that one of the reasons for the astonishing statistics is that many people in the neighborhood are temporary residents. Many, for example, moved into the neighborhood after arriving in Brownsville from Mexico, and will move to other areas of the city once they have found opportunities to do so. In 2004, the university's office of civic engagement applied for a grant from the Compassion Capital Fund to address poverty in Buena Vida. The application proposed a variety of efforts to improve the quality of life in the neighborhood, including the provision of sub-awards to some of the city's churches in order to enhance their capacity to provide social services and to help residents to find employment.

After receiving the grant, the university's office of civic engagement hired a small staff to administer the grant and to initiate contact with churches with which the office could collaborate. One member of the staff explained that she sought to "reach out to" and to "grow" faith-based organizations, while keeping in mind federal prohibitions again funding "inherently religious activities." The staff was initially more interested in La Iglesia del Pueblo than any other church in Brownsville because it was centrally located in the Buena Vida neighborhood, had a sizeable congregation, occupied a respectable building, and had more fi-nancial resources than any other church in the neighborhood, which it had dem-onstrated by buying surrounding plots of land to expand its parking area. One day, two members of the staff walked through Buena Vida—a mix of rundown houses and businesses, whose major landmarks include the county jail—and made their way to La Iglesia del Pueblo Pentecostal. They went up the broad staircase in front of the church and found the door of a small office, beside the main entrance to the sanctuary. They knocked at the door, and the pastor, José Becerra, answered. The representatives of the university introduced themselves, provided information about Buena Vida and the grant, and invited the congrega-tion to apply for a sub-award.

Like most members of his congregation, Pastor Becerra does not reside in the Buena Vida neighborhood—a complication that often confronts efforts to engage congregations in the provision of services to the neighborhood where they meet, as sociologist Omar McRoberts (2005) has noted—and he interpreted the visit by the university's representatives by recalling a tale, or parable, that has become foundational for him. According to the tale, the members of a church were assembled for one of their regular meetings when they heard an angry crowd gathering outside of their building. The crowd shouted ominously, "¡Fuera iglesia! Get out church!" The congregants feared that they were under siege and that the crowd intended to shut down the church, but once they ventured outside they found that their fears had been misplaced. In fact, the crowd was demanding that the congregants get out of the building so they could provide help and bring the message of salvation to the desperate people in the streets and homes around the church. For Pastor Becerra, the tale points to a spiritual problem that should trouble the conscience of many believers: Some congregations have become so engaged in their routines and so estranged from the world that they often fail to appreciate the needs of people beyond their fold.

In a conversation with me, Pastor Becerra—who grew up and pursued a modest political career in Matamoros before resettling in Brownsville in the 1980s—explained that the appeal from the university's representatives resonated with the cries of the angry crowd in the parable. He recognized that involvement in the project would lead members of the church into unfamiliar spaces and pursuits, but refusal was not an option. He explained,

> I see it from God. One day they knocked on the door. I didn't go to the office. I didn't go to the university. They knocked on this door . . . For a minute there was uncertainty. My daughter said, "Maybe they're going to evaluate us." I said, "Look they already helped us. They opened our eyes to the great needs here." I even said, "With or without the funds, we are going to do this work. We have to do this work as a church, as a believer." The best thing that this people could desire is that you don't shut yourself in.

For him, the invitation to join the project had occurred at God's direction, and it promised to redress the isolation and inattentiveness that had hampered the congregation's growth.

In the years that followed, the church solicited and received small sub-awards from the grant, which it used to purchase materials for two programs that served a handful of residents in the Buena Vida neighborhood.[11] The congregation was one of many organizations that offered programs with the support of sub-awards, and while its programs played only minor roles in the university's larger initiative, its involvement was deeply meaningful. For the university, it represented an effort to strengthen mediating institutions in the heart of the Buena Vida neighborhood, and for the congregation, it was an affirmation of their spiritual aspirations and a point of entry into other partnerships with professedly secular nonprofits and government agencies. Nevertheless, as Pastor Becerra indicates, a certain degree of unease attended the congregation's transition into a realm where its spiritual interests could converge with the narrower campaigns of civic activists and social service providers. I contend that this unease points to the ambivalence, as well as the nimbleness, with which it probed the meanings and purposes of community service.

Ambivalent Engagements in Community Service

Pentecostalism, which has become increasingly interconnected with evangelicalism in recent years, originated with revivals in the first decade of the twentieth century and quickly achieved a presence throughout the Americas and around the globe. Many Pentecostals maintained elements of the holiness movements, such as the pursuit of personal sanctification, while promoting emotional and enthusiastic forms of worship and the exercise of charisms through the Holy Spirit. To many observers, their practices seemed to insist upon strict separation between spiritual and mundane pursuits (Robbins 2004, 126), but closer examination reveals that distinctions between the two pursuits, while allowing Pentecostals to position themselves within larger fields of human action, are not always clear or easy to maintain. Indeed, one of the most important features of Pentecostal churches is their ability to pursue an exclusivist faith while remaining flexibly engaged with the world.[12] According to anthropologist Joel Robbins, this flexibility is often readily apparent in the content and forms of discourse that Pentecostals employ. He notes that Pentecostalism "avails itself of locally meaningful idioms for talking about the past and about current social problems" (Robbins 2004, 129). His observation is helpful for charting the relationship of Pentecostalism to secularism in the United States, suggesting that Pentecostal praxis can adapt to and adopt secular initiatives even while maintaining antagonistic relationships with them.

In conversations with the leaders of La Iglesia del Pueblo Pentecostal and observations of its church services, I found many examples of the flexibility of Pentecostal praxis, which, in my view, has rested upon "habitando en la Palabra," or "inhabiting the Word," the realm of intertextual practices that insists upon a thorough appreciation of the Bible and its applicability in one's life. Pastor Becerra explained to me that the emphasis on studying the Word and assimilating its truth has been the aspect of his congregation that has distinguished it from churches of other denominations.[13] He was able to receive the invitation to collaborate with the university—and effectively participated in the transvaluation of faith—because the invitation coincided with the action of the Word in his life. He recalled that after the awkward yet momentous meeting on the threshold of his office, he testified about it in a gathering with other pastors of churches in south Texas, turning the university's initiative into the source and means for an evangelical awakening. He noted,

> I asked them to pray for us because we are in a time when God is showing his interest but in a very, very strong way that in a community, thanks to the university, we are waking up to the enormous needs that there are here. I said something that a fellow told me, I think it was last year or the year before last,

one of those years, there was a total of thirty-two reported rapes in Brownsville, in this neighborhood twenty-nine of those occurred. . . . This is so that you can say, "Wow, what am I doing? What am I doing? How are we affecting a community so lost?"

Through his testimony, Pastor Becerra confirmed that civic activists had been able to exert pressure on his faith, so he could find within it the inspiration to participate in the provision of social services; but even as he admitted to the principle of faith-based initiatives, he turned it on its head. He pointed out that faith-based initiatives have served to refocus the spiritual pursuits of the church, by bringing information and resources to the church that can illuminate and reinforce its beliefs. To this end, he incorporated into his call to evangelism a statistic that reveals the vulnerability of women in the neighborhood and an attempt to redefine the Buena Vida neighborhood as a community that can be saved and reconstituted.

Before La Iglesia del Pueblo Pentecostal began to solicit sub-awards for programs that could address the needs of the neighborhood, the pastor's daughter attended meetings and workshops organized by the university, where she learned how to strengthen a nonprofit organization and became more familiar with the formation of faith-based initiatives. The workshops also introduced her to the technical language of grant applications and administration, and she began to consider whether and how their practices could be rendered in this language. The pastor's daughter once suggested to me that the emphasis on "pre- and post-tests" and "measurements," for example, was almost too foreign to be useful to the church, but the growing sense that the church was a community within a community—a sentiment endorsed in public discourse about faith-based initiatives—proved compelling. Working with other members of the pastoral team, she reformulated a mission for the church that attempted to reestablish the relationship of their faith to the wider community, and the potential for this relationship to effect change. In a conversation with me, one of the church leaders offered a concise summary of this mission by noting, "Our job as a church is to serve the community." She explained that the application for sub-awards was consistent with this mission because the sub-awards "are for the benefit of the community."[14]

The congregation's first application for sub-awards yielded support for a formal, although short-lived, outreach program to alcoholics and addicts to illicit drugs. The application explained that the church had already rescued many people from alcoholism and addiction through its usual evangelistic services, and noted that these people, as a result, "have the pleasure of having a beautiful family, are completely healthy and are actively serving the community." According to Pastor Becerra, the elements of the outreach program began to emerge a few months before his meeting with the university's representatives, after a young addict showed up at the church's doorstep and was converted. This young man, working with other church members, invited his friends, who were in the same situation as he had been, to a meeting at the church where they received a meal and listened to his testimony. A sub-award allowed the congregation to continue with this program on a weekly basis for a few months.

The second successful application for sub-awards was concerned with the girls' club, a better established and multi-faceted program. Since its first encounter with civic activists, the pastoral team insisted that the girls' club should be the logical focus of civic interest because of the curriculum that the girls' club employed and the fact that the club included a few members who lived in the Buena Vida neighborhood.[15] Presumably, the club also responded to the church's understanding of the nature of the problems that afflicted the neighborhood—problems that were tied to the reconstitution of gender orders in the era of neoliberal governance, by which women faced the loss of social supports and became more involved in the labor market, especially the informal market, while simultaneously finding themselves in situations where their domestic responsibilities were greater than they had been for previous generations (Bakker 2003). According to the church's application, the club addressed the challenges that the girls faced by gaining their trust "through love and acceptance," helping them with their "spiritual and intellectual development," and providing them with "motivation, support and responsibility through healthy and stable relationships." Conversation with church leaders revealed that the main focus of the club's program has been building self-esteem. The woman who leads the club, for instance, explained that her measure of success is "if the participants understand their real worth as persons" and their "self-esteem is improving." By engaging the girls in a variety of exercises and lessons, the club has helped the girls to "construct a self to act upon and govern" (Cruikshank 1993, 330), but in contrast to programs in secular realms, it has done so largely by reestablishing and strengthening their Pentecostal faith. In this regard, it has relied upon the action of the Word.[16]

One of the club's sessions that I observed in 2005 was dedicated to the question "How can I guard my attitude?" The session was one in a series that sought to help the girls to develop a positive attitude and to maintain it; in this way it exemplified how the congregation adopted the neoliberal technologies of self-governance associated with building self-esteem. By teaching the girls to guard their attitude—by developing timelines that track changes in their attitude, for example—the session engaged them in the kind of subjective work that is consistent with self-governance, but it also made clear that successfully guarding their attitude depended on reinforcing their faith. One of the principal references for the session was Hebrews 4:12: "For the Word of God is living and active . . . it judges the thoughts and attitudes of the heart." The club's leader explained that girls should resist "selfish, sinful desires," and, on the verge of tears, she appealed to them, "As Christians, we should be different from the rest . . . We should not be anxious." She adds, "People are getting involved in drugs, girls getting pregnant, there is prostitution, homosexuality, suicide. Why do these things happen? They don't have the peace of God in their hearts . . . You have no excuse, no excuse to turn to those things. God speaks to you, and cares for you. You already know him, and you need to reach out to those who need help, who need the peace of God." In effect, the club's leader revealed one of the principal ways in which the church community sought to reach and connect to the community beyond the church: by employing the Word to create the conditions for the transmission of a fortified and fortifying faith. [17]

On this point—where Pentecostals have attempted to serve the community by building self-esteem (along with faith)—I reconsider the mutual constitution of neoliberal governance and evangelical transformations (Sharp 2009). To begin with, I find that the congregation in Brownsville has fully endorsed neoliberal and market-oriented technologies of governance, especially as they are related to gender orders, yet it has insisted that such technologies remain subject to the spiritual relationships and processes in which church members have traditionally been engaged. As a consequence, neoliberal regimes have not always found strong reinforcement amid the spiritual pursuits of evangelical communities, especially Pentecostal congregations of Latinas/os, which are often just as easily led away from civic engagement as they are led into it. My conclusions resonate with observations made by other scholars of Pentecostalism, who have noted, for example, that Pentecostal Latinas/os have more experience with a range of social problems that have commanded public attention than many other church communities, and have been more inclined to engage in types of informal mutual aid and formal social ministries (Ramírez 1999; Sánchez Walsh 2003; Ríos 2005). At the same time, Pentecostal Latinas/os have attempted to maintain a critical distance from the problems around them and the regimes that have helped to generate the problems, by relying on the "praxis of refuge" (Ramírez 1999, 591).

The Future of Faith-Based Initiatives in Brownsville

By 2009, members of La Iglesia del Pueblo continued to believe that their involvement in civic partnerships had strengthened the congregation. In the intervening years, the church had added several members. At one of the services that I attended, the church secretary joyfully announced that attendance on that day had been 201, suggesting that it had crossed an important threshold in its growth. In conversations with me, Pastor Becerra observed that there had not been a tremendous growth in membership, but the congregation had, in fact, experienced a "growth in transformation" since it had developed its programs in conjunction with the university's initiative. According to him, the congregation had "opened its eyes" and reached a state of "spiritual maturity." After their involvement in the university's initiative concluded, the church pursued other opportunities to expand the range of services that it could provide, and members of the pastoral team became involved in another type of federal grant project focused on strengthening marriages. The project, coordinated by a private counseling center based in the Dallas metropolitan area, trained the team to provide counseling sessions to couples planning to get married. Couples who completed the session could receive a significant reduction in the cost of their marriage license in the county.

On the other side of the street, the Good Neighbor Settlement House also continued to attract increasing numbers of people. Although it had suffered a loss of funding, especially because it could no longer use the grants that it received from the Department of Housing and Urban Development to cover its major expenses, one of Good Neighbor's administrative assistants explained that they had been able to continue providing services because of private donations and the profits that they made from the store where they sell secondhand clothes and other items. Happily, she noted that the settlement house had also received funds from the stimulus package that Congress had authorized earlier in the year, although these funds were subject to the same limitations as the grants from the Department of Housing and Urban Development. I asked her if she knew that La Iglesia del Pueblo Pentecostal had recently received small federal grants, while the settlement house struggled with a change in its funding scheme, and she nodded, noting that faith-based organizations were allowed "more flexibility." She stopped, and then attempted to clarify, "Well, we are also a faith-based organization, but we're more of a service agency, really." In that moment, in which she attempted to determine how the settlement house fit within the current political and cultural configurations, she opened the possibility for more conversations. The challenge for social scientists, especially cultural anthropologists, is to engage in these conversations in ways that can not only influence the formation of policy but also formulate critiques of the basic terms that make the conversations possible.

64 Ethan P. Sharp

Notes

1. One of the means by which Protestants engaged the civic realm in the early twentieth century was the formation of settlement houses. Methodist churches in the southwestern United States built settlement houses in order to reach and instruct people of Mexican descent (Ruiz 2006, 347).

2. Anthropologist Talal Asad's critique of the categories of religion and secularism provide a strong basis for this kind of analysis (cf. Brittain 2005).

3. For this reason, nonprofit organizations that originated many decades ago through a very clear commitment of faith, including Catholic charitable organizations that have long received public funds to carry out their work (cf. Mapes 2004), did not begin to describe themselves as faith-based organizations until recently.

4. This speech was delivered in Indianapolis on July 22, 1999. A text is available at: http://www.cpjustice.org/stories/storyreader$383, last accessed January 20, 2010.

5. Political scientist Michael Leo Owens notes, for example, that there was "significant growth between 2003 and 2005 in overall federal discretionary allocations to faith-based organizations," yet continued growth was not guaranteed (Owens 2007, 60).

6. Since succeeding Bush, President Barack Obama has kept the OFBCI open, although the name of the office has changed, and has continued to endorse the notion that government can and should pursue partnerships with faith-based organizations (Johnson 2009).

7. Leading social scientists, who helped to open debate about faith-based initiatives and to generate more studies of them, have only recently begun to address the confusion in the terms that they have used. They have attempted to define, for example, what are *congregations* and what are *social services* (see McGrew and Cnaan 2006).

8. Some ethnographers working outside of the United States have reinforced the arguments offered by politicians and prominent social scientists. For example, having documented the growth of Pentecostal churches in Africa, together with the increasing marginalization of poor communities in the region, anthropologist James Pfeiffer argues for a broader recognition of the importance of Pentecostal churches for civil society and suggests that scholars should look for possibilities for collaboration with them, "given their ongoing sustainable activities around mutual aid, health education, and community support" (Pfeiffer 2004, 369).

9. The subjugation of people of Mexican descent in the region also became more severe during this period (see Paredes 1970).

10. For an ethnographic reflection on the barriers and crossings that make up the border, see Heyman (2008). With only a few exceptions, the gap in wealth between the United States and Mexico is much greater than the gap that can be found between two other neighboring nations on any continent. Economists James Peach and Richard Adkisson report, for example, that in 2000 the median household income in the United States was about $42,000, and the median household income in Mexico approached $5,000 (Peach and Adkisson 2002, 428).

11. The only other congregation to receive a sub-award in 2005 was a suburban, multi-ethnic congregation with well over 1,000 members. In its application, it proposed in a colonialist fashion to help clean up the neighborhood by "building relationships through faithfully communicating with families in the area," and to demonstrate to residents that "we love them and are there to serve them."

12. Sociologist Omar McRoberts (1999) describes Pentecostal churches in the inner cities of the United States as highly committed communities, organized against a range of potential adversaries, which pursue points of contact with people and forces beyond the world in flexible ways. Taking a broader view of Pentecostalism, anthropologist Joel Robbins (2004) notes that Pentecostal practice and discourse interact directly with indigenous religions in many sites around the world, often accepting indigenous spiritual entities as real beings that must be suppressed.

13. In my first conversation with the pastor, he gave a lengthy description of his faith which made clear his opposition to Catholicism, humanism, and materialism. He offered criticism of capitalism, the United States, and its imperialism, and ended by clearly distinguishing himself from the rest of society. He welcomed the collaboration with the university, saying that "our purposes coincide," but made clear that the government's aim is to keep people happy by "giving them a goodie," and his aim is to get to Heaven.

14. In their first application for a sub-award, they explained, "Since our beginning as an organization of faith, our desire and prayer has been that this community and this neighborhood where we find ourselves can be witnesses to and participants in great results and changes for good that can happen when a community of faith puts faith in the hearts of others and when society receives it." This explanation provided a direction for the congregation in terms that were widely acceptable, while endeavoring to assert the distinctive power of their Pentecostal faith.

15. Professional educators employed by the national office of the Assemblies of God have prepared the curriculum for the girls' club in ways that respond to initiatives outside of the church, including not just faith-based initiatives, but also the more general movement to promote self-esteem and responsible citizenship. The curriculum, for example, is a flexible plan that churches can adapt to their needs, even choosing one that limits references to God and the Bible for use in "after school" programs. The professionalization and versatility of the programs suggest that the interplay of faith and civic engagement within the Assemblies of God has reached a point at which they have developed glosses for evangelistic principles.

16. Sociologist David Smilde notes that Latin American Pentecostals understand social problems as the result of the "wrong relations between humans and the supernatural" (Smilde 1998, 298). The girls' club reveals ways in which Pentecostal praxis has relied upon supernatural agency to resolve social problems.

17. In 2005, one of my students conducted observations of the meetings of the girls' club, as well as observations of a boys' club that took place in the church on the same night. She noted that the boys' club was more focused on fun and practical activities, while the girls' club was more concerned with talking to them and addressing challenges to their self-esteem.

66   Ethan P. Sharp

Works Cited

Adkins, Julie, and Robert V. Kemper. 2006. Oasis Housing Corporation: From solutions to dissolution in a faith-based organization. *Urban Anthropology* 35(2-3):237-61.

Arispe y Acevedo, Baltazar, Ignacio Rodríguez, and Oralia de los Reyes. 2003. *The Buena Vida barrio: A Brownsville transitional neighborhood.* University of Texas at Brownsville and Texas Southmost College: Cross Border Institute for Regional Development.

Bakker, Isabella. 2003. Neo-liberal governance and the reprivatization of social production: Social provisioning and shifting gender orders. In *Power, production and social reproduction: Human in/security in the global political economy,* ed. Isabella Bakker and Stephen Gill, 66-82. New York: Palgrave Macmillan.

Brittain, Christopher Craig. 2005. The "secular" as a tragic category: On Talal Asad, religion and representation. *Method and Theory in the Study of Religion* 17(2):149-65.

Cisneros, Henry. 1996. Higher ground: Faith communities and community building. *Cityscape: A Journal of Policy Development and Research.* Special Edition: A Collection of Essays by Henry Cisneros, Secretary of Housing and Urban Development.

Cnaan, Ram. 1999. *The newer deal: Social work and religion in partnership.* New York: Columbia University Press.

Cruikshank, Barbara. 1993. Revolutions within: Self-government and self-esteem. *Economy and Society* 22(3):327-44.

Daly, Lew. 2009. *God's economy: Faith-based initiatives and the caring state.* Chicago: University of Chicago Press.

DiIulio, John J., Jr. 2007. *Godly republic: A centrist blueprint for America's faith-based future.* Berkeley: University of California Press.

Farnsley, Arthur. 2003. *Rising expectations: Urban congregations, welfare reform, and civic life.* Bloomington, IN: Indiana University Press.

———. 2007. Faith-based initiatives. In *The Sage Handbook of the Sociology of Religion,* ed. James Beckford and N. J. Demerath III, 345-56. London: Sage Publications.

Goode, Judith. 2006. Faith-based organizations in Philadelphia: Neoliberal ideology and the decline of political activism. *Urban Anthropology* 35(2-3):203-37.

Hall, Peter Dobkin. 2005. The rise of the civic engagement tradition. In *Taking faith seriously,* ed. Mary Jo Bane, Brent Coffin, and Richard Higgins, 21-60. Cambridge, MA: Harvard University Press.

Heyman, Josiah. 2008. Constructing a virtual wall: Race and citizenship in U.S.-Mexico border policing. *Journal of the Southwest* 50(3):305-34.

Hirschberg, Victoria. 2004. Census ranks Hidalgo, Cameron poorest urban counties in US. *The Monitor.* August 27.

Johnson, Carrie. 2009. Obama cautious on faith-based initiatives. *Washington Post.* September 15.

Kirshenblatt-Gimblett, Barbara. 1998. *Destination culture: Tourism, museums, and heritage.* Berkeley: University of California Press.

Mapes, Mary. 2004. *A public charity: Religion and social welfare in Indianapolis, 1929-2002.* Bloomington, IN: Indiana University Press.

McGrew, Charlene, and Ram A. Cnaan. 2006. Finding congregations: Developing conceptual clarity in the study of faith-based social services. *Journal of Religion and Spirituality in Social Work* 25(3-4):19-37.

McKenzie, Ana. 2007. Census: Brownsville population surging. *The Brownsville Herald.* July 14.

McRoberts, Omar. 1999. Understanding the new black Pentecostal church activism: Lessons from ecumenical urban ministries in Boston. *Sociology of Religion* 60(1):47-70.

———. 2005. H. Richard Niebuhr meets "The Street." In *Taking faith seriously,* ed. Mary Jo Bane, Brent Coffin, and Richard Higgins, 94-112. Cambridge, MA: Harvard University Press.

Morgen, Susan, and Jeff Maskovsky. 2003. The anthropology of welfare reform: New perspectives on U.S. urban poverty in the post-welfare era. *Annual Review of Anthropology* 32:315-38.

Owens, Michael Leo. 2007. *God and government in the ghetto: The politics of church-state collaboration in black America.* Chicago: University of Chicago Press.

Paredes, Américo. 1970. *With his pistol in his hand: A border ballad and its hero.* Austin: University of Texas Press.

Peach, James, and Richard V. Adkisson. 2002. United States-Mexico income convergence? *Journal of Economic Issues* 36(2):423-30.

Pfeiffer, James. 2004. Civil society, NGOs, and the Holy Spirit in Mozambique. *Human Organization* 63(3):359-72.

Ramírez, Daniel. 1999. Borderlands praxis: The immigrant experience in Latino Pentecostal churches. *Journal of the American Academy of Religion* 67(3):573-96.

Ríos, Elizabeth. 2005. "The ladies are warriors": Latina Pentecostalism and faith-based activism in New York City. In *Latino religions and civic activism in the United States,* ed. Gastón Espinosa, Virgilio Elizondo, and Jesse Miranda, 197-218. New York: Oxford University Press.

Robbins, Joel. 2004. The globalization of Pentecostal and Charismatic Christianity. *Annual Review of Anthropology* 33:117-43.

Ruiz, Vicki. 2006. Confronting "America": Mexican women and the Rose Gregory Houchen settlement. In *American dreaming, global realities: Rethinking U.S. immigration history,* ed. Donna Gabaccia and Vicki Ruiz, 343-60. Urbana, IL: University of Illinois Press.

Sánchez Walsh, Arlene. 2003. *Latino Pentecostal identity: Evangelical faith, self, and society.* New York: Columbia University Press.

Sharp, Ethan. 2009. Waging the war on drugs: Neoliberal governance and the formation of faith-based organizations in urban Mexico. In *Bridging the gaps: Faith-based organizations, neoliberalism, and development in Latin America and the Caribbean,* ed. Tara Hefferan, Julie Adkins, and Laurie Occhipinti, 35-50. Lanham, MD: Lexington Books.

Smilde, David A. 1998. "Letting God govern": Supernatural agency in the Venezuelan Pentecostal approach to social change. *Sociology of Religion* 59:287-303.

Urban, Greg. 2008. The circulation of secularism. *International Journal of Politics, Culture and Society* 21(1-4):17-37.

Vila, Pablo. 2005. *Border identifications: Narratives of religion, gender, and class on the U.S.-Mexico border.* Austin: University of Texas Press.

Chapter 4
Faith-Based Development and Community Renaissance: Tradition and Transformation in South Memphis

Katherine Lambert-Pennington and Julie Pfromm

Introduction

We entered St. Andrew through the back door, just as we had for our project meeting with the pastor earlier in the week. Today was different; it was Sunday. The pastor, Dr. Kenneth Robinson, had invited us to come to this service to hear "Brother Tavis" and "Brother West" speak. As uninitiated church attendees we were unsure where to go, much less the protocols of where to sit, when to stand, or what to do. A greeter directed us to the sanctuary, and everyone we passed welcomed us with a smile and "Hello. Welcome to the Saint." Guided by an usher, we took our place in a pew near the back of the church. Members all around us introduced themselves, and welcomed us to the church with hugs and handshakes. The service was electric, with music from BeBe Winans, testimony from a member on the power of faith and tithing, and a "pass the mic" sermon from Cornel West, Tavis Smiley, and Michael Eric Dyson, who had stopped in to worship at St. Andrew in the process of traveling across the country.[1]

As this ethnographic moment suggests, St. Andrew African Methodist Episcopal (AME) Church is no ordinary church.[2] The presence of these special guests is not only emblematic of Robinson's—and by extension his congregation's—accumulation of social capital, but also the church's engagement with broader discussions about the role of African American spirituality and religious tradition in social reform and community change (West 1982; 1988; 2004; Dyson 2002; Smiley 2004). Saint Andrew AME Church (also known as "the Saint"), like many African American churches located in impoverished urban neighborhoods (Chaves and Higgins 1992; Day 2001; McDougall 1993), is committed to improving the quality of life and physical conditions of the predominantly African American neighborhood around the church.

Described by its pastor as a contemporary, twenty-four/seven church, St. Andrew sponsors a constellation of social service programs known as the Enterprise. This multi-pronged approach is comprised of five components that encompass a range of services for persons from birth through senior years. The Enterprise includes: (1) twenty-six Congregational Ministries ranging from a food pantry to the Women's Missionary Society to a clothes closet; (2) a Childcare Center, which provides care for 84 children, 25 percent of whom reside in South Memphis, with 90 percent receiving childcare subsidies; (3) a community life center that offers programs for at-risk youth, health education, a homework center, and a gymnasium; (4) a Community Development Corporation (CDC) that provides homebuyer and foreclosure education, a minor repair program, new home construction, and rental opportunities for low-income renters; and (5) a charter school serving 140 children in grades K-5. The success of these programs is attributable to the AME church's tradition of mutual aid, strong institutional leadership, and an active congregational volunteer base, as well as St. Andrew's commitment to using its collective social capital and position to improve its local community.

While much has been written about the increasingly important role that faith-based organizations play in filling the gaps between government funding and programs and private philanthropy (Chaves 1999; Cnaan 2002; Kemper and Adkins 2005; Hefferan, Adkins, and Occhipinti 2009), Vidal (2001) has suggested there is a lack of critical analysis of the reasons, approaches, and impacts of faith-based social service efforts. Anthropologists are well suited to pursue these avenues of research; however, as Kemper notes, our absence from the conversation "reflects the failure of many anthropologists to engage in current debates about the roles of faith-based organizations in American life" (2006, 145). This chapter builds on the anthropologically grounded discussion of faith-based organizations started by Kemper, Adkins, DeTemple, Goode, Hill, and Woodrick in a special issue (2006) of *Urban Anthropology and Studies of Cultural Systems and World Economic Development*. In doing so, it turns its lens on the Enterprise's model of community development in an effort to respond to a gap identfied by Vidal, who suggests that "the issue of whether services are offered in a way that helps households *get ahead* as opposed to *getting by* (i.e., whether they are developmental in character) is rarely raised" (2001, 14). In particular, we ask, where does the Enterprise fit in the continuum from charity (get by) to empowerment focused (get ahead) faith-based community development approaches (Kemper and Adkins 2005), and what does the latter approach require?

Bringing Katie Day's (2001) analysis of the tensions and parallels between community economic development (CED) and church based community organizing (CBCO) strategies practiced among African American churches in Philadelphia into conversation with the Kemper and Adkins (2005) continuum of approaches, we examine how St. Andrew manages its tendency toward CED strategies and charity and its desire for CBCO and empowerment outcomes. Our analysis focuses on four key aspects of St. Andrew's model of community development: mission and goals, leadership, congregational involvement, and partnerships. We conclude with recommendations about what it would take to bring the full transformational potential of the Enterprise's community development model to reality.

Methods

The query that inspired this paper was first posed by Rev. Robinson when he invited our university team to be part of the South Memphis Renaissance Collaborative (SMRC). With the goals of catalyzing a neighborhood renaissance and making the Enterprise a model of community transformation, Robinson brought together a consortium of stakeholders, including representatives of government agencies, local and national foundations, and educational institutions, to assist the Enterprise in the design and implementation of the organization's long-term community development plans. To this end, he asked the university team for an assessment of the Enterprise and the socioeconomic and social service status of the community.[3]

In an effort to begin answering Robinson's questions, Katherine Lambert-Pennington, an anthropologist, partnered with Ken Reardon, an urban planner, to bring together a research team that included five faculty members and more than fifty students from the departments of City and Regional Planning, Anthropology, Architecture, and Civil Engineering.[4] Reflecting the interdisciplinary mix of the team, our research methodology ran the gamut of qualitative and quantitative techniques, including a comprehensive land use survey, thirty-five in-depth interviews, and two focus groups. Additionally, the anthropologists on the team did systematic participant observation at local events sponsored by the church and Enterprise programs, including numerous informal conversations with Robinson and other Enterprise staff members, as well as a lecture Robinson gave at the university in which he laid out his life trajectory and the evolution of his ideas. Seeking to learn more about the history of the church's involvement in community development efforts, we interviewed seventeen church members and leaders, asking questions about why they chose St. Andrew as their church, what social ministries they were involved in, their perceptions of the neighborhood, and what they saw as St. Andrew's biggest contribution to the community. Additionally, we interviewed six key staff members of the Enterprise, asking them about their programs, whom they served, how they were connected to St. Andrew, and what they saw as their program/organization's biggest contribution to the community. We also interviewed a sample of twelve community stakeholders to get their perceptions of the strengths and needs of the neighborhood and St. Andrew's programs. Finally, we conducted focus groups with one of the area's longest standing neighborhood associations and with parents of children attending the Enterprise-affiliated charter school. We draw on this data to explore the model of community development employed by the Enterprise and the potential for this model to have a transformative impact on the neighborhood.

South Memphis

An interstate overpass is the doorway into St. Andrew's home neighborhood, an area geographically and colloquially referred to as South Memphis. Just beyond the overpass the grassy, tree-lined parkway divider gives way to an ordinary but overly wide street. Along the parkway, the number of sturdy brick bungalow-style homes from the 1920s and 1930s signal the once middle class status of the neighborhood and remain a widely recognized neighborhood asset. Down side streets, brick homes stand beside wooden frame homes built in the 1940s and 1950s in the era of urban renewal. Like many neighborhoods across metro-politan America, South Memphis was a victim of the dynamics of commercial and residential disinvestment that began as white residents left the "inner city" for post-WWII suburban developments. Whites' fears about school integration following Brown vs. Board of Education (1954) and successful block busting campaigns, coupled with redlining and lending practices that discriminated against African Americans, meant that formerly white middle class neighborhoods like the one around St. Andrew were the first to be re-inhabited by working and middle class African Americans who wanted to own their own home (Pattillo-McCoy 1999).

The shifts from manufacturing electronics to a service economy to a knowledge economy, coupled with continuing local public and commercial divestment in South Memphis during the 1970s and 1980s (Hyland 2005), had a severe impact on the quality of life and economic viability of the neighborhood that has continued into the present. From 1990 to 2000 the population of South Memphis declined 21 percent. Although about 50 percent of residents own their homes, of the approximately 9,000 people that make up the neighborhood, 40 percent are living at or below the poverty level (Lambert-Pennington and Reardon 2009, 54-8). The slow decline in this South Memphis neighborhood is visible and varies by area. In the southwest quadrant, there are many vacant houses and overgrown lots woven between well cared-for family homes. The successful work of the Enterprise's CDC is most apparent in the area to the south of St. Andrew, as fresh paint and sapling shrubbery accentuate recently constructed and rehabbed homes.

Although a core group of residents have lived in the neighborhood over twenty years,[5] the mix of commercial and economic decline and an increase in rental property has resulted in the loosening of what were once dense social and civic networks and left the neighborhood with only a few organized and functioning neighborhood associations and block clubs. Nonetheless, as we spent time in the neighborhood and talked with residents, it became clear that residents are major assets in the community. Elders are the established eyes and ears of the neighborhood, while the children are what make the community come alive, playing ball in the streets, riding bikes, playing in one of the few parks, and walking with friends (resident elders, men and women over 65, make up 15 percent of the population; residents under the age of eighteen make up 35 percent of the population) (Lambert-Pennington and Reardon 2009, 51). Educationally, more than 54 percent of adult residents hold less than a high school diploma, while 20 percent have some college or a college degree (Lambert-Pennington and Reardon 2009, 54-8). Currently, most school aged children attend one of the ten area schools. Other neighborhood assets include a dozen non-profits, a neighborhood association, several block clubs, twenty-one churches,[6] and two public parks, as well as the youth and health focused programs offered by the community life center at St. Andrew. Together, these assets and challenges contribute to a complex social fabric and provide an ideal ground for innovative community and economic development projects.

Paradigms of Faith-Based Community Development

As the chapters in this volume attest, approaches to faith-based development are diverse, varying by denomination, forms of engagement, types of organizations, and modes of change, all of which inform the model of community development that faith-based organizations ultimately adopt. Kemper and Adkins (2005) suggest that faith-based activities fall along a continuum from charitable assistance to community transformation, and are informed by the role of faith and whether or not the locus of control is local, national, or international. Vidal, borrowing from Bastelli and McCarthy, suggests three major types of faith-based organizations that engage in community development: denominational organizations and national networks, congregations, and freestanding organizations (Vidal 2001, 6). Falling along the continuum of faith-based activities articulated by Kemper and Adkins (2005), national networks like The Salvation Army often benefit from having a large, professional staff, and tend to receive both public and private funding to provide a wide range of human and social services, including housing and economic development activities. Often closer to the charity end of the continuum, congregations, like St. Andrew, primarily provide human services that address immediate, basic needs such as food, clothes, housing, and shelter (Chaves 1999). Most frequently their support for community development activities takes the form of task-oriented, periodic volunteerism, rather than large monetary donations (Chaves and Tsitsos 2000).

Within this general congregational trend, Katie Day has identified two types of faith-based development predominant among African American churches: community economic development (CED) and church based community organizing (CBCO). Notably, congregational involvement in CED and CBCO strategies creates opportunities to move beyond the provision of charity, with the former focusing "on the economic well-being of a community" and the latter utilizing "development projects only as the means to the larger goal—the empowerment of the people for self-determination" (Day 2003, 322). Thus, some congregations, like St. Andrew, have engaged in housing development in their local communities by forming independent nonprofit CDCs in order to address the housing, economic, and educational needs of neighborhoods under their purview. Such freestanding faith-based organizations, according to Vidal, "are much more likely to provide direct services to individuals than to engage in broader community development activities" (2001, 14). Complicating this view, Day argues that the CDC approach allows African American churches to "preserve ownership of projects that are 'in,' 'of' and 'for' the African American community" (2001, 193).

While congregational efforts are largely linked to CED (also referred to as traditional economic development), denominational networks like Sacramento Area Congregations Together and Valley Interfaith are frequently linked with faith-based community organizing (FBCO) approaches. With roots in People Improving Communities through Organizing (PICO) and the Industrial Areas Foundation (IAF), this approach focuses on advocating for local communities by building broad-based coalitions and leveraging their political power to obtain political support for policy changes and projects that address local concerns (Kemper and Adkins 2005). Sharing the elements of relationship building and social capital with the community organizing approach, asset based community development (ABCD) engages residents and local stakeholders such as CDCs, schools, and other nonprofits in the collection of systematic, detailed ethnographic, spatial, and sociocultural information about the community's assets in order to mobilize them for the purpose of community development (Kretzmann and McKnight 1993). In contrast, CED, which currently dominates St. Andrew's community based development approach, tends to be deficiency or needs-focused and often results in faith-based organizations doing "for" their community, while ABCD and CBCO pay attention to assets and building the capacity of a community to "do" for itself. The asset-based approach combined with community organizing principles has emerged as a best practice, and has become prerequisite in the funding arena (Reese and Clamp 2002). Granting agencies' interest in supporting sustainable community development efforts has not been lost on Robinson, as the SMRC attests.

That CED and CBCO strategies tend toward different ends of the continuum of faith-based development is reflective of the key differences between the two strategies with respect to leadership, collaboration, power distribution, and ideas of change (Day 2001). In their approach to leadership, CEDs are more top-down and clergy driven, while CBCOs rely on grassroots leadership. In terms of collaboration, CBCOs have an expanding network of partners and a larger geographic focus, while CEDs are church-centric and have a bounded area of service. Likewise, power is distributed broadly in CBCOs, while access to power is more guarded in CEDs. Finally, each approach creates change in a different way: CEDs tend to use the status quo to access resources without challenging structural inequalities, while CBCOs will confront and seek to change the underlying unjust policies and practices that inform the ways resources are distributed (Day 2001). Ultimately, Day's research suggests "the vernacular culture of many African-American churches seems more naturally suited to CED than to CBCO" (2001, 324). This insight seems true of St. Andrew's model of community development with its deep roots in AME teachings, hierarchical organization, a strong, centralized pastoral leader, and an active congregation. However, the Enterprise's multi-pronged approach to community development, which spans the continuum from charity to empowerment, suggests that there may be space for CBCO strategies. Further analysis of the key aspects in the model—mission and goals, leadership, congregational participation, and partnerships—reveals the ways that St. Andrew negotiates and struggles with the tensions between largely top-down congregational and more bottom-up coalitional strategies of community development.

Works of Faith: Mission and Goals

A mission statement says a great deal about an organization. In the nonprofit world, mission statements guide the actions of the organization and officially set its purpose, values, and beneficiaries. In the analytic world of organizational analysis, a mission statement can be read as a text (Smith 2006), that is, a discursive device that reveals the ideas and ideology that an organization is trying to reproduce. In keeping with the spirit of its early work as a mutual aid society, the mission of the AME church is: to preach the gospel, feed the hungry, clothe the naked, house the homeless, cheer the fallen, provide jobs for the unemployed, administer to the needs of those confined to prison, home, or hospital, and encourage thrift and economic development (Henning 2001, 13). The Enterprise, then, serves "as the vehicle for St. Andrew to accomplish its mission of works in the world . . ." Although the Enterprise could best be characterized as a "faith-affiliated" organization—sharing the AME faith is not a requirement to receive services, the faith content of the programs is minimal, and the focus is not on conversion (Hefferan, Adkins, and Occhipinti 2009)—the AME church's history, theological tradition, and hierarchical organization provide a foundation for St. Andrew to vitalize the mission of the Enterprise.

"Faith without works is dead," asserts Rev. Robinson from the pulpit, a theme repeated in the church's literature. For members and leaders at St. Andrew, community and economic development, in both their broadest and most limited senses, are seen as an extension of the AME faith. Robinson highlighted the significance of the African American church's "history of community healing" in a talk he gave to an anthropology class at the university. He said the church has:

> [H]istorically been a significant value convening institution . . . [it has] traditionally restored land and provided services that support African-American community life and bring wholeness, relieving [the] dis-ease of economic distress, political impotence, and racial marginality . . . It has always had a holistic presence [and] been a ubiquitous and uniform messenger. . . . It is indigenous in its action; [it is] owned by the people, [has] an affinity with the community and credibility in the community. . . . It has networks and linkages through members, and created a community-based interdependence.

Robinson identifies St. Andrew as a servant church, which, according to Dulles, "asserts that the Church should consider itself as part of the total human family, sharing the same concerns as the rest of men" (1991, 91). Moreover, Robinson clearly positions the church as a source of spiritual and social uplift and social capital, which are further reflected in the goals of the Enterprise: "Transforming South Memphis from a place of lack to a place of provision; Stabilizing and sustaining families in South Memphis and beyond; Inspiring and empowering people of all ages to reach their full potential, and have the knowledge, skills and resources to sustain their own success."

Within the goals we hear both a call for personal change and responsibility and a recognition of the connection between social determinants and well-being. It is crucial to note that this blend of personal and structural conditions not only represents potentially divergent social service paths (Bradshaw 2006), but also reflects the underlying differences between CED and CBCO strategies. On the one hand, the goals move from broad to specific—community, family, and individual—suggesting the connection between and the need for multi-pronged, "wrap around" strategies of community development (Galster and Hill 1992), which the Enterprise strives toward. On the other hand, drawing on a language of deficiency, dependency, and individualism, they suggest an alchemy of charity and personal change is the emphasis of Enterprise programs. The latter is reinforced by the absence of references to assets in the goals statement, which suggest a "do for" rather than "build on" or "do with" approach to community development.

As the Enterprise has worked to achieve its goals, St. Andrew has gained a reputation for helping those in need. Echoing the suggested "do for" sentiment of the mission and goals statements, one church member characterized it this way: "People in this community already know Saint Andrew. They know when they need food they can go to the CDC. They know when they need clothing they can go to the clothing closet . . . We have been doing it for so long in the community that they know what our services are."

Although proud of the work they do for the neighborhood, some congregants recognized the potential of fostering the kinds of dependence-based relationships that can accompany charity driven strategies. As one member explained:

> The community can depend on us being able to give away, or helping to meet the needs. The greatest need, that some disadvantaged kids just don't have, shoes, school uniforms, things of that nature at the start of the school year. I think the community has come to rely on the fact that we are going to have our doors open on Labor Day giving that away for free.

The distance between need-based programs and the goal of self-sufficiency was reflected in several interviews. One of the social ministry leaders reflected:

> The greatest challenge is getting the community to commit . . . it can't work if it's one sided. Now we can keep giving to you . . . we can keep feeding you, but if you won't come and learn how to feed yourself then, it won't ever develop into room or chance or time to go to the next one because you're always needing us to feed you.

Even as some congregation members expressed frustration and anxiety about the potential for dependency, their explanations echoed the goals' movement between personal responsibility and empowerment programming. One interviewee saw community members' dependence on St. Andrew as something that the ministries could address by paying "[a] little bit more personal attention toward those people that we serve. You know we have people that we've been helping for years, and so giving a more personal aspect to what they really need to help them to become totally self-sufficient, at a comfortable place in their life."

While still focused on the realm of the individual, we begin to see how congregants are attempting to appreciate the difference between providing generalized charitable help to the less fortunate and understanding the particulars of people's struggles and desires for the future. Implicit in the speaker's suggestion is a call for the social ministries to get to know the people they are serving and to advance community development activities that lead to independence and sustainable change in the lives of individuals and, by extension, in the community.

Regardless of whether the Enterprise programs utilize CED or CBCO strategies, the efforts of the church are a substantiation of the Enterprise's mission and goals. Congregation members' works in the world are not simply personal expressions of their faith; they make the church's commitment to and role in the neighborhood visible to the community outside. As a representative of a neighborhood organization reflected, "Saint Andrew is a good example of progressiveness because they have come in and done a lot of things. I see the future for them being very bright . . . the pastor is very involved in what he is about and I just feel like he is going to do things." As this stakeholder suggests, the church's status as an anchor in the neighborhood's social service network is due in no small part to its pastor.

"Healing the Land": Leadership

Although faith-based community development is often articulated as a natural extension of the AME tradition of service in African American communities, the way in which it is carried out at the local level varies from church to church and pastor to pastor. Importantly, Rev. Robinson's vision for the Enterprise and approach to community development have been shaped by the church's leadership structure and his training as both a doctor and a minister. These influences shed light on Robinson's embrace of a CED model and desire for CBCO results.

As a leader, Robinson shares many of the qualities of clerical leaders involved in traditional community development, described by Day as "charismatic, entrepreneurial pastors" who "have spearheaded enormously complex development projects single-handedly, not collaborating with other clergy or lay people, but occasionally working with a consultant" (2001, 8). He is the driver of St. Andrew's community development effort, and the assistant pastor talks of Robinson's personality and past as being a major asset to the church:

> When you think of a pastor . . . certainly personality drives a lot of things. It's innately a part of who you are so it comes out wherever you are, in whatever capacity you are functioning in. So who Pastor Robinson, who [he] is, is a driving force behind the major progression of Saint Andrew.

More than personality, Robinson's role as the driving force behind the Enterprise is due in part to his position within the church structure. Reflecting the hierarchical organization of the AME church, Robinson sits at the nexus of the church and the Enterprise. He presides over pastoral staff and the church's social ministries in his role as pastor, and serves as the President of the Enterprise and Executive Director of the CDC. As President of the Enterprise, he oversees the community life center and the childcare center, which fall under the church's nonprofit status, as well as the CDC and the charter school, which are independent 501(c)(3) organizations. Operationally, professional staff members support the Enterprise; they are responsible for providing leadership in the day-to-day activities associated with their programs. Robinson acts as both the internal conduit that links the Enterprise's executive team together and the public representative and spokesperson for the Enterprise and St. Andrew.

Called to preach during medical school, Robinson spent the last three years of his training exploring the relationship between faith and health, a relationship that continues to be part of his vision for the Enterprise. The connection between the physical and spiritual came together for Robinson during his residency. He credits his experiences taking detailed patient histories with showing him how the presentation of illness was informed by complex social determinants of health. Additionally, through his work with a group of patients struggling with drug and alcohol addiction, he found that treatment techniques like twelve-step programs enabled him to "really explore the issue of alcoholism and chemical addiction and the interface, the interaction and the interrelationship of faith and healing." Robinson not only came to view healing as a process of creating bodily and spiritual well-being, but also saw the need to actively intervene in the conditions that led to illness in the first place. Likewise, in the context of the church, he explained, "I think what the church does best is prevention." Keeping with this medical and spiritual focus on intervention/prevention, one of his first projects was a health initiative. In an entrepreneurial move, Robinson took advantage of the loosening of federal restrictions on grants to faith-based organizations and became one of the first leaders of a congregational faith-based organization to seek and receive federal funding for youth focused HIV prevention education and training programs. Additionally, he founded a day care center at the church to "immunize children from their harmful environment." These initial programs provided a template for Robinson's approach to social service provision at St. Andrew.

Robinson describes the growth of St. Andrew's community development efforts over the last seventeen years as "organic," yet his experiences and vision have been instrumental to the Enterprise's success. From the outset, he recognized that the church's main physical asset, a 31,000 square foot building, "was a well-kept, concrete anchor in the community." Revitalizing the childcare center was his first strategic step in reconnecting St. Andrew to the neighborhood, formally initiating the church's community development efforts, and attracting new members to the church. The level of trust given to him by his congregation has allowed Robinson to grow St. Andrew's community development programs. Maintaining an emphasis on prevention, he intentionally added community minded social ministries geared toward disrupting the effects of poverty, like health and educational programs for at-risk youth (which later became the charter school) and a job counseling program, which later became a housing-focused CDC. Additionally, as the congregation grew and programs expanded, Robinson raised congregational and public funds to support church building expansion and increases in the operating costs of Enterprise programs.

While Robinson's leadership of the Enterprise is consistent with the hierarchical structure and social gospel of the AME church, he also recognizes that he brings a unique set of experiences, networks, and skills to the Enterprise's community development efforts. Both factors have shaped the scope and delivery of Enterprise programs. Additionally, Robinson's focus on prevention has the potential to take either the form of outside intervention (do for) or individual and community empowerment (do with). His commitment to "healing the land" has inspired his congregation to action; as one congregation member reflected, "He's the visionary, but that has been our mission to do these things and change these things."

From Pulpit to Pew: Congregational Involvement

Rev. Robinson's "beyond-the-sanctuary approach" (Day 2001, 154) has been a key factor in the congregational growth of St. Andrew from seventy-five members in 1991 to 1,700 in 2009. Attracting African Americans from across the socioeconomic and geographic spectrum of Memphis, the congregation's diversity provides a key source of capital and power to the church's community development agenda: human capital (people and skills), social capital (in national, state, and local arenas), and financial capital (tithes). Members draw on these resources as they connect spiritual teachings they hear from the pulpit to their social ministries both within and beyond the church. As one congregation member said:

> Every Sunday he's giving us something as far as the Word is concerned . . . so that we can go back out in the community. . . . He teaching us the Word and teaching how to study the Word, but also teaching us how to take that same Word and spread it out. . . . You don't just take it and keep it in here.

The ways members engage with the community are not only tied to the AME church's commitment to mutual aid, but also reflect who the congregation is as a group and what they interpret as the purpose of community outreach. Notably, the forms their engagement takes often reinforce the spatial, social, and economic differences between congregation members and the residents of the neighborhood they serve.

Drawn to St. Andrew by its aggressive community development agenda, wide-ranging programs, and charismatic pastor, the congregation comes from across Memphis. Fourteen percent of the congregation shares St. Andrew's zip code and another 35 percent live one to five miles away. The remaining 51 percent live anywhere from five to twenty miles away from the church and the surrounding neighborhood (St. Andrew AME Church 2009, 25). Research suggests that residential distance from a church does not correlate with a congregation's commitment to community development activities (Cnaan 2002; Day 2001). Nevertheless, in Memphis, where the geographic diversity of congregation members also signifies differences in class, education, and profession, where congregants live does have economic implications for St. Andrew.

Through strategic use of congregational tithing and grants, the church serves as a vehicle for bringing significant "outside" dollars into the immediate community. Over the past seventeen years, the congregation has raised $13.8 million in tithes and donations, and for some members, seeing this money spent on the community is part of what keeps them at St. Andrew. As one church steward said:

> I do have a desire that where I deposit my money, where I put my money into the storehouse, that the storehouse are good stewards of those monies and are

willing to do something for the community at large. So I think that being at the church allows me to actualize a lot of the principles and values that I have.

The socioeconomic diversity of the congregation is a double-edged sword. On the one hand, tithing provides a strong and consistent financial foundation for the Enterprise's community development activities. On the other hand, many congregants are Sunday-only members of St. Andrew's neighborhood. They are familiar with the area immediately around the church, but have limited experience in other parts of the neighborhood or with many of the issues that neighborhood residents face on a day-to-day basis. Moreover, members' willingness to donate money does not guarantee their interest in being actively involved in outreach activities and community change.

Congregational participation in social ministries falls on a continuum from passive to active engagement, but is concentrated in need-based, task-driven events and activities. When asked what they saw as St. Andrew's most significant contribution to the community, congregants identified the church itself as a marker of St. Andrew's investment in the community. Several members pointed to the fact that the church stayed in the community. One interviewee explained: "We're here. We stayed as we grew. Many large churches left, but we wanted to affect this community and so everything that we have done has been to increase our opportunity for programs and development that affect the community."

Other interviewees pointed to the CDC as the church's most significant accomplishment. They noted that the CDC has brought visible and positive changes to the look of the neighborhood with an apartment complex for low-income renters and several new houses. Moreover, of all of the Enterprise programs, the CDC facilitates sustainable change in people's lives through new homebuyer education, credit counseling, and ultimately home ownership. Significantly, while both recent church expansion and housing development have provided very visible and important physical improvements, neither requires members to be actively engaged with community residents or other community stakeholders.

For twelve of the seventeen congregation members we interviewed, their involvement in community outreach was primarily channeled through church sponsored social ministries like the Women's Missionary Society's provision of Thanksgiving and Christmas baskets, the Labor Day Shoe Give Away, the annual community baby shower, health education and services, or prison outreach. As a result of their efforts in 2008, St. Andrew's social ministries provided 1,300 school aged children with school shoes and school supplies, and 1,034 households with food from the food pantry. As members described their engagement in these activities, their comments often reflected the social distance between congregation members and the community.

Some participants went into their social ministry assuming residents shared their norms and life experiences; however, they discovered that this was not necessarily the case. For example, the congregational coordinator was both moved and surprised that a mother of five attending the community baby shower had never had a baby shower. Others that we interviewed expressed astonishment at the level of need in the community. Reflecting on the Shoe Give Away, another congregation member explained:

> Sometimes these children don't have any shoes at all, so that was a major eye-opener to me and being over there and just not, you know, just seeing the need and not caring, [that] you have to touch feet. It didn't bother me, you know. Just making sure they got a shoe was my purpose.

The children's need for shoes was also a major eye-opener for other volunteers, one of whom reflected, "That just blew me away . . . I had no idea, I didn't understand the need . . . I did not understand what parents would go through . . . it hit me how important that it was to the families we gave the shoes away to." Although congregants did not always go into these activities fully understanding how the challenges of poverty shape community members' everyday lives, through events like the Shoe Give Away congregants were able to see how their participation in direct service delivery made an immediate difference.

Over time these experiences have defined the relationship between the church and the community as one in which congregants give and community members receive. Just what they are giving and receiving is subject to church members' own interpretations, ranging from charity to self-sufficiency to salvation to all of the above, which again draws our attention to the connections and tensions between faith, outreach, and community development. Although many members stressed the importance of outreach for drawing residents to God and the church, interviewees' opinions of the role that faith should play in the church's community development efforts varied from implicit to aggressive. For some congregants, participating in social ministries is part of giving back to the church. As one interviewee explained, "St. Andrew has helped us get to this point, so we can get involved . . . we want to get you to a point where you're self-sufficient, where you want to help someone else because you got help." For others, the explicit purpose of the social ministries is to bring people to the church. Taking this more evangelistic stance, a lifelong church member and South Memphis resident asserted, "We're in the business of winning souls. There's a lot of souls to win out here. So the bounty is plentiful, we just need to go in and reap the harvest. And so our ministries, that's the purpose. That's what we're trying to do." Falling right in the middle, another member identified both the physical and spiritual benefits of receiving help from the social ministries, saying, "the more people we feed, the more people we help. I would like to see them sitting in service with me and helping them to partake in all the benefits we have at St. Andrew as well as spiritual benefits." Each of these positions, we note, suggests a potentially different outcome: from self-sufficiency to salvation to immediate assistance with the potential for more.

Regardless of whether a congregant took a more passive interest in St. Andrew's community outreach efforts or actively participated in "doing for" activities like the food pantry, the community baby shower, or the Shoe Give Away, congregation members were committed to the neighborhood and saw the church's community development effort as something that makes St. Andrew unique. And while they differed on the degree to which spiritual healing of individuals was the goal of the church's work in the community, they all saw it as an important part of enacting their faith.

Beyond the Church: Partnerships

Collaboration and partnerships are an explicit part of the Enterprise's mission, and Rev. Robinson's strategy has been to cultivate limited but strategic partnerships in the neighborhood and to invest heavily in developing assets and relationships external to the local community. Locally, the church has built some relationships with other stakeholder groups; for example, one of the social ministries has adopted a local public school and the youth ministry occasionally partners with two other neighborhood congregations for youth activities and holiday events. Additionally, the church works with local healthcare providers to sponsor an annual screening and check-up event (primarily attended by congregants). Outside of South Memphis and the faith community, Robinson has forged a wide ranging network of relationships with secular organizations that do not normally partner with traditional churches. This approach to collaboration is perhaps most revealing of the Enterprise's tendency toward traditional community development and the tension between CED and CBCO.

Robinson's cultivation of social and cultural capital in the government and philanthropic funding arenas on behalf of the Enterprise has not only increased the resources available in the community, but also built the capacity of St. Andrew to administer grant monies and direct programs, both of which he sees as drawing "the distinction between the St. Andrew Enterprise and the other 2,999 [churches in Memphis]." As an organization they have demonstrated an ability to provide services in a secular manner that allows them to access state funds. Such experiences have provided St. Andrew with a level of status and reputation that are not available to other local churches. While Robinson sees the Enterprise as a replicable model of community development that could be shared with other churches, he is hesitant to collaborate with other churches at a programmatic level. He worries that other churches lack the capacity to undertake the kind of community development that he envisions, and might jeopardize the effectiveness of the programs and funding sources. Instead, the Enterprise primarily looks to its own assets to achieve its community development goals, namely the pastor and the congregation.

Leaving local partnerships and collaborations largely undeveloped has had both benefits and liabilities. On the one hand, it has enabled Robinson to be a strategic and efficient leader, avoiding competition and compromise with other local organizations. Additionally, he has been able to focus on developing a new generation of leaders within the church. On the other hand, it has limited his participation in developing and mentoring new leaders within the broader social service community or neighborhood. Moreover, the lack of relationships between St. Andrew and other community organizations has restricted the amount of promotion and knowledge generated about the Enterprise programs.

The importance of partnership and collaboration is not lost on Robinson or his congregation, as one of the church members we interviewed powerfully articulated. She said:

> So while we can make provisions for them—we can feed them, we can put clothes on their backs, we can put shoes on the children, we can tell them about HIV and AIDS and tell them how to protect themselves—we can do all this. We are one entity . . . we only have them for that time frame or it may be that we only get them on Labor Day, we only get them when we have an HIV/AIDS promotional. That's the one time out of a window of 365 days, so many hours that's going against the world or the community or the environment in which they're living that speaks totally different to that. . . . That's why it becomes imperative that other organizations, community outreach programs, state funding programs, work in conjunction, hand in hand with the church because first, most have the resources that the church doesn't have and secondly has a greater impact on the external.

As this congregant recognizes, one point of contact is not sufficient to change a neighborhood. Community empowerment and transformation occur when a critical mass of individuals, organizations, and service providers come together to address community challenges at the collective and systemic levels. The questions remains: how?

Transformative Potential

Like faith-based organizations across the country, the St. Andrew Enterprise is helping people in its neighborhood: children are being cared for and educated, mothers-to-be have been "showered" with gifts in preparation for the birth of their child, and families have the roofs of affordable homes over their heads. The church's commitment to community development has helped to resurrect St. Andrew and given rise to the Enterprise's model of community development. Their approach blends a congregational type of faith-based organization with traditional CED strategies (Day 2001) and is powered by the pastor's and congregation's collective social and financial capital. As a result, the church has become a trusted anchor institution in the community, and congregational participation in social ministries has become the cultural norm. Likewise, Rev. Robinson has been able to blend his professional training as both a doctor and AME minister to do good works in the world and "heal the land." Even with its successes, however, the Enterprise has yet to create the "renaissance" that Robinson envisions. As he looks ahead, Robinson asserts:

> I do want to really begin to allow what the Enterprise has done to catalyze others' active engagement in the rest of the story . . . Much of what we've done for the past seventeen years has been driven around the core of the church in terms of our service delivery, but it has been centripetally-driven. It started at the core and continued to spin to impact the community, but, clearly, for it to be sustainable, it is probably high time, certainly a good time for us, even as a major stakeholder to catalyze the rest of the story with the community's engagement.

Catalyzing the kind of community engagement that Robinson desires will require that the Enterprise consider not only what aspects of the current model of community development best support community empowerment, but what aspects of the ABCD and CBCO approaches they are willing to adopt.

The strengths of St. Andrew's current model are its theological imperative, effective accumulation and use of social capital, visionary and entrepreneurial leadership, working organizational infrastructure, physical space, and socio-economically diverse congregation. Amid these strengths, however, the ways the church has engaged with the community have inadvertently encouraged a relationship of dependence between church and community. While the mission of the AME Church remains an unchanging and guiding principle for its local congregations and for community development efforts like the Enterprise, the methods St. Andrew uses to achieve the goals of the Enterprise can be shifted. Any move from community deficits and "doing for" strategies to ones that "build on" existing community assets and resources would require expanded opportunities for leadership, increased congregational involvement, and active engagement with neighborhood residents and stakeholders.

The Enterprise has flourished under the leadership of Rev. Robinson. His personal experiences, professional training, and personality, as many of his congregants recognize, have catapulted St. Andrew into a leading role in the community. While centralized, entrepreneurial leaders like Robinson are often effective and necessary early in the planning and execution of community development activities, the organizations they help create may not be sustainable in the long run. In their absence and without their vision, drive, and direction, organizations can lose their way, a reality that Robinson is trying to avoid by carefully considering his succession plan. The Industrial Areas Foundation (IAF) model teaches that one of the most effective ways of sustaining an organization beyond the tenure of a charismatic leader is to develop a strategy for identifying and growing leaders from within. Shared leadership cultivates shared ownership in the organization and facilitates the growth and sustainability of community development programs and activities.

St. Andrew has also built administrative and fiscal capacities, which makes the pastors and key congregational leaders ideal mentors for other faith-based organizations. Although area churches may not have the resources to be able to take on the types of wrap-around community development Robinson has envisioned, both congregants and key community stakeholders recognize that local churches still have great community influence and are important assets. A community stakeholder and South Memphis resident talked about the power the churches within the community could have if they joined together:

> I think that the churches in that area are not as viable as St. Andrew. St. Andrew is good, they got a lot of money. You know [CB Church] try to do little things as they can. I just think that the churches in the area could pull their funds together and make one big change, maybe a big community center . . . or something like that.

There is no doubt that the congregation is an enormous asset in St. Andrew's community development efforts, particularly with regard to the church's social ministries. Increasing congregational involvement in extra-church Enterprise programs would further connect congregants to the neighborhood in an ongoing rather than event driven fashion, and increase the programs' local impact. One of the church members we interviewed spoke of the need for more coordination between lay leaders and other church ministries/Enterprise programs. She suggested that having a staff position dedicated to community outreach and volunteer coordination would help facilitate an increase in volunteers. Additionally, the creation of a community advisory committee composed of congregation members who are also residents of the neighborhood would increase congregational involvement, bring community residents into more of a leadership role, and steer the church's community engagement in a more informed direction.

The Enterprise has begun to focus on the need for collaboration through the creation of the South Memphis Renaissance Collaborative (SMRC). To date, the SMRC's efforts have followed the pattern of looking outside the community for assistance, advice, expertise, and support to implement the Enterprise's development agenda. In contrast, a collaboration built on asset-based principles would bring all the relevant stakeholders from within the community together to collectively discuss resources and challenges, devise solutions, and implement programs. Such a process is currently underway through South Memphis Revitalization Action Plan Project (SoMe RAPP), a grassroots participatory planning process facilitated by the University of Memphis team.[7] Importantly, this effort has planted the seeds of community organizing, coordination of services, and collaboration between community organizations and stakeholders, including the Enterprise. Implementation of the comprehensive plan will require partnerships and drawing on resources from within the community, as well as philanthropic and government sources from outside. Additionally, residents and other stakeholders, like St. Andrew, will have to stay involved—from discussions and brainstorming to decision-making and leadership to programmatic implementation and advocacy.

St. Andrew's path to creating a community renaissance lies ahead, but their approach is still undecided and important questions remain. What role will St. Andrew and the SMRC play in the implementation of the South Memphis Revitalization Action Plan? How can St. Andrew build the capacity of the congregation to participate in the resulting neighborhood organizing efforts? How does what the Enterprise is currently doing fit into the plan? Can a coalition of congregations and faith-based organizations come together to support and take ownership of the revitalization plan? What other forms will community ownership take? Perhaps St. Andrew's participation in the revitalization planning process will prove an opportunity for the Enterprise to begin to move its approach to FBCD toward a church based community organizing strategy.

Notes

1. We would like to acknowledge St. Andrew AME Church and its affiliated programs for providing us an opportunity to work with them and for their support of this research, especially Revs. Kenneth and Marilynn Robinson and Curtis Thomas. We are also indebted to the congregants and community stakeholders for their willingness to answer numerous questions and share their insights with us. Additionally, we want to especially recognize two of our colleagues for their assistance and insights:

We are grateful to Stan Hyland and the volume editors for reading and offering invaluable feedback on earlier versions of this chapter. We would also like to thank Ken Reardon, as the co-director of SoMe RAPP, for sharing his experience and mentoring, listening and questioning us as our argument evolved. Finally, none of the data that we draw on in this paper would have been possible without the students in Kenneth Reardon's Fall 2008 and Spring 2009 Introduction to Planning and Planning Studio classes, Katherine Lambert-Pennington's Spring 2009 American Communities class, and her team in the Fall 2008 Applied Anthropology class. We are grateful for all the hours and hard work they put in on this project. Any mistakes or misinterpretations are the responsibility of the authors.

2. With the permission and encouragement of Rev. Robinson, we have not changed the names of the church or the pastor. However, to ensure the anonymity of other participants we have identified them in general terms by their relationship to the church and/or community (i.e. congregant, resident, lay leader, key stakeholder, etc).

3. The questions that guided our work included: What are the Enterprise's programs doing? How have they impacted the community? Are there administrative or programmatic changes or expansions that need to occur moving forward? What are the current demographic and land use trends in the community? What services are key community stakeholders providing and what are their perceptions of St. Andrew's activities? What neighborhood challenges are not currently being addressed?

4. Our participation in the SMRC reflects the University of Memphis's commitment to building university-community partnerships through engaged scholarship.

5. In subsequently conducted door-to-door interviews with 174 residents, 65 percent of those we interviewed had lived in the neighborhood more than twenty years.

6. To calculate this number, we searched using Google maps and the church's zip code, and then counted the number of churches shown on the map in St. Andrew's self-defined service area.

7. Committed to participatory action research (PAR) and with the knowledge that successful community development projects require direct input, buy-in, and leadership from the community, the University research team ultimately expanded its role beyond the SMRC to the neighborhood as a whole to facilitate a participatory planning process (Reardon, Green, Bates, and Kiely 2009). Working with a neighborhood advisory board, we interviewed an additional twenty-six community stakeholders and leaders representing local nonprofits, government, residents, and clergy, and conducted 174 door-to-door survey-interviews with residents. In addition, we recruited a community-based steering committee, held four open community forums, and held a series of house meetings hosted by residents and accountability sessions with representatives of the local government. This process of data collection and community dialogue was the basis of the comprehensive revitalization plan that was submitted to the city.

Works Cited

Bradshaw, Ted. 2006. Theories of poverty and anti-poverty programs in community development. Working Paper No. 06-05. Columbia, MO: Rural Poverty Research Center.

Chaves, Mark. 1999. Congregations' social service activities. *Charting Civil Society* 6:2-5.

Chaves, Mark, and Lynn Higgins. 1992. Comparing the community involvement of black and white congregations. *Journal for the Scientific Study of Religion* 31(4):425-40.

Chaves, Mark, and William Tsitsos. 2000. Are congregations constrained by government? Empirical results from the National Congregations Study. *Journal of Church and State* 42(2):335-44.

Cnaan, Ram. 2002. *The invisible caring hand: American congregations and the provision of welfare.* New York: New York University Press.

Day, Katie. 2001. *Prelude to struggle: African American clergy and community organizing for economic development in the 1990s.* New York: University Press of America.

———. 2003. The renaissance of community economic development among African-American churches. In *The Blackwell companion to sociology of religion,* ed. Richard Fenn, 181-95. New Jersey: Wiley/Blackwell.

Dulles, Avery. 1991. *Models of the church.* New York: Random House.

Dyson, Michael Eric. 2002. *Open mike: Reflection on philosophy, race, sex, culture, and religion.* New York: Basic Civitas.

Galster, George, and Edward Hill. 1992. *Metropolis in black and white: Place, power and polarization.* New Brunswick, NJ: Center for Urban Policy Research.

Hefferan, Tara, Julie Adkins, and Laurie Occhipinti. 2009. *Bridging the gaps: Faith-based organizations, neoliberalism, and development in Latin America and the Caribbean.* Lanham, MD: Lexington.

Henning, (Bishop) Cornal Garnett. 2001. *The doctrine and discipline of the African Methodist Episcopal Church 2000-2004.* Nashville, TN: AMEC Publishing Co.

Hyland, Stan. 2005. Evaluation of HOPE VI College Park Initiative. Memphis Housing Authority, 2001-2004. Memphis, TN: Division of Housing and Community Development.

Kemper, Robert V. 2006. Anthropological perspectives on faith-based organizations. *Urban Anthropology And Studies Of Cultural Systems And World Economic Development.* 35(2-3):141-53.

Kemper, Robert V., and Julie Adkins. 2005. The world as it should be: Faith-based community development in America. In *Community building in the twenty-first century,* ed. Stan Hyland, 71-100. Santa Fe, NM: School of American Research Press.

Kretzmann, John P., and John L. McKnight. 1993. *Building communities from the inside out: A path toward finding and mobilizing a community's assets.* Chicago: ACTA Publications.

Lambert-Pennington, Katherine, and Kenneth Reardon. 2009. South Memphis Revitalization Action Plan: A people's blueprint for building a more vibrant, sustainable, and just community. Memphis: University of Memphis, Departments of Anthropology and City and Regional Planning.

McDougall, Harold A. 1993. *Black Baltimore: A new theory of community.* Philadelphia: Temple University Press.

Pattillo-McCoy, Mary. 1999. *Black picket fences: Privilege and peril in the black middle class*. Chicago: University of Chicago Press.

Reardon, Kenneth, Rebekah Green, Lisa Bates, and Richard Kiely. 2009. Commentary: Overcoming the challenges of post-disaster planning in New Orleans. *Journal of Planning and Education Research* 28(3):391-400.

Reese, Davis, and Christina A. Clamp. 2002. Faith-based community development: Principles & practices. Produced by Federal Reserve Bank of Boston, Public and Community Affairs Department. www.bos.frb.org/commdev/faith/index.htm.

Saint Andrew AME Church. 2009. St. Andrew Enterprise Business Plan: 2009. Concilience Group, LLC.

Smiley, Tavis. 2004. *Keeping the faith: Stories of love, courage, healing, and hope from black America*. New York: Anchor Books.

Smith, Dorothy. 2006. *Institutional ethnography as practice*. Lanham, MD: Rowman and Littlefield.

Vidal, Avis C. 2001. Faith-based organizations in community development. U.S. Department of Housing and Urban Development Office of Policy Development and Research. Washington, DC: The Urban Institute.

West, Cornel. 1982. *Prophesy deliverance: An Afro-American revolutionary Christianity*. Philadelphia: Westminster/John Knox.

———. 1988. *Prophetic fragments: Illuminations of the crisis in American religion and culture*. Grand Rapids, MI: Eerdmans.

———. 2004. *Democracy matters: Winning the fight against imperialism*. New York: Penguin Press.

Chapter 5
Bricks Without Straw: Faith-Based Responses to Homelessness in the Hostile City
Julie Adkins

For more than three decades, the Stewpot has served as a hub of activity for the homeless and hungry in Dallas, Texas. Begun in 1975 in response to hungry people literally on the doorstep of the First Presbyterian Church, the Stewpot has grown from its origin as a soup kitchen in a downstairs church dining room to a separate facility located across the street. Its programming has expanded from providing a mid-day meal to include casework services, a dental clinic, assistance with obtaining legal identification, AA and NA meetings, art classes, Bible study, monthly birthday celebrations, and space where outside providers such as Legal Aid, the Veterans Administration, local AIDS outreach workers, and others can meet on a regular basis with their clients. It also shares the second floor of its building with Crossroads Community Services, a ministry of the First United Methodist Church that helps prevent homelessness by assisting individuals and families with rent, utilities, food, and clothing.

When I began my hybrid volunteer/research work at the Stewpot in 2004, I had been a pastor for almost twenty years, seven of them in an urban congregation in Dallas. I knew the faith-based homeless shelters in the city fairly well; I had from time to time referred people to them and had even served on the board of the first transitional housing facility/agency in the city. However, I had also read Hopper (2003), Dordick (1997), and others with their vivid depictions of varied kinds of shelters, particularly the warehouse-like and rather frightening city-owned facilities their informants described. I knew nothing about similar facilities in Dallas, and was looking forward to learning about them, to expanding my vision beyond the faith-based world in which I had operated for so long. But on one of my first afternoons "on the job" at the Stewpot, when a client asked for information about overnight shelters and I dutifully dug through the files to find him a printed list, I was astonished to find that I already knew every shelter on that list. There were six, all of which will be described in greater detail below, and every one of them was a faith-based organization. Until 2008, the City of Dallas had no overnight shelter at all, despite a homeless population of nearly 6,000 and shelter beds for fewer than half that number.

Based on my work at the Stewpot, and in Dallas in general, my argument in this chapter is twofold. First, I argue that the city-as-context (Rollwagen 1975) is crucial to understanding the phenomenon of homelessness and, even more, the solutions available. Brettell (2003) has cogently argued that the experience of immigration differs depending on the city to which an immigrant arrives; that is, we should not assume that patterns discovered in New York City will necessarily hold true for immigrants arriving in Kansas City. I suggest that the same is true for homelessness: the experience of being homeless is different in a city that accepts responsibility for providing shelter—even if it is pretty awful—than in a city that assumes no such responsibility. Being homeless is different in a city where one is arrested for sleeping on the sidewalk than in one where the courts have ruled that public spaces are indeed for the public. Being homeless is different in a city that has adequate public transportation than it is in a city without such transport. And, I argue, being homeless in a city such as Dallas, which is shaped by a larger-than-life myth of its own origin and destiny, is a more *difficult* experience because of how that myth shapes the city's responses to the poor.

Second, I argue that Dallas, because of its dependence on faith-based organizations to perform key social services with relation to the homeless, may provide an object lesson for the rest of the United States as the country continues to move toward having the private nonprofit sector take on the role of social welfare agencies. Cities as contexts are unique, as noted above; nevertheless, I believe there are lessons to be learned from a setting in which the public sector has *never* assumed a critical role in the provision of social services. If Dallas were successful in giving over care of the homeless to the faith-based sector, then it *might* work in other locations. But if it turns out *not* to work, even in a large and perennially conservative[1] Bible belt city, then, I argue, it hasn't a prayer (literally!) of working in other settings.

The City: Present Imperfect[2]

Ninth-largest city in the United States, Dallas is home to a population of slightly more than 1.2 million;[3] of these, at least 5,000-6,000 are homeless at any given time.[4] While stereotypes of Dallas abound—from fictional tycoon J. R. Ewing to real-life billionaires H. Ross Perot and Mark Cuban, and from "urban cowboys" to Dallas Cowboys—the reality on the ground is neither as white nor as wealthy as these icons suggest (cf. Kemper 2005). Dallas's population is 29.0 percent white, 22.3 percent African American, and 44.6 percent Hispanic/Latino. Among current residents of Dallas, 27 percent are foreign-born. However, in the midst of what appears to be diversity on a large scale, there are long-entrenched patterns of residential and economic segregation. The table below illustrates the differences in ethnic makeup of Dallas as a city, the children enrolled in the Dallas Independent School District (DISD 2009), and Dallas's homeless population (MDHA 2009).

	City of Dallas	DISD student population	Dallas homeless population (2009)	Dallas chronically homeless (2009)
White	29.0 %	4.6 %	30 %	27 %
African American	22.3 %	27.7 %	59 %	65 %
Hispanic/Latino	44.6 %	66.5 %	7 %	4 %

Table 5.1 – Ethnic differences in Dallas constituencies

The under-representation of whites in the public schools is indicative of two trends: first, that Dallas's white population is, on the average, older than its minority populations, and thus less likely to have school-age children living in the home. It also indicates that white families are for the most part unwilling to entrust their children to the Dallas public school system, with the exception of a handful of highly ranked magnet schools. However, there are also numerous private and charter schools serving Dallas's minority populations, so the exodus from DISD is not solely a white phenomenon.

Income is also distributed unevenly across the landscape. Approximately 22.6 percent of Dallas residents live at or below the poverty level. The Gini coefficient[5] for Dallas is strikingly high at 0.542, and would be even higher were it not for the fact that the wealthiest parts of the city (Highland Park, University Park) are separately incorporated and therefore not included in the data for Dallas as a whole. Table 5.2 offers comparisons for Dallas's Gini index figure:

City of Dallas	**0.542**
Dallas County	**0.497**
United States as a whole	**0.466**
Other U.S. cities with a high degree of racial/ethnic segregation	
Chicago	0.512
Detroit	0.478
Other major cities in Texas	
Austin	0.481
El Paso	0.474
Fort Worth	0.444
Houston	0.519
San Antonio	0.480
Inequality comparable to that in Dallas[6]	
Honduras	0.538
Chile	0.549

Table 5.2 – Comparison of Gini coefficients

While Dallas's population continues to grow numerically, primarily as the result of immigration, the city is landlocked geographically, surrounded on all sides by suburbs which began their lives as isolated farming and/or railroad communities. The inner ring of suburbs received the first wave of "white flight" in the 1960s-1970s, as many Dallas residents who could afford to do so fled the court-ordered desegregation of their neighborhoods and schools. In recent years, these inner suburbs have become home to an increasing number of ethnic minorities who have chosen, as did their white neighbors before them, to pull their children out of a perennially dysfunctional urban school district. Even "ethnic flight" has remained largely segregated, however. African Americans have mostly moved southward, to the towns/cities of DeSoto, Duncanville, Cedar Hill, and Lancaster. Hispanics have spread to other points of the compass: Garland and Mesquite on the east; Carrollton, Farmers Branch, and Richardson on the north; and Irving and Grand Prairie on the west. And as those suburbs have become increasingly "majority minority," a new wave of flight has sent their most affluent residents—mostly white, though not exclusively—still farther outward into a second and even third ring of suburbs (Frisco, Allen, McKinney, Rockwall, and others). Thus, as is true in many other large American cities, the business elite who work in downtown Dallas generally do not *live* in Dallas; they do not shop in Dallas; they mostly do not pursue social and recreational opportunities in Dallas. Even the "Dallas" Cowboys football team has not played in Dallas since the opening of Texas Stadium in Irving, in October 1971.

The City: Past Perfect?

Perhaps not since the great cities of Renaissance Italy has there been such a striking example of an oligarchy in action (McCombs 1949, 101).

Only in Dallas would being called an "oligarchy in action" count as praise (Graff 2008, 126).

Founded on the prairies in the 1840s, on the banks of the Trinity River, Dallas has since its earliest days wrestled over questions of how to cope with the "unfortunate" in its midst. In this, Dallas is hardly different from other American cities. By the 1870s, and in particular with the arrival of the railroads, the city was growing rapidly and drawing to itself settlers and entrepreneurs from other parts of the United States. Dallas was fortunate to escape the worst of the 1873-74 depression that affected most of the nation, and during these years hundreds of unemployed men came to the area seeking work. Newspaper accounts of the time note the presence of "tramps" living in the Trinity River bottoms—men who had come and sought work with varying degrees of success. In 1876 the County established a "poor farm," intended as a shelter for "law-abiding paupers"—the assumption being that the "able-bodied" would be given farm work to do—and as a place for prostitutes to work off their fines for "vagrancy" (Enstam 1998).

Dallas flirted with Progressivism in the 1910s, and in 1915 the newly-elected mayor, Henry Lindsley, announced that one of his primary goals for the city was the establishment of "an overnight shelter for the homeless." He tapped a former Sears, Roebuck executive to organize and to head the city's first municipal welfare department (Hill 1996). The reaction of Dallas's business elites was all too predictable: Lindsley was voted out of office at the earliest available opportunity, and the 1920s saw a violent backlash against progressives and socialists who had dared to push for change during the previous decade. By 1923 the Ku Klux Klan controlled both city and county government—with overt support from mainline Protestant churches, at least at the beginning—and continued to win elections for nearly a decade, until the sheer number of lynchings finally turned public opinion against them (Hill 1996; Payne 1994).

Thus, Dallas elites have a long history of opposition to public spending on social programs. Rather, city leaders preferred to make donations—often quite generous ones—to local charitable organizations, which allowed them to maintain some degree of control over spending. Hill suggests that the funding of local charity rather than public social programs "did not jeopardize one's commitment to capitalism" (Hill 1996, 99). This pattern has largely held to the present day. Philanthropy in Dallas is strong; the *Dallas Morning News* maintains a regular column in its business section that details various charity events and lists the name of significant supporters and donors from among the city's elites. The *News* also holds its own annual fund drive, Dallas Morning News Charities, from November through January each year. In the campaign just completed—its twenty-fourth—over $1.2 million was raised in support of twenty-four local nonprofits that help the needy. Fully half of these are aimed specifically at the homeless and their needs (Dallas Morning News 2010).

The Myth of Exceptionalism

One of Dallas's core origin myths holds that Dallas is "the city with no reason to exist." This myth received nationwide articulation in a 1949 article in *Fortune* magazine, which I quote at some length for its astonishing chutzpah:

> Properly, it never should have become a city. Founded, for no ascertainable reason, in 1841 on a flat piece of blackland soil that grew nothing but cotton, Dallas was set aside no natural routes of trade. The nearest railhead was hundreds of miles away. There was no port nearby. Beneath the city were none of the raw materials—the oil, gas, and sulfur—that made other Texas cities rich. Water is still in short supply; the Trinity River, alternately a flood or a trickle, has been such a mean affair that there is now some sentiment for piping the thing underground to get it out of the way. The climate in summer is practically unendurable.

Yet there Dallas stands—its skyscrapers soaring abruptly up from the blackland like Maxfield Parrish castles, and so wildly, improbably successful that the stranger leaves it feeling as if he had been suspended in a vast hyperbole. It is the Athens of the Southwest, the undisputed leader of finance, insurance, distribution, culture, and fashion for this land of the super-Americans, and now it is becoming a great manufacturing center as well. . . . Everything in Dallas is bigger and better; the parties are plusher, the buildings more air-conditioned, the women better dressed, and the girls more fetching. And in all of these things it is, finally, *a monument to sheer determination.* Dallas doesn't owe a thing to accident, nature, or inevitability. It is what it is—even to the girls—because the men of Dallas damn well planned it that way (McCombs 1949, 99-101, emphasis added).

The author of the hyperbole above was *not* a Texan—having been born in Tennessee in 1905—but became one in later life. Nor did he invent the myth, but, as an outsider, he appears to have articulated it more clearly than the insiders who lived and believed it—and still largely believe it (cf. Graff 2008). Later writers note the hegemonic quality of this origin myth, citing as evidence of its power the fact that even Dallas's minority populations tend to believe in the city's exceptionalism, though they have benefited little from it (Graff 2008; Hanson 2003).

It is within the context of the myth that we can begin to understand the city's chosen pattern of responses to its homeless citizens. The implicit argument runs something like this: if early settlers arrived to a virtual "nowhere" with "nothing," and yet somehow created a world-class city on the plains, how can having "nothing" in the present possibly be an obstacle for any person already privileged enough to live in such a place? If the entire city of Dallas somehow managed to create itself *ex nihilo*, how is it that an individual human being cannot take control of his or her own life and destiny? The homeless cause distress for Dallas elites not so much because of their misery as because their continued presence calls the city's whole story of itself into question. Ultimately, what the homeless cannot be forgiven is their power to tarnish Dallas's glittering image of itself (Graff 2008). Thus, for the elites who govern and work in Dallas's downtown, it is *the homeless* who are the problem, not the reality of *homelessness.* Their preferred solution, therefore, is to make the homeless go away—indeed, this has historically been the *only* use of tax dollars considered "appropriate" for confronting homelessness.

Exceptionally Mean?

In January of 2006 the National Coalition for the Homeless and the National Law Center on Homelessness and Poverty ranked Dallas as the sixth "meanest" city in the United States (NCH/NLCHP 2006). This ranking was based specifically on the presence, the number, and the degree of enforcement of laws that criminalize behaviors commonly engaged in by homeless people (and *not* generally engaged in by people who are housed). In Dallas's case, specific actions which led to its ignominious spot in the rankings were: (1) the passage in 2005 of a city ordinance making it illegal to taking a shopping cart off store property; (2) a Texas Department of Transportation sweep of homeless encampments that took place on the day after the HUD-mandated homeless census; (3) a May 2005 sweep of one of the city's largest and most elaborate homeless camps, with the rationale given by the City that this would give the residents incentive to deal with their problems of addictions and/or mental illness; (4) a September 2005 ordinance penalizing any organization that feeds the homeless outside of specifically designated areas; and (5) the suggestion, by then-mayor Laura Miller, that the city begin ticketing any person who gave money to panhandlers, since the blanket ban on panhandling that had been passed two years earlier was having little to no effect.[7]

Although the report and ranking do not consider this as a factor, readers should also be aware that at the time of the ranking Dallas did not have (and had never had) a city-owned and -operated nighttime shelter—Mayor Lindsley's 1915 dream having failed to reach fulfillment. Thus, police and city social workers were, in 2005 and again in the fall of 2007, bulldozing homeless camps and arresting people sleeping on sidewalks in order to "encourage" people to seek treatment and shelter, without there being any guarantee that such services were actually available at the time of the sweeps.

In the City But Not Of the City: Faith-Based Groups Respond

The earliest homeless shelter in Dallas, the Union Gospel Mission, was founded in 1949 by the "Christian Businessmen Breakfast Club" that met in downtown Dallas; it still operates with no government or United Way funding. UGM now operates two separate shelter facilities, one for men, with a capacity of 330 per-night, and one for women and children, with space for 235. Although the shelters' physical locations are no longer in downtown Dallas, UGM sends a bus downtown every afternoon to pick up anyone wishing to stay there for the night. Its self-description reflects a curious blend of motivations—on the one hand, the sense of a faith-rooted obligation to provide shelter for anyone who seeks it; on the other, the deep belief that real change in people's lives will only come about through adopting faith for themselves:

> Since 1949 the Union Gospel Mission has been reaching out to the homeless in Dallas. We provide food, shelter, clothing and faith to 500+ men, women and children nightly. For many the mission is a place to enter, to seek shelter from the storm. For many others it's a place to stay, to live, to become a healthy member of society with a deep and abiding faith in Jesus Christ (Union Gospel Mission n.d.).

The Dallas Life Foundation, which began in 1954, is an outreach of the downtown First Baptist Church. Like UGM, it depends entirely on donations from the private sector, primarily churches and individuals; and receives neither United Way nor government funding. Dallas Life operates a 100,000 square-foot shelter in downtown Dallas, with space for up to five hundred men and ninety women (on separate floors), with an additional fifty units for families. Its mission statement is slightly more assertive about the role of faith in its programming: "Dallas Life reaches out to homeless men, women and children with food, clothing, shelter, education and long-term rehabilitation programs founded on spiritual principals [sic] and the teachings of Jesus Christ" (Dallas Life Foundation n.d.). One hears stories, however, which suggest that the "spiritual" component is more mandatory than the above language suggests. I was told by one family seeking shelter that they had been kicked out of Dallas Life for missing a 9:00 p.m. chapel service, even though they had been at their own church and could prove it. And in 2008, a shelter resident claimed to have been kicked out of Dallas Life's drug rehabilitation program because he continued to atttend the Cathedral of Hope (Dallas's largest GLBT congregation) even after having been counseled that the Cathedral was doing "the devil's work" and teaching "false doctrines" (Wright 2008).

Austin Street Centre was founded in 1983 by a partnership between First Presbyterian Church and several Episcopal churches. Its facility, located about a mile from downtown, is able to house up to 425 men, women, and children each night. Because the sleeping space is one large gymnasium-like room, with only a flimsy partition separating men from women and children, the shelter only admits males over the age of forty-five (who, they feel, are less volatile). Austin Street's mission statement reads as follows:

> The Centre's primary purpose for existence is to offer emergency shelter and related services to the homeless person in a compassionate Christian community, so that the person in need might be better able to make responsible choices and changes in their lives. The Centre has a particular ministry of caring for those who suffer from various physical and mental disabilities, unable to care for themselves, with few or no available alternatives. This includes 24-hour shelter care for those persons recovering from serious illness or injury (Austin Street Centre 2006-2010).

Austin Street has a chapel adjacent to the shelter building, where residents *may* attend services if they choose; they are never required to do so. In addition, the chapel is available for baptisms, weddings, and funerals—and since the shelter's director is herself an Episcopal priest, these can be fairly easily accomplished. Like UGM and Dallas Life, Austin Street is supported entirely by donations, with no government or United Way funding. They also maintain connections with the Dallas faith community by providing the opportunity for congregations to prepare and serve an evening meal for shelter residents, on a rotating basis.

It begins to sound as a familiar refrain. Interfaith Housing Coalition was formed in 1985 by First Presbyterian Church; it now provides transitional housing[8] as well as emergency shelter. Family Gateway, a families-only shelter, was begun in 1986 by a coalition of congregations representing several denominations; it, too, now provides transitional housing in addition to emergency services. The Salvation Army, whose shelter is located several miles north of downtown, is, obviously, also a faith-based organization . . . and they, too, now offer transitional housing.

The *first* transitional housing facility and program in Dallas, opened in 1987, was Oasis Housing Corporation, a ministry of Trinity Presbyterian Church (Adkins and Kemper 2006); both Oasis and Trinity have since closed. Genesis Woman's Shelter, for victims of domestic violence, was formed by the same Presbyterian-Episcopalian partnership that founded the Austin Street Centre. The agency that provides daily child care for homeless children, along with family counseling and other services, is the Vogel Alcove, a project of the Dallas Jewish Coalition. The Stewpot was the first agency to provide meals to the hungry and homeless in downtown Dallas. If it were not for churches and synagogues, congregational partnerships and other religious organizations, there would until recently have been few to no services for the city's homeless. A number of these FBOs do receive federal funding for some portion of their programming, but all are deeply dependent on local foundations, congregations, and individuals for the majority of their support, as well as for volunteers to supplement the activities of professional staff.

Of course, services that are generally available to citizens of the City of Dallas and Dallas County are available to the homeless, provided they have the means to make use of them. Parkland, the county hospital, treats hundreds of homeless patients every year, and has instituted a homeless-outreach medical service with mobile clinics that park themselves in different locations where the homeless are known to congregate. Since the city-owned shelter, The Bridge, opened in 2008, Parkland has provided onsite clinical and medical care at that facility.

Until the Bridge opened its doors in May of 2008, the only facility resembling a shelter that the City of Dallas provided was a daytime-only location called the Day Resource Center, where restrooms and showers were available, and where numerous social-service providers kept weekday office hours to meet with and assist the homeless (e.g., the Veterans Administration, county mental-health providers, etc.). But significantly, this city agency, opened in 1989, was designed and originally operated *by the Stewpot and First Presbyterian Church*, whose staff members had far more knowledge about the needs of the homeless than did anyone at the city level. Unfortunately, this did not keep city officials from interfering in Day Resource Center operations. Homeless persons quickly learned that, if they had been told "no" by someone at Day Resource, all they had to do was walk a couple of blocks to City Hall and make enough of a nuisance of themselves that *someone* would pick up the phone, call Day Resource, and attempt to intervene on their behalf. After just a few months of this, the Stewpot withdrew itself from the Center's operations and it became entirely a city-run entity.

In addition to the Day Resource Center, in recent years the city has fielded a Crisis Intervention Team, consisting of both trained social workers and formerly homeless persons, whose job it is to make contact with the homeless in places where they like to congregate, to encourage them to begin the process of getting into treatment for their mental illness and/or addiction challenges, and to offer them referrals to shelters and other helping agencies. While these teams have met with some success with individual homeless persons, the fact remains that until recently they had only very limited services to offer. They also labor with the constant knowledge that the City's primary motivation for getting the homeless off the streets is not concern for the homeless themselves, but concern over the City's "image" and friendliness to business.

The Stewpot: An FBO in Detail

As noted above, the Stewpot was begun in 1975 as a ministry of First Presbyterian Church in downtown Dallas. Despite having grown to a staff of more than fifteen, with an annual budget of over $1 million, the Stewpot has never been incorporated as a 501(c)(3) separate from the church. Staff and building expenses are line items in the church's budget, and while the Stewpot has an advisory board which meets on a regular basis, ultimate control rests with the elders of the congregation. This has not been an accidental choice; church leaders have felt that the congregation as a whole would remain much more engaged and interested in the Stewpot's work—along with the church's other community ministries—if they retained more of a structural "buy-in." Since the Stewpot has never sought federal funding for its work, its non-separation from the church has caused no problems in that regard.

To anyone unfamiliar with the church's history and connection to the Stewpot, its faith-based roots are not immediately visible. The main room, where guests congregate and where the noon meal was served until recently, is decorated with charcoal-sketch portraits of former clients; there is no religious art apparent. A prayer was always offered before the mid-day meal, but clients could easily enough avoid it by not being among the first in line. The only regularly scheduled activity that qualifies as "faith-based" is the one-hour daily Bible study, which draws twenty to thirty participants not only for the religious content but also for the coffee and donuts which accompany it. (Clients *have* been "banned" from Bible study if they repeatedly take the food and then leave without remaining for the lesson.) These hour-long studies are led by a different person each weekday—some lay, some clergy—and are nearly always lively and interactive. An annual event, held on or near All Saints' Day, is a brief worship service which commemorates the lives of the homeless who have died in the previous year. Few clients attend this service, which is held in a small chapel at First Presbyterian, but those who do invariably express appreciation that someone has remembered their friends.

Faith-based content is far more evident in the Stewpot's communication with its supporters and donors. The quarterly newsletter is titled *Inasmuch*, taken from Matthew 25:40: "Inasmuch as you have done unto one of the least of these my brethren, you have done it unto me" (King James Version), a verse that appears on the newsletter's first and last pages. Fundraising letters invariably cite the Bible, often in direct juxtaposition with a story drawn from daily experience at the Stewpot:

> One of the enjoyable events at The Stewpot is our winter and summer concerts for the homeless. Besides the classical music, modern dance, and contemporary vocalists (and bagpipes!), door prizes are awarded. The most popular one is a two-night stay at a local hotel. After one recent winter concert, I asked the winner of the hotel stay how he had enjoyed his weekend. He said he didn't go. He saw my surprise. Then he told me he had given his prize away to a newly-married homeless couple so that they could have a honeymoon. I would like to think that I would have done the same, but I wonder.
>
> *Such giving models true charity.* Perhaps this story is a modern-day applied example of the vision of the banquet found in Luke 14:12-14—"But when you give a feast, invite the poor, the maimed, the lame, the blind, and you will be blessed, because they cannot repay you" (Fundraising letter, November 2006; emphasis in original).

For the most part, the Stewpot's faith-rootedness shows up in ways that are quite subtle, but might best be described as "addressing both body and soul." By this I mean not only obviously religious activities such as Bible study, but also activities that are not "useful" at all, but designed to bring joy and to celebrate people's lives and gifts. Weekly art classes encourage clients to express themselves and to develop their talents; a handful of them have been able to leave homelessness through the sale of their art. When guests are invited to a birthday celebration in the month on which their birthday falls, one of the usual activities is the sharing of favorite birthday memories. It is simultaneously heartbreaking to hear any number of participants say, "This is the first time anyone has ever celebrated my birthday," and heart-healing to see how much it means to them that strangers have brought them refreshments and gifts. The Stewpot hosts an annual event on Halloween each year complete with a costume contest; essay, poetry, and art contests; a talent show; and prizes for all the winners. Staff and volunteers usually end up standing through the whole afternoon, as homeless guests fill all the available chairs to celebrate one another's talents in a world which sees them as undesirables. Twice a year, Stewpot guests are invited across the street to First Presbyterian's sanctuary[9] for an hour-long concert given just for them by professional musicians from all over the city; attendance is frequently more than 200. This event is followed by a party with more door prizes. Stewpot programs do everything possible to treat the homeless as whole persons, individuals who not only have tremendous needs but also have tremendous gifts to offer.

Bricks Without Straw

> That same day Pharaoh commanded the taskmasters of the people, as well as their supervisors, "You shall no longer give the people straw to make bricks, as before; let them go and gather straw for themselves. But you shall require of them the same quantity of bricks as they have made previously; do not diminish it . . . " So the taskmasters and the supervisors of the people went out and said to the people, "Thus says Pharaoh, 'I will not give you straw. Go and get straw yourselves, wherever you can find it; but your work will not be lessened in the least.'" So the people scattered throughout the land of Egypt, to gather stubble for straw (Exodus 5:6-8a, 10-12; New Revised Standard Version).

Though there is no such thing as an exact analogy, the biblical story of the Hebrew slaves being forced by Pharaoh to "make bricks without straw" seems to me a useful parallel to the situation of faith-based groups who are asked to take on tasks "devolved" to them by reigning political institutions: A task needs to be done. Those who hold political power make a choice about who is to be asked (ordered) to do the work. Yet they also withhold at least some of the resources necessary to accomplish the work that is being asked or demanded. The Hebrew people are forced to begin gathering straw themselves in order to make the bricks Pharaoh has compelled them to make, yet the daily quota of bricks is not reduced. Faith-based organizations may be provided with some federal dollars—this is, after all, the entire point of the Faith-Based Initiatives program—but it is not enough money to provide the homeless with what they truly need, namely, a permanent and safe place to live. The primary reason that FBOs often appear to be more "efficient" than governments is that they "gather their own straw," i.e., they have little choice but to supplement the tax dollars they receive with donations, grants, volunteers, in-kind gifts, and so on.

Dallas is an object lesson for what happens—and doesn't happen—when FBOs alone are expected to figure out how to care for the homeless. Millions of dollars have been spent year after year to provide shelter beds, food and clothing, job training and placement, drug and alcohol rehab, mental health services. Yet the number of homeless in the city remains essentially the same. The homeless may well be less miserable because of the aid offered to them by FBOs in Dallas, but they don't appear to be any less homeless.

Not until the City of Dallas became actively involved on behalf of the homeless, rather than in opposition to them, has the situation begun to turn. Having somewhat bravely disobeyed the wishes of downtown business owners by not situating the Bridge somewhere other than downtown, city leaders are now faced with the question of how to address their own success. In the weeks after the Bridge opened, its sleeping areas were filled to overflowing with homeless persons who were quite willing to come in off the streets if there was just space for them somewhere. In partnership with the faith-based shelters, the Bridge managed to deal with the overflow before winter made it impossible for people to sleep in its enclosed courtyards. The city is now faced with figuring out how to find permanent housing for its homeless citizens—a situation which it is taking much more seriously now that *it* is carrying responsibility for sheltering them. Previously, city council members were loath to approve options such as group housing, permanent supportive housing, and public housing within their own districts; and made it nearly impossible for the faith-based groups (and others) who tried to establish such facilities. Now, with several hundred homeless persons living in *their* facility, they are beginning to resist the NIMBY ("not in my back yard") complaints of constituents who do not want "those people" as neighbors.

While a city is a smaller-scale stage on which to observe government and nonprofit action and/or inaction than is the federal government, I suggest that the lesson of Dallas is a crucial one for the United States as a whole in the ongoing dicussion about whose responsibility it is to offer care for those within society who cannot care for themselves. And regardless of the question of whose task it "ought" to be, the Dallas story addresses the issue of *capacity* for doing the work. In a politically conservative city where the preference has always been for private dollars rather than public funds to address human need, nonprofit organizations ought to have the resources they need to fix problems rather than just softening their blow. They do not. In one of the largest cities in the "Bible belt," faith-based organizations should have all the resources they need to do whatever it is that needs doing. They do not. Without the involvement and commitment of governments, FBOs have neither the political, the economic, nor the social capital to do the work that we as a society are asking them to do. I do not suggest that government involvement guarantees that social problems will be solved—witness the truly awful city-run shelters cited in the first section of this chapter. I *do* suggest that government abdication guarantees that such problems will *not* be solved.

Notes

Thanks are due to the staff and volunteers of the Stewpot, who welcomed me into their midst and tolerated my many questions—and who, indeed, continue to ask when I am going to come back as a volunteer!—and to Robert V. Kemper and Laurie Occhipinti for their comments on this chapter as a work-in-progress.

1. I.e., not "neo"conservative.
2. Section adapted and expanded from Adkins (2010).
3. Unless otherwise noted, all population and demographic data are taken from the 2008 American Community Survey (ACS), available online through the U.S. census portal at www.factfinder.census.gov.
4. The U.S. Department of Housing and Urban Development mandates that all cities receiving HUD funding for homeless services conduct a census of their homeless population at least biennially. Nationwide, the count is normally conducted on a single night in January—the theory being that more people are likely to seek shelter during cold weather and thus be easier to find and to census. However, since many homeless do not seek shelter even in the worst of times, census-takers must also make an effort to count the unsheltered homeless in the myriad locations where they settle in for the night. It is impossible to locate all of the unsheltered homeless; therefore, the HUD census count must always be understood as a minimum number of homeless in a given city.
5. The Gini coefficient measures inequality of income or wealth for a given region. The mathematics are complex, but results are expressed on a scale that ranges from 0 to 1, where 0 represents a (hypothetical) group in which all people have exactly the same resources and 1 represents a group where one individual has all the resources and everyone else has nothing. Thus, the higher the Gini index number, the greater the economic inequality in a given society.
6. Gini coefficient data on other countries come from the CIA World Factbook, available online at https://www.cia.gov/library/publications/the-world-factbook/rankorder/2172rank.html. Comparable figures are also available from the United Nations Human Development Report.
7. I note that a more recent report (NLCHP/NCH 2009) no longer includes Dallas among its "Ten Meanest." Careful reading of the text, however, makes clear that Dallas has not improved its treatment of the homeless; rather, other cities have become even "meaner" in the interim.
8. Transitional housing is an intermediate step for persons or families who are ready to leave an emergency shelter but who cannot yet afford market-rate housing. During a one- to two-year stay in a transitional housing program, participants receive reduced rent and are expected to participate in programs such as job training, budgeting, and other life skills. Many are waiting for Section 8 (federally subsidized) housing to become available.
9. Lest this sound like homeless persons are welcome in First Presbyterian's sanctuary *only* twice a year, let me hasten to add that numerous homeless worship at First Pres. every Sunday, where they are welcomed and invited into membership along with the elites of Dallas.

Works Cited

Adkins, Julie. 2010. Helping the homeless in Dallas: Lessons and challenges from a faith-based nonprofit. *Practicing Anthropology* 32(2):11-16.

Adkins, Julie, and Robert V. Kemper. 2006. Oasis Housing Corporation: From solutions to dissolution in a faith-based organization. *Urban Anthropology* 35(2-3): 237-64.

Austin Street Centre. 2006-2010. Our mission. Available online at www.austinst.org/ (last accessed March 8, 2010).

Brettell, Caroline B. 2003. Bringing the city back in: Cities as contexts for immigrant incorporation. In *American arrivals: Anthropology engages the new immigration*, ed. Nancy Foner, 163-95. Santa Fe: School of American Research Press.

Dallas Independent School District (DISD). 2009. 2008-2009 Facts. Pdf file available as a link from www.dallasisd.org/about/geninfo.htm (last accessed January 27, 2010).

Dallas Life Foundation. n.d. About us: Mission. Available online at www.dallaslife.org/about-us/mission (last accessed March 8, 2010).

Dallas Morning News. 2010. Hunger can show up on the sweetest faces (DMN Charities homepage). Available online at charities.dallasnews.com/ (last accessed March 7, 2010).

Dordick, Gwendolyn A. 1997. *Something left to lose: Personal relations and survival among New York's homeless*. Philadelphia: Temple University Press.

Enstam, Elizabeth York. 1998. *Women and the creation of urban life: Dallas, Texas, 1843-1920*. College Station, TX: Texas A & M University Press.

Graff, Harvey J. 2008. *The Dallas myth: The making and unmaking of an American city*. Minneapolis: University of Minnesota Press.

Hanson, Royce. 2003. *Civic culture and urban change: Governing Dallas*. Detroit: Wayne State University Press.

Hill, Patricia Evridge. 1996. *Dallas: The making of a modern city*. Austin: University of Texas Press.

Hopper, Kim. 2003. *Reckoning with homelessness*. Ithaca, NY: Cornell University Press.

Kemper, Robert V., ed. 2005. Communities old and new in the Dallas-Fort Worth metropolitan area. A special issue of *Urban Anthropology* 34(2-3).

McCombs, Holland. 1949. The dydamic [sic] men of Dallas. *Fortune*, February.

Metro Dallas Homeless Alliance (MDHA). 2009. 2009 annual "point in time" homeless count and census, Dallas County. Available online at mdhadallas.org/ homelesscount.aspx (last accessed March 7, 2010).

National Coalition for the Homeless and National Law Center on Homelessness and Poverty. 2006. A dream denied: The criminalization of homeless in U.S. cities. Report available for download at www.nationalhomeless.org/publications/crimreport/ 2006_index.html (last accessed February 10, 2010).

National Law Center on Homelessness and Poverty and National Coalition for the Homeless. 2009. Homes not handcuffs: the criminalization of homelessness in U.S. cities. Available for download at www.nationalhomeless.org/publications/crimreport/ index.html (last accessed February 10, 2010).

Payne, Darwin. 1994. *Big D: Triumphs and troubles of an American supercity in the 20th century*. Dallas: Three Forks Press.

Rollwagen, Jack. 1975. The city as context: The Puerto Ricans of Rochester. *Urban Anthropology* 4(1):53-59.

Union Gospel Mission (UGM). n.d. About us. Available online at www.ugmdallas.org/
     about.html (last accessed March 8, 2010).
Wright, John. 2008. Faith-based eviction? *Dallas Voice*, April 11.

Chapter 6
Muslims, Medicine, and Mercy:
Free Clinics in Southern California[1]
Lance D. Laird and Wendy Cadge

The UMMA Community Clinic inhabits a small, flat-roofed building with stucco walls painted battleship gray. The name "University Muslim Medical Association" is prominently displayed alongside a crescent/star/family logo on the "Welcome – *Bienvenido*" signage in this densely populated South Central Los Angeles neighborhood. The clinic sits on a wide commercial street behind a black iron fence, the edges of its small parking lot neatly landscaped with palm trees, shrubs, and patches of green grass. The "annex" building, a modular unit in the parking lot, houses two Muslim administrative assistants and the CEO, Yasser Aman, whose Honda parked alongside has license plates reading, "ONE UMMA."[2] The waiting room of the clinic is neat, clean, and generically clinical in appearance, the reception window providing a glimpse into a cramped room full of patient files. The white interior hallway is lined with framed quotations from the Qur'an and Sunnah, in Arabic with English translation. The staff room displays a prominent *Āyat al-Kursī* (Verse of the Throne) from the Qur'an, gold embroidered on black, like those often seen in traditional Muslim homes. The majority of UMMA clinic's governing board, however, is now non-Muslim, and all of the paid clinical staff, including the medical director, are non-Muslim.

In contrast, the stark white mobile unit with green awning that houses Al-Shifa Clinic stands on the grounds of a mosque, Masjid Ulum, its parking lot dotted with palm trees, against the backdrop of rocky hills in the Muscoy section of San Bernardino. The mosque is home to a largely South Asian Muslim community in a predominantly Hispanic and African American neighborhood. The mosque behind and the name *Al-Shifa*, Arabic for "healing," are the only markers inside or out that this clinic is a Muslim space. The sign out front reads, "Free Health Clinic for Everyone." In this organization, the board is entirely Muslim and the physician volunteers are nearly all Muslim, and yet the administrator, Mr. Saab, disclaimed repeatedly, "We do not mention Islam here."

The physical spaces of these two clinics provide the first indication to a client or observer of the ways in which each manifests its Muslim identity. The geographic locations, the names of the clinics, and the adornment of interior spaces are held in tension with personnel and governance choices that demonstrate subtle differences in how Muslim identity is expressed and maintained in these organizations. In 2007, the authors interviewed leaders of ten Muslim community-based health organizations (MCBHOs) in four major metropolitan areas with large Muslim populations: Chicago, Detroit, Los Angeles, and Houston. In this chapter, we focus on the role and expression of religious identity in the narrative accounts of two Muslim clinics in the greater Los Angeles area: the University Muslim Medical Association Community Clinic (UMMA), in Los Angeles; and Al-Shifa Clinic, in San Bernardino. Our analysis of the tales, the founding narratives of these new American Muslim charitable healthcare institutions, enables a grounded discussion of how clinic leaders are actively constructing the identity of these faith-based health service organizations and charting new paths for Muslims in American society.

Muslim community-based health organizations (MCBHOs) first appeared in the United States in the early 1990s in Los Angeles, though most of the approximately twenty organizations have emerged in a range of North American cities during the past decade. We include in this category only organizations that provide ongoing professional physical or mental healthcare in their local communities *and* publicly identify their organizations as being Muslim, being led by Muslims, or having developed out of Muslim teachings or traditions. They include a range of groups, from domestic violence shelters and family counseling centers to medical clinics and networks of private healthcare professionals. The organizations inhabit upper rooms, trailers, free-standing commercial buildings, renovated storefronts, or a virtual chain of private offices. Taken together, they represent a significant form of Muslim participation in the American public square.

Most studies of the growth of Muslim communities in the United States have focused on the rapid progress of mosque-building, the emergence of Islamic schools, the formation of regional and continental organizations like the Islamic Society of North America and Islamic Circle of North America, and, more recently, the emergence of Muslim political action groups. In assessing the historical development of these institutions, Schumann argues that "mainstream" immigrant and post-migrant Muslims in the United States constitute a "Muslim diaspora" that evolved an identity discourse in the 1980s-1990s which enables them to embrace political participation in the American public sphere while maintaining a sense of connection to the wider "Muslim world" (i.e., the *umma*). He attributes the emergence of this discourse to "the universalistic desire to contribute Islamic values and norms to a wider notion of American civilization as well as to improve the situation of the Muslim community in the U.S. with lobbying and public relations work" (2007, 24). Schumann thus depicts a U.S. Muslim diaspora in a "fateful triangle" of political communication among their own communities, the American public, and Muslims outside the United States.

American Muslims are also one religious community (or, perhaps more accurately, several communities of faith and practice sharing a body of tradition) among others in the United States. Studies of societal shifts in American religious groups identify a renewed spirit of voluntarism and increasing congregationalism (Ammerman 1997; Edgell 2006). They indicate a pluralism of organizational styles, decision-making processes, and interplays between individual piety, communal identity, service provision, and public religion (Cnaan 2006; Cnaan and Boddie 2002). The role of non-"church" religious organizations in the United States often complements, supplements, or challenges the religious practices within more official institutions (Edgell 2006). In addition to documenting the rapid proliferation of mosques, Bagby and colleagues' Mosque Study notes several different models of membership and governance, and a range of social services offered to members and neighborhoods. They note that African American mosques have a stronger tendency toward community service than their immigrant counterparts (Bagby 2004). How might Muslim-initiated community services represent an integration of individual piety, communal identity, and public religion? How might these MCBHOs complement, supplement, or challenge official American Muslim institutions and the discourse of participation in American society?

With increasing governmental support for faith-based organizations in the provision of social services in the United States since the 1996 Welfare Reform Act, scholars of religion and of constitutional law have devoted significant attention to the nexus of church-state relations these organizations represent (Cnaan 2006; Cnaan and Boddie 2002; Solomon 2003). Research on the relationship between religion, spirituality, and health has also grown, though studies have focused mainly on the individual as the unit of analysis rather than the institution. Important exceptions examine the role of African American churches in mental health service and other health ministries (Taylor et al. 2000; Thomas, Quinn, Billingsley, and Caldwell 1994). The relative dearth of research on the role of religious identity in health organizations is surprising, as many major hospitals, nursing homes, free clinics, substance abuse facilities, and other organizations that address basic healthcare needs today were founded and influenced by religious people and organizations. In the nineteenth century, religion shaped the process of American hospital expansion as Catholic and Jewish hospitals opened to accommodate patients and health practitioners who experienced mistreatment or exclusion from mainstream, predominantly Protestant institutions (Lazarus 1991; Rosenberg 1995; Vogel 1980). These religiously affiliated hospitals were open to everyone and, until the mid-twentieth century, cared for more than one quarter of all hospitalized patients (Numbers and Sawyer 1982). The evolving religious values and shifting identities of these faith-based institutions continue to shape current administrative structures and social norms in the hospitals (Swartz 1998).

Free healthcare clinics also have a particular history in the American healthcare landscape, first emerging in the mid-1960s in San Francisco (The Haight-Ashbury Free Clinic), Cleveland, Seattle, Cincinnati, Detroit, and other cities. Street clinics, neighborhood clinics, and youth clinics provided healthcare services to drug users, racial and ethnic minorities, youth, and others not well served by existing healthcare organizations. Though many clinics struggled to survive, they multiplied through subsequent decades, and there were an estimated 800 free clinics in operation in 2004. While many are completely secular in their origins and mission statements, many others are supported by religious leaders and volunteers, and some have close connections to local religious, particularly Christian, organizations (Weiss 2006).

Many successful church-based programs develop into semi-autonomous religious service agencies, which can appeal both to religious donors, based on their values, motivations, and historical roots; and to secular donors, based on the quality of human services provided. Jeavons has developed a set of multidimensional criteria for evaluating the degree of religious or spiritual identity in faith-based organizations. He suggests that scholars examine the relevance of faith identity to an organization in its self-identity, the mix of participants, the sources and nature of its material resources, its products and their delivery, its decision-making, its distribution of power, and its primary partners within the organizational field (Jeavons 1998). (See also chapter 1 of this volume.) Studies of faith-based social service organizations, however, note that they often struggle to maintain their religious identity as they deal with the growing pains of expanding services, hiring staff, and qualifying for public and private foundation funding (Chambre 2001). In the current climate of federal funding for faith-based social services, it is vital to consider the experience of minority religious organizations. Our study of Muslim clinics offers a unique window into the role of religious identity in faith-based service organizations and into the process of contemporary Muslim American identity formation.

Collecting and Analyzing the Clinic Narratives

During a field visit in April 2007, we toured both clinic facilities and gathered reports, publications, and other relevant media. We conducted individual interviews with four UMMA clinic leaders and two Al-Shifa clinic leaders, in addition to a group interview with six other members of the Al-Shifa board and staff. Each interview explored the organization's history, relations with Muslim constituents, reasons for identifying as "Muslim," and lessons learned. Interviews with multiple leaders of each organization elicited multiple versions of the developmental narrative and perspectives on the identity of the organizations.

Narrative analysis enables identification of common plotlines between narrators, disruptions to these plots, and thematic connections within an individual's account and between accounts (Riessman 1993). In order to examine organizing metaphors and structures that frame the meaning of participation in the clinic for these individuals, we re-transcribed selected accounts into poetic stanzas, breaking lines at critical junctures in meaning and shifts of vocal intonation

(Gee, Michaels, and O'Connor 1992). Attending to the framework and structure, thematic shifts, organizing metaphors, repetitions, and cadences, even within such mundane stories of groups gathering to sort out the logistics of running a medical clinic, we hope to present a fuller, more contextual social portrait of the organizations and their meanings for participants.

Narrative Plotlines

After analyzing the separate accounts of each narrator, we identified a common institutional narrative for each organization:

UMMA was initiated by second-generation (a majority of South Asian and some Arab immigrant parents) medical students who were leaders of the progressive Muslim Student Association at UCLA. They originally envisioned a mobile van that would offer basic health screenings throughout impoverished South Central. The students received significant mentoring and organizational assistance from UCLA and Drew Schools of Medicine. Los Angeles city councilor Rita Walters helped them secure a building and federal funds to support the all-volunteer clinic for its first four years (1996-2000). The founders reached a financial crisis point, at which time they held a highly successful fundraiser in the local Muslim community. They have since diversified their funding sources, including major public support through grants and limited billing, private foundation support, and a donor base of predominantly Muslim individuals. The clinic has expanded its specialty services and medical education programs, hired paid professional staff, and reorganized its board of directors in order to be eligible for Federally Qualified Health Clinic status.

Al-Shifa Clinic began with a group of mid-career, mostly immigrant physicians from various hospitals and practices who prayed together on Fridays at Masjid Ulum. A Muslim county architect and Muslim county hospital cardiologist convinced the county to donate a used modular clinic for their use as a free clinic in an underserved neighborhood. These physicians raised funds in the Muslim community, secured permission to place the building on the grounds of the mosque, and received significant grants from the county government to open the clinic in 2000. Restrictions imposed by malpractice insurance policies limit the number of volunteers and hours of this half-time clinic, which has nevertheless expanded to include dental and eye clinics. The clinic is moving from primarily public sources of funding to a Muslim donor base and private foundations.

These developmental narratives have much in common. Each clinic was organized by a group of Muslim medical professionals who encountered each other in religious settings, whether on campus or in a mosque. Both groups saw a gap in primary health services for a large population of uninsured or underinsured populations in their local area. Both groups then utilized connections to secular universities, hospitals, and local government in order to secure large donations of infrastructure and operational funding.

The narratives of both clinics present them as institutions that have an important educational mission for training and mentoring the next generation of health professionals. UMMA has striven from its inception (as the brainchild of medical students) to integrate its services with prominent local medical schools in order to train hundreds of medical students and residents in cross-cultural community medicine. Al-Shifa board members speak of the clinic as a "resource for the youth," where student volunteers can be exposed to "how medicine works" and can develop job skills. Dr. Mohammed Aslam recounted that they had helped several students, at least one of them Christian, to get into medical school. Both clinics tout the fact that some residents choose to return as volunteers after their training.

The founding groups seem to have mobilized support from their local Muslim community at different points and in different ways. UMMA initially mobilized an existing informal network of Muslim medical students who were committed to volunteer, as did Al-Shifa. At the beginning of their project, Al-Shifa Clinic's founders approached the mosque director to acquire land and solicited donations from the Muslim community toward a county matching grant that would enable them to transport the building and open the clinic. UMMA CEO Yasser Aman confirms what the narrative suggests, that initially the founders "didn't really have a strategy of, 'Okay, let's make sure the Muslim community is invested.'" They focused on civic and community partnerships, and turned to the local Muslim community for financial support at a later crisis point. UMMA narrators are very conscious, however, of the pride they now inspire in Muslims across the country and how significant the story of the "first Muslim clinic" has become.

The Al-Shifa Clinic continues to operate with an all-volunteer Muslim physician staff, and malpractice insurance policies emerge in their story as the significant barrier to expansion. While UMMA continues to use volunteer physicians, many of whom are Muslim, it has employed sixteen non-Muslim staff to carry out its basic mission. Challenges that emerge in UMMA's narrative include maintaining the "volunteer spirit" and changing governance patterns to meet the mandates of public funders.

Organizing Themes

The organizing theme for the narratives collected in this study is that these community-based health organizations are "Muslim," "local," "for everyone," and "in America." These themes emerge in a number of intersecting ways.

Muslim Obligations to/in America

The Al-Shifa developmental narratives begin with a group of physician friends who happen to be Muslim, "looking at opportunities to help people" (Khan l.51-

52).[3] The intersection of professional, religious, and "American" motivations for community service is illustrated in a narrative from board member Dr. Mohammed Aslam, which we have entitled, "What we can do for our country" (Narrative 1.3-58):

3 You do your job
4 and take care of things
5 which have to be
6 and that's obviously
7 where we did start.
8
9 It was very interesting.
10 Obviously a lot of people were
11 thinking about this project
12 for some period of time
13
14 and my involvement
15 was basically that,
16 you know,
17 I always think about
18 what President Kennedy said:
19 "Ask what you can do
20 for your country,
21 not what your country
22 can do for you."
23
24 So when, thinking about
25 that one, that
26 we are physicians,
27 we are Muslims,
28 we happen to be
29 in this area.
30

31 And the United States is
32 the richest country,
33 but poorest in healthcare.
34
35 So this is a
36 perfect opportunity
37 which we can contribute
38 for this society
39 as a Muslim
40 and being present
41 over here,
42
43 people go
44 to all over the world,
45 missionaries,
46 yet there are a lot of
47 things to be done
48 right over here.
49
50 [L: True]
51
52 R: Perfect opportunity.
53 And to have the resources
54 to utilize the local resources
55 helped the people.
56
57 So that's what I think,
58 that's how we got started.

In this narrative, framed by "how we got started," Aslam, who appears to be in his late fifties, places his volunteer activities at the clinic late in his medical career. He has "done his job" and "taken care of things which have to be," fulfilled his basic obligations to complete an education, establish a career, and provide for his family. Aslam is well-established as a cardiologist in a supervisory role at the large county hospital. This job provided the foundation for his involvement in starting the clinic, which involved negotiating with the county's board of supervisors in order to secure the donation of the building. During the group interview, a member of the clinic's board joked that, when Aslam had performed a heart operation on one of the county supervisors, he had had to "put something in." The second stanza indicates that he entered the clinic planning process after the initial group had developed the idea.

In the third stanza, Aslam links his personal involvement in Al-Shifa Clinic with Kennedy's famous patriotic call for Americans to engage in volunteer service. By so doing, he lays claim to an American icon and the spirit of volunteerism inherited from the 1960s that gave birth to both free clinics and the Peace Corps. The following three stanzas serve to deepen this sense of duty to country and to link it with his identity as Muslim. Stanza four includes three "we" statements, establishing the identity of the founders as physicians, Muslims, and local. In the fifth stanza, he states the underlying social issue to which the clinic is a patriotic response: though "your country" is seemingly the richest, it is "poorest in healthcare." Given this situation, the sixth stanza repeats the refrain of "we can contribute" (as physicians), "as a Muslim," and "over here" (local). The seventh stanza repeats the refrain "over here," contrasting the clinic's charitable mission with "missionaries" who "go all over the world." Such comparisons may be important for narrators to establish Muslim charity work as part of normative mainstream religion in the United States.

The penultimate stanza provides a coda to the narrative. Aslam repeats the phrase "perfect opportunity," indicating that, as Muslim physicians who have fulfilled their obligations, they "have the resources" and can "utilize the local resources" to help "the people." The opportunity to fulfill one's obligations to one's country, to do your job in contributing "for this society as a Muslim," may resonate in amplified ways for immigrant professionals who have adopted the United States as home. The repeated variations of the theme "being present over here" drive home the point of local loyalty and commitment, as opposed to involvement in "homeland" or foreign causes. This almost certainly reflects social pressure on immigrant Muslims in particular to justify and defend their Americanness by service to their country, imbuing the words of President Kennedy with an added layer of meaning. Notably, Kennedy's assassination had occurred two years prior to the Immigration Reform Act of 1965, under which a large wave of immigrant Muslim students and professionals from South Asia and the Middle East arrived.

External social forces have considerable weight in shaping the self-presentation of these American Muslim faith-based health organizations. Several narrators expressed their awareness that the clinic's work was representing "Muslims in general." A member of the Al-Shifa board narrates this sense in a segment we labeled, "The call to do something" (Board Narrative 2.19-46):

19 You know we always felt	31 or sometimes an offensive side,
20 obligated	32 a hostility issue,
21 to do something	33 that was raised a lot
22 for the community	34 of times in the past,
23 and that was the main	35
24 motive behind it all.	36 and we thought the minimum
25	37 we can do
26 Back then there was also	38 is to proceed and establish
27 a lot of, unfortunately,	39 a project like this one
28 stigmatizing about the Muslim	40
29 community being like either passive	41 and not only
30	42 to clean that image

43 but to actively get involved
44 in the community

45 and maybe we can do
46 something good

In the first and last stanzas of this passage, the board member provides the narrative frame: the obligation to "do something/something good" "for/in the community" was the fundamental motive for establishing the clinic. The middle stanzas, however, call attention to external social forces. The second stanza refers to the stigma arising from the public impression that Muslims were "passive," uninvolved in the local public sphere, placing this stigma "back then," at the time of the clinic's founding. The third stanza, however, refers to the stigma of Muslims' offensiveness or hostility, a stigma that has assumed increasingly shrill tones role in public discourse about Muslims in Western societies after 9/11. In the fourth stanza, then, the narrator proposes that the clinic is a rebuttal—though perhaps minimal—to both the "passive Muslim" and "hostile Muslim" images. In the final stanza, the clinic "cleans" the image of Muslims, who now "actively get involved in the community" and "do something good."

UMMA Clinic leaders have assumed with alacrity the mantle of "representing" Muslims in America. The promotional DVD "Healing Our Community" opens with the dramatic title, "As the nation watches . . ." then cuts to footage of the U.S. Congress. The title ". . . History unfolds in the House of Representatives" appears as Los Angeles's Representative Maxine Waters reads an official commendation for the UMMA Clinic in Congress:

If you want to see
what Muslim Americans
truly represent,
go to the UMMA community clinic,
and you will see it there
          (UMMA Video Narrative 1.1-12)

Identification with South Central Los Angeles is particularly strong in the UMMA video. Dr. Stock, a European-American physician volunteer, says that the clinic is located in "the exact spot where the L.A. riots happened," and founder Dr. Rushdi Cader continues:

131 We found that
132 this particular area,
133 which was right on
134 the same street
135 where Reginald Denny was beaten
136 during the civil disturbances
137 of 1992,
138

139 it's a place,
140 that had showed
141 historic intolerance,
142
143 and it should be
144 a place that shows
145 historic mercy
146 and historic compassion.

In this brief passage, Rushdi Cader contrasts the image of violent streets, an infamous beating, and "historic intolerance"—reinforced on the video with visual images of police in riot gear—with the clinic image of "historic mercy and historic compassion." This latter phrase is significantly an allusion to the *basmala*, "In the Name of God, the Compassionate, the Merciful," the opening phrase for chapters of the Qur'an, recited by pious Muslims when they initiate any new activity. Shirani points out that Rushdi Cader often used the phrase "civil disturbances" rather than "riots" in Muslim Student Association magazine articles to describe the 1992 events, as a marker of political solidarity with progressive Third World and African American student groups (Shirani 2008).[4] The UMMA Clinic narratives seem to locate their work very intentionally as Muslims in a specific place, as each stanza above emphasizes "particular area" and "place."

This background provides the context for interpreting Dr. Rumi Cader's extended narrative of the turn toward the local Muslim community during UMMA's financial crisis, which forms the final episode of the narrative we entitled "Infancy and growing pains." After describing the dire financial situation in 2000, Cader continues,

268 And what we did was
269 we went out to
270 our Muslim population
271 here in Los Angeles county
272 and we got upward of I think
273 $350,000
274 and I'm probably underestimating
275 from a Muslim population,
276 right here in LA!
277
278 And the beauty of it was,
279 you know the Muslim population
280 in general,
281 I think in most first world countries,
282 there are a lot of immigrants
283 in the Muslim community
284
285 and the majority of charity
286 money that they give,
287 you know I'm from Sri Lanka,
288 it goes toward the local
289 orphanage in Sri Lanka,
290
291 and that's, generationally,
292 that has been a thing,
293 you know the Italian Americans
294 traditionally donate
295 to stuff out there.

296
297 But to make them aware
298 of a Muslim project
299 right here at their back door
300 and have people donating
301 people donating money to that
302 to a clinic where 98 plus percent of
303 the patients are non-Muslims,
304 that's a statement.
305
306 That's showing Muslims care
307 not just the people in the clinic,
308 but the people
309 in the community too—
310
311 [L: The people funding it.]
312
313 R: Exactly, exactly
314 and that was a big thing for us
315
316 and we've always tried to keep
317 the Muslim identity of the clinic
318 and let Muslims know that,
319 hey, this is a Muslim organization
320 that's put together a clinic
321 to help people,
322 not just Muslims.

The narrative here is framed by stanzas that situate UMMA clearly within the local Muslim population of Los Angeles. The first stanza (268-276) stakes a claim to "our Muslim population." The repetition of "here in Los Angeles county" and "right here in L.A.!" in reference to the Muslim population adds emphasis to the claim of local belonging. The final stanza (316-322), with its fourfold use of "Muslim," puts the emphasis on the other end of this equation: the "Muslim identity" of the "Muslim organization," about which "Muslims" need to know. It returns, however to the local: the goal of the clinic is to "help people, not just Muslims."

The second through fourth stanzas (278-295) drive home both of these themes, while drawing a contrast with traditional immigrant patterns of charitable giving. Cader casts this event of tremendous local Muslim giving as a historic one, marking a generational shift in immigrant identity, similar to that of Italian Americans, to whom he alludes in lines 291-293. The second stanza (278-283) identifies "the Muslim population in general" as primarily immigrant minorities in the West ("in most first world countries"), thus locating himself in the center of a particular portion of the Muslim world. In the third and fourth stanzas (285-295), he compares his own experience of Sri Lankan Americans donating money toward "the local orphanage in Sri Lanka" to Italian Americans who "traditionally donate to stuff out there." In this verbal portrait, we see the shift that UMMA leaders would like to see in the Muslim community, a shift in the meaning of "local" from "out there" (295) to "right here" (276, 299). Other UMMA leaders offer similar analyses of previous generations of immigrant Muslims being concerned with building "basic structure" like mosques and schools, such that "the message around a social service institution was just not really there yet" (Aman 2.29-31). UMMA is part of this generational shift in Muslim immigrant communities toward claiming an American identity by donating to local causes.

In the fifth stanza, Cader represents UMMA as an active agent of this shifting identity process. UMMA "make[s] them aware" of an opportunity to donate to "a Muslim project right here at their backdoor," contrasting the "right here" (299) with the "out there" of the previous stanza (295). UMMA raises awareness of the local within a traditionally homeland-focused immigrant Muslim community. Cader preserves some tension in this stanza, though, as the shift is not only away from donating to Muslim projects abroad but also away from projects that primarily benefit Muslims. Both of these shifts seem to be included in "that's a statement" (305).

UMMA's leaders consistently mention that 98 percent of their patient beneficiaries are non-Muslim, that they are "caring for those neighbors who are most needy" (UMMA Clinic 2008). In Rumi Cader's sixth stanza, UMMA's representative function emerges clearly, as we hear echoes of the Congressional commendation in "That's showing Muslims care," including not just UMMA's staff, "but the people in the community, too" (307-310). Cader reiterates that this is important for UMMA, a "big thing" (316), to represent Muslims as caring for others. This vision of accomplishing the shift in Muslim identity is reinforced with a coda in the final stanza of Cader's narrative, as the "Muslim organization" creates a clinic "to help . . . not just Muslims." Such proclamations by leaders of Muslim faith-based service organizations are significant, as they are responding directly to external negative social forces that other FBOs may not face. These forces include discrimination and prejudice against both immigrants and Muslims in the United States, or forms of xenophobia and Islamophobia. As we have seen in the narratives examined in this section, the leaders of both clinics articulate the identity of their organization, and of themselves individually, in ways that emphasize their local community involvement *as* first- or second-generation immigrants as an *American* duty. They both also highlight the need to represent Muslims in a positive light, particularly as people who give generously, care for, and serve non-Muslims.

Religious Obligations to Serve

Thus far, we have treated Muslim identity in these clinics as a matter of responding to external social factors. Jeavons notes that while an organization's name may have religious connotations, and its members may share religious convictions, one must nevertheless ask how relevant the name and religious convictions are for the mission of the organization. Participants may also share and articulate "core values" that are religious. He further suggests that scholars need to examine not only the products an organization delivers but also the manner in which these products are delivered; for instance, whether they are personally or impersonally delivered and whether they are mass-produced or relationship-promoting (Jeavons 1998).

The stated mission of both of these clinics is to provide high quality, free or affordable healthcare for underserved communities. Whether this service is distinguishable from mainstream "secular" healthcare may depend on intangible factors. For instance, medical staff in the UMMA video claim to be "creating relationships" (161), offering a "setting of acceptance, tolerance, friendship and love" (215-220). Patients bear testimony that UMMA staff treat them like people instead of numbers, and that the clinic is "like a little piece of heaven in the middle of chaos" (170-172). Stories of personal transformation and compassion fill out the picture of how UMMA is "Healing Our Community" as a first step "to heal the world" (307). Several of the staff and storytellers who make these statements on the video are non-Muslim. Al-Shifa board members speak of feeling an extraordinary sense of conscientiousness about their work at the clinic, and of treating patients more humanely than at other clinics or even at their own outside practices. Is religious identity of the clinic or its staff germane, however, to the provision of compassionate care?

We have already seen that the "Muslim identity" of these organizations is significant for the secondary mission of each: to present a positive image of Muslims in American society. In this section, we examine key narratives to discern internal forces shaping these Muslim faith-based clinics. Unlike mosques and PACs, these clinics demonstrate an Islamic identity not only for outsiders, but also for participants and supporters themselves.

One emerging theme is that Muslims have a religious obligation to serve others. One narrator in the group interview with the Al-Shifa board developed the theme of "Discharging a Muslim obligation" (Board Narrative 7.41-61) as he described the founding of the clinic:

41 Also many of us,	52 We think
42 and that comes back	53 it's an obligation
43 to the Muslim physician	54 and we feel pride in that.
44 and the philosophy,	55
45	56 So many of
46 all of us have	57 the physicians here
47 the want to do charity	58 feel guilt
48 and we don't expect	59 if they cannot come
49 thanks or, you know,	60 for any reason,
50 gratitude for that.	61 they feel guilty
51	

The narrator speaks for the collective "we" in this passage. In the first stanza, he connects to his fellow board members as "many of us . . . Muslim physician[s]" who share a "philosophy." The second stanza elaborates on this philosophy, which includes a desire to "do charity" without expecting thanks. The third and fourth stanzas juxtapose the concepts of obligation and guilt. The common bond is reiterated in the final stanza, where the "many" are linked as physicians who may "feel guilty" if they cannot fulfill their Muslim obligation to serve at the clinic. Earlier in the interview, another narrator said, "service to the underserved would be a form of worship . . . [It is] to your own benefit, to erase your bad deeds and shortcomings." Another added that Muslims needed to "establish that call," to devote "your work, also your effort, free of any return, free of any charge" (Board Narrative 2.60-64). For these narrators, Al-Shifa Clinic is a practical expression of their Muslim devotion, and represents a purification of motives for practicing medicine as a vocation.

In two UMMA sources, narrators expressed similar ideals for Muslim service. Dr. Altaf Kazi recalls being a part of the "idealistic group of students" with an idea but no resources, but "we had our Islamic faith in common, which compelled us to put our faith in action and provide services for a community in need" (Video 73-85). The following passage from the interview with Dr. Raziya Shaikh, UMMA's first clinic manager, illustrates this claim (Shaikh 4.1-33):

1 Um, well,	13 serve the underserved
2 the bottom line was that . . .	14 and provide them with the needs
3 the founders had seen	15 that they're not provided with
4 a need to serve the indigent—	16
5 medically indigent population	17 and with the medical education
6 of Los Angeles,	18 it just seemed like the needs
7	19 a perfect fit
8 and the underlying,	20 that you provide—
9 or the backdrop behind all this	21
10 was the Muslim faith—	22 if you're being trained
11 in Islam we were taught	23 in the medical sciences
12 that you're supposed to basically	24 it's a perfect fit—

25 you use your training   30 that was probably the ideology
26 to help those who can't   31 behind starting a clinic.
27 afford medical care   32 I mean just at a very basic level
28   33 to help those in need.
29 So that was the,

Shaikh frames this portion of the narrative, like Kazi's comment above, with a discourse of "need," though the subject of the need in the first and last stanzas is different. In the first stanza, it is the "founders" of the clinic who have a "need to serve." In the final stanza, their "ideology" is "to help those in need." The second stanza locates Islam as the "underlying . . . backdrop" behind the clinic, as Shaikh identifies the "Muslim faith" with a sense of obligation ("you're supposed to"), which clinic founders "were taught." The presentation of binary opposites, "serve . . . underserved" and "provide . . . not provided" adds emphasis to this sense of religious obligation. The terminology of underlying/backdrop/basically in this stanza is repeated in the coda: "at a very basic level" (32). The next two stanzas link this religious mandate to "medical education." In both stanzas, she proclaims medical education/training as a "perfect fit" for fulfilling this obligation to "provide," then shifts the language to "help," which she repeats in the final line of the passage (33). Thus, in this narrative, Shaikh portrays Islam as nurturing a need . . . to help those in need, to serve the underserved, to provide what is not provided; and medical training as a perfect vehicle for doing so. Undoubtedly, the founders and volunteers in other faith-based health initiatives articulate their own religious motivations for service in similar ways to these Muslim providers.

Islam and Decision-Making

When we ask Jeavons's question about how religious or spiritual information influences decision-making in the faith-based organization, some uniquely Muslim resources and issues come into play. The best illustration of this is a narrative from UMMA's Yasser Aman, which we have entitled "Being faithful Muslim stewards" (4.1-202). Because of its length, we will summarize the contents of each section before analyzing selections from it.

Aman introduces the two sections of his narrative with the phrase, "as a Muslim institution." In an earlier narrative, by contrast, he had suggested that we "look at UMMA as an institution, not necessarily religious, but it has its identity found in the Muslim community" (Aman 1.10-15). In the present narrative, however, Aman demonstrates that UMMA's Muslim identity means taking seriously the constraints imposed by the principles of Islamic economic jurisprudence concerning zakāt (obligatory charity, alms tax), sadaqa (charitable giving), and ribā (interest).

Zakāt is frequently discussed as the third of the five pillars of Islam, an annual act of worshipful giving required by God. The legal formula for zakāt on cash and precious metals is calculated at 2.5 percent of an individual's net income, after deducting family expenses. Dr. Muzammil Siddiqui, a nationally prominent American Muslim jurist in Southern California who is mentioned in Aman's narrative, declared in a popular published sermon that "Zakāt is also to help the needy Muslims only. Non-Muslims can be helped from *Sadaqat* [sadaqa] and other charities" (Siddiqui 2007). Sadaqa is a broader term for voluntary charity, and it may include a range of activities, from offering a smile to general charitable giving and forms of public service. Ribā is a financial practice prohibited in Islamic law. It is alternately defined narrowly as usury, prohibiting the excessive accumulation of wealth at the expense of another; or as simple interest, thus prohibiting most forms of banking and finance common in Western capitalist societies. Muslim financial institutions and organizations have designed ribā-free mortgages and profit-sharing cooperative investment plans to avoid engaging in the interest economy.

Returning to Aman's narrative, we can see a reflection of the debate and its effect on UMMA as a "Muslim institution." Each section of the "Being faithful Muslim stewards" narrative ends with unresolved tension, as the organization is "trying to strategize" (4.80-85) or finds the situation "hairy when it comes to just how do you come up with a decision" (4.198-202). The first section focuses on the use of zakāt funds, which UMMA receives from individual donors. Aman questions Siddiqui's restriction of zakāt beneficiaries to Muslims; rather, he suggests that UMMA needs "as an organization [to] come up with . . . our methodology . . . because there's no one mouthpiece [on such issues]" (151-164). The monitoring of which funds went to Muslims would certainly be difficult to accomplish in a clinic that serves 98 percent non-Muslim patients. He nevertheless suggests that "we need to educate our donors . . . this is how we're going to use it . . . call it sadaqa, don't call it zakāt" (4.63-78). The need to "create a policy," "figure that out," and "strategize" reflects significant scholarly and lay debates about the principles of zakāt and the proper methods for its collection and distribution that are frequent in contemporary Muslim diaspora communities.

In the second section Aman defines ribā as "no interest in banking" (91). He characterizes this issue as something that may come up in the future, as UMMA expands and runs capital campaigns. Aman states, in "Being faithful Muslim stewards":

93 you know, even though	97 we still hold true
94 the majority of our funds	98 to the actual principles
95 are not from the	99 of financing.
96 Muslim community,	

In this stanza, Aman qualifies his statement about UMMA belonging within the Muslim community with "even though . . . we still." He returns to this in the stanzas immediately following these (107-149), with the hypothetical "argument" that, whereas Islamic schools and mosques may be bound by such Islamic finance principles, UMMA clinic may be exempt, because it serves the general public.

The final section of this narrative outlines the current strategy that UMMA has in place to remain faithful to Islamic economic jurisprudence. Aman says that, before they brought in non-Muslim board members, the founders wrote bylaws that state, in carefully chosen language (Aman 4.179-202):

179 when we make decisions	191
180 around what is a Muslim issue	192 We specifically didn't use
181 and a non, it that—	193 the word scholar or imam
182 and we chose a language	194 or anything like that
183	195 because any board
184 that the board shall strive to,	196 10, 15, 20 years ago [sic]
185 the wording is really,	197 can—it's just like today,
186 the board shall	198
187 make their decisions	199 so it gets very hairy
188 in line with the majority	200 when it comes to just
189 or the consensus of	201 how do you come up
190 the Muslim community.	202 with a decision.

Here, the first, second and fourth stanzas repeat the framing phrase, "make" or "come up with" a "decision." The terms "language" and "word" recur in the first three stanzas, coupled with Aman's hesitating speech (181, 185), indicating the delicate nature of the issue at hand. The "Muslim issue" of the first stanza is parallel to "the majority or consensus of the Muslim community" in the second, and the latter is deliberately contrasted in the third stanza with "scholar or imam." In traditional Sunni Muslim jurisprudence, the concept of "consensus of the community" (*ijma'*) as a source of law is often interpreted as a consensus among qualified scholars This section of Aman's narrative reveals two important positions: first, that he sees contemporary American Islamic legal authority as disputed and in flux ("years ago . . . just like today"); second, that the predominantly non-Muslim board of the clinic must abide by the current understanding of "Muslim issues" such as zakāt, sadaqa, and ribā in making its financial decisions. UMMA as an organization clearly takes into account religious and spiritual information as a part of its decision-making processes, though it remains "hairy" and not fully worked out.

One interesting part of UMMA's story, however, is how it is striving to maintain this Muslim identity as it has grown and adapted. The people making decisions on the board are now predominantly non-Muslim, and the paid clinic staff is completely non-Muslim. The executive staff and many volunteers are Muslims, but many non-Muslim students and physicians also volunteer. In Kadri's and Aman's narratives of the clinic's development, they mention two factors that account for this shift from an originally all-Muslim staff and volunteer base. Aman attributes the change to a need to be relevant to the community being served. He emphasizes in his opening narrative that the founders did not see themselves as doing something *for* the community, but rather *with* the community, in a partnership (Aman 1.17-32). Subsequently, they recognized a need to employ staff who could speak Spanish and who "understood our community better." The clinic decided to expand its staff significantly in 2005-2006, resulting in "the majority of our staff [being] not from the Muslim community." (Aman 2.99-114). Kadri explains the shifting make-up of the governing board in an extended passage, which we have entitled, "Muslim identity markers," abbreviated below:

> In order for us to get the money, to become . . . a Federally Qualified Health Clinic . . . our board used to be predominantly Muslim before . . . we have to change the dynamics of the board. . . .The people that started UMMA were not on the board anymore, a few people switched to advisory status . . . and our board has changed. . . .We had to get other people from outside of it . . . the majority of them have to be [local] community members. . . . We're not a Muslim board, I would say, overwhelmingly, at all. . . . It was mandated . . . It's been very difficult [to find Muslim board members, because] they have to be living in that community.

> We try to do prayers before we start rounds, in our meeting, so that we establish our identity in a similar way that other [faith-based] hospitals do . . . And I think we're much more conscientious now of that than we were before. Now we have the translation of the *surah*, you know the *al-hamdulillah*, which is just "in the name of God" to begin . . . And we will have a translation when we end our session, too. And I think they're aware . . . that we'll go off to prayers in the middle of our talk or if we're having a meeting, [to perform] the prayer of the sunset . . .

> If you go to UMMA, it would be nice to see women who are covered who are working in the front, so people would realize these are Muslim people and not everybody is awful and trying to do awful things. But we have non-Muslim office workers. I mean, it's hard enough getting nurses or MAs [medical assistants]. I mean it's, like, the reality of life. (Kadri 4.1-162)

This narrative is a poignant reminder of the ways in which faith-based organizations evolve in response to their own success as service institutions and in response to the demands of funding agencies. In this case, the federal program that is designed to support community clinics, through subsidizing prescription drug purchases and medical training staff, "mandated" changes in the composition and dynamics of the organization's governing board. Whereas Aman's narrative depicts UMMA staffing decisions as pragmatic adjustments to the linguistic and cultural environment in which the clinic functions, Kadri laments the difficulty in finding community-based Muslim board members and the loss of the clinic's founders on the board. He also refers to the changes in staff composition, alluding again to UMMA's secondary but important mission: "so people would realize these are Muslim people and not everybody is awful and trying to do awful things" (Kadri 4.151-155).

Kadri's narrative likewise points to ways in which the organization tries to preserve its Muslim identity in the face of such external forces. The use of translated phrases of Muslim piety and Qur'ān verses at the beginning of meetings, as well as the regular interruption of meetings for ritual prayer (*salah*), are reminders of the Muslim-ness of the organization. These rituals, along with the physical embellishment of the walls of the clinic with Arabic calligraphy and translations of the Qu'rān and sayings of Muhammad, are efforts to maintain an environment that, as Aman says, "remind[s] people of the background" of the organization (Aman 2.128-129).

Conclusion

These narratives illuminate the dynamic interplay of important aspects of Muslim identity for these two clinics as faith-based service organizations. Both Al-Shifa and UMMA clinics represent an important claim of Muslim immigrants on American identity and local belonging for their founders, boards, and some volunteers. The leaders present themselves (or perhaps *perform their selves*) as fulfilling a religious obligation, purifying their motives for professional care provision, and representing Islam and the broader Muslim community in a public square where the stigmatization of Islam has taken a personal and a communal toll. These performative claims of identity constitute a refusal to accept an external self-definition.[5] Dr. Aslam of Al-Shifa Clinic interprets the emergence of Muslim community-based health organizations in this way: "I think Muslim people feel that their participation in the local communities, to help the local communities, is also important. Not to remain isolated, [but] to become part of the mainstream—and I think this is—you'll have to come with something. When somebody invites you to come to a party, you have to bring something" (interview, 2007).

These Muslim faith-based clinics are the dish that American Muslims are bringing to the party of U.S. healthcare services. There is nothing particularly exotic about the shape of the dish or its contents. The founders and volunteers share with those in other mainstream faith-based community clinics a combined sense of religious and professional vocation to care for the needy neighbor. Like other faith-based organizations, they mobilize resources that are within their sphere of influence, and these include religious entities and individuals as well as academic and governmental resources, to accomplish their primary mission. The effects of growth in services and increasing reliance on public and private funding sources, as illustrated by UMMA's adjustment to the FQHC standards, may be shared by many FBOs. The difficulty of finding appropriate community members of a governing board who also share the religious affiliation of the organization is likely less of a problem for Catholic and Protestant FBOs than it is for religious minority groups. The particular concerns of Muslim clinics about religiously appropriate financial decision-making may set them apart from many

Christian organizations, though it is possible that some Jewish faith-based organizations might share similar concerns.

What does set these Muslim clinics apart is how public the presentation of the dish might be at the party. The public sphere in which Muslim FBOs operate is much more highly charged than for most other religious groups. The secondary purpose of these organizations—to present a positive image of American Muslims as a compassionate, generous, local healing presence—provides a unique motivation and shapes organizational decisions (though in diverse ways, as we have seen) about physical space, staffing, location, and alliances with religious authorities. Both of the clinics examined here maintain a strong sense of autonomy from any specific religious congregation, sect, or leader, and they provide an outlet for independent charitable action in a culturally and ideologically pluralistic Muslim *ummah* (community). So, to adapt the words of U.S. Representative Maxine Waters, "If you want to see what American Muslims really represent," let us listen to the emerging stories of Muslim faith-based health organizations. While this is only one window on American Muslim identity, it represents a growing movement of influential and energetic Muslim Americans.

Notes

1. This research study was funded by a collaborative grant from the Association of Muslim Health Professionals Foundation and the Institute for Social Policy and Understanding. It was reviewed and exempted by the Institutional Review Board of Boston Medical Center. The present essay is a slightly abridged version of one originally published as Laird, Lance D., and Wendy Cadge. 2009. Constructing American Muslim Identity: Tales of Two Clinics in Southern California. *Muslim World* 99(2):270-93. Republished here by permission of *Muslim World*.

2. The clinic's acronym is intentional. The Arabic term *umma* or *ummah* literally means "community, nation." It is used by religious Muslims to designate the worldwide community of followers of Islam.

3. Each of our interviews yielded several continuous narrative segments, which we have retranscribed into poetic stanzas for analysis. Throughout this article, we cite each narrative by name, narrative number, and line number. The narrator is named first, the only exceptions being the group "Narrative" from Al-Shifa and the UMMA video, which do not carry names of individual narrators. The reference in the text here is thus to two short "lines" (51-52) of the first narrative from an interview with Dr. Khan.

4. As a Harvard undergraduate, Nir Shirani analyzed the archives of the Muslim Student Association at UCLA during the late 1980s and early 1990s, when UMMA's founders began to take leadership. He contends that these largely middle-class, second-generation immigrant Muslim students created a distinct American Muslim identity, espousing "a radical critique of the world which was embodied domestically in the struggles of African American Muslims against racism and internationally by the struggles of Muslims abroad against non-Muslim governments." The MSA under their leadership allied with Third World political activists on campus, and specifically with African American groups, frequently adopting the rhetoric of Malcolm X. An important part of their construction of an American Muslim identity was a critique of the assimilationist tendencies and lack of social engagement in their parents' generation, and the inclusion of African American racial and economic justice concerns.

5. I am indebted to my colleague, Kambiz Ghanea-Bassiri (personal communication, May 22, 2008) for pointing out the "performative" nature of these claims in response to an earlier version of this essay.

Works Cited

Ammerman, Nancy Tatom. 1997. *Congregation and community*. New Brunswick, NJ: Rutgers University Press.

Bagby, Ihsan. 2004. The mosque and the American public square. In *Muslims' place in the American public square: Hope, fears, and aspirations*, ed. Zahid H. Bukhari, Sulayman S. Nyang, Mumtaz Ahmad, and John L. Esposito, 323-46. Walnut Creek, CA: AltaMira Press.

Chambre, Susan J. 2001. The changing nature of "faith" in faith-based organizations: Secularization and ecumenism in four AIDS organizations in New York City. *Social Service Review*, September, 435-55.

Cnaan, Ram A. 2006. *The other Philadelphia story: How local congregations support quality of life in urban America*. Philadelphia: University of Pennsylvania Press.

Cnaan, Ram A., and Stephanie C. Boddie. 2002. Charitable choice and faith-based welfare: A call for social work. *Social Work* 47(3):224-35.

Edgell, Penny. 2006. *Religion and family in a changing society: Princeton studies in cultural sociology*. Princeton, NJ: Princeton University Press.

Gee, James Paul, Sarah Michaels, and Mary Catherine O'Connor. 1992. Discourse analysis. In *The handbook of qualitative research in education*, ed. Margaret Diane LeCompte, Wendy L. Millroy, and Judith Preissle, 227-92. San Diego: Academic Press.

Jeavons, Thomas. 1998. Identifying characteristics of "religious" organizations: An exploratory proposal. In *Sacred companies: Organizational aspects of religion and religious aspects of organizations*, ed. N. J. Demerath III, Peter Dobkin Hall, Terry Schmitt, and Rhys H. Williams, 79-96. New York: Oxford University Press.

Lazarus, Barry A. 1991. The practice of medicine and prejudice in a New England town: The founding of Mount Sinai Hospital, Hartford, Connecticut. *Journal of American Ethnic History* 10(3):21-41.

Numbers, Ronald L., and Ronald C. Sawyer. 1982. Medicine and Christianity in the modern world. In *Health/medicine and the faith traditions*, ed. Martin E. Marty and Kenneth L. Vaux, 133-60. Philadelphia: Fortress Press.

Riessman, Catherine Kohler. 1993. *Narrative analysis*. Qualitative research methods series, vol. 30. Newbury Park, CA: Sage Publications.

Rosenberg, Charles E. 1995. *The care of strangers: The rise of America's hospital system*. Baltimore: Johns Hopkins University Press.

Schumann, Christoph. 2007. A Muslim "diaspora" in the United States? *Muslim World* 97(1):11-32.

Shirani, Nir. 2008. The formation of an American Muslim radicalism: An intellectual history of the Muslim Student Association at UCLA, 1989-2001. Unpublished essay. Cambridge, MA: Harvard University.

Siddiqui, Muzzamil H. 2007. Zakat and charity—our gratitude to Allah. In *Encyclopedia of Islam in the United States*, ed. Jocelyne Cesari, 741-2. Westport, CT: Greenwood Press.

Solomon, Lewis D. 2003. *In God we trust? Faith-based organizations and the quest to solve America's social ills*. Lanham, MD.: Lexington Books.

Swartz, David. 1998. Secularization, religion, and isomorphism: A study of large nonprofit hospital trustees. In *Sacred companies: Organizational aspects of religion and religious aspects of organizations*, ed. N. J. Demerath III, Peter Dobkin Hall, Terry Schmitt, and Rhys H. Williams, 323-39. New York: Oxford University Press.

Taylor, Robert Joseph, Christopher G. Ellison, Linda M. Chatters, Jeffrey S. Levin, and Karen D. Lincoln. 2000. Mental health services in faith communities: The role of clergy in black churches. *Social Work* 45(1):73-87.
Thomas, Stephen B., Sandra Crouse Quinn, Andrew Billingsley, and Cleopatra Caldwell. 1994. The characteristics of northern black churches with community health outreach programs. *American Journal of Public Health* 84(4):575-9.
UMMA Clinic. 2008. UMMA Community Clinic 10 Year Video. Los Angeles: University Muslim Medical Association.
Vogel, Morris J. 1980. *The invention of the modern hospital: Boston, 1870-1930*. Chicago: University of Chicago Press.
Weiss, Gregory L. 2006. *Grassroots medicine: The story of America's free health clinics*. Lanham, MD: Rowman and Littlefield.

Chapter 7
Culture, History, and Discourse at Tree of Life: A Faith-Based Relief Agency in Mission, South Dakota
Janet G. Brashler

Introduction

This chapter describes the work of one faith-based relief agency called Tree of Life, located in Mission, South Dakota, which works with the Sicangu Lakota of the Rosebud Sioux Reservation. Tree of Life (TOL) has a permanent presence in the community of Mission, a mostly white enclave within the Rosebud Reservation. Tree of Life is one of a number of faith-based (and other) non-governmental organizations that provide various kinds of assistance to the Lakota, coupled with different intensities and varieties of Christian evangelism. The permanent presence of Tree of Life is unusual in Mission, as many other organizations and volunteers come to the area only during the summer. Tree of Life maintains a year-round presence through a food and clothing distribution center, and through hot meal and home repair programs that provide assistance to significant numbers of Lakota people each year. In addition, a major portion of TOL's time and energy is given to coordinating participation in its various programs for short-term mission volunteers, primarily during the summer months. However, providing assistance to the Lakota is only part of the work of TOL. Tree of Life creates opportunities for volunteers who come from churches and colleges across the United States to understand the historical and cultural contexts of the Lakota as well as to witness the relative deprivation and poverty experienced by many Lakota people, and this is perhaps as important a function of TOL as are the services provided to the Lakota people. In the course of their one-week stay, volunteers have opportunities to interact with Lakota staff, clients, and cultural presenters who introduce Lakota culture and history through evening presentations and daily interactions.

A primary objective of this chapter is to understand the nuances of culture, history, faith, and development as they play out in the interactions between and among volunteers, staff, and the Lakota with whom they interact on a daily basis. I first briefly summarize the historical and cultural contexts that shape relationships between Sicangu Lakota (Rosebud Sioux) and the staff and volunteers at Tree of Life. Then, I critically examine the goals and objectives of this agency in light of the intersections of culture, history, and development as they play out in the daily interactions I have observed, using several examples from fieldwork conducted over the last two years on the Rosebud reservation and with mission volunteers.

Framework

The framework discussed by Paul Farmer (2003), in which he identifies charity, justice, and development as three overlapping but different approaches to social issues and problems, influences my approach with this project. In this model, Farmer and others (e.g., Freire 1986; Poppendieck 1998) find charity and development solutions for responding to health care among the poor "deeply flawed" (Farmer 2003, 153). Those who subscribe to charity models see the poor as powerless, inferior, and "always with us"; that is, part of a hierarchical social structure that is historically constituted and supported by the "proliferation of charity" (Farmer 2003). While acknowledging that there is a place for charity, Farmer warns that charity should "avoid at all costs, the temptation to ignore or hide the causes of excess suffering among the poor" (Farmer 2003, 154), and that charity too often involves the distribution of "second-hand, castoff services . . . doled out in piecemeal fashion" (Farmer 2003, 155).

In Farmer's opinion, development as a model is equally flawed in that it assumes the poor are "backward" and in need of modernization, a western view that has been adopted throughout much of the world (Farmer 2003; Sachs 1992). Farmer notes that development efforts have been perceived as successful on some scales of measurement in the so called "nations of the south," but only a narrow examination of aggregate data permits such a view. A closer examination of class differences (Farmer 2003, 156) and, I would argue, differences in racial/ethnic and gender groups within a country, reveals that development in health care and other areas benefits primarily the wealthy, and only occasionally, in a piecemeal manner, the poor. That leaves justice—a preferential option for the poor as defined by liberation theology—as the way to improve health care and/or other aspects of life among the poor. Farmer (2003) concludes his discussion of charity, justice, and development models by acknowledging that each is necessary to address the problems of health care among the poor. But in order to understand how best to serve the poor or "the least among us," any faith-based or other effort at analysis of "the problem" must be "historically deep" and "geographically broad" (Farmer 2003, 158). To that end, the research presented in this chapter extends the analysis of faith-based development efforts beyond interactions between North and South and focuses on the Sicangu Lakota of Rosebud, an indigenous group within the United States whose culture and history profoundly impact efforts to provide assistance to them by organizations such as Tree of Life.

Historical and Cultural Context

The Sicangu are one of seven subgroups of the Lakota (also known as the Teton Sioux), the westernmost of the three groups known as Sioux, which include the Dakota, Nakota, and Lakota language groups. Contacted in the eighteenth century through Euro-American fur trade forays into their territory, the Lakota quickly adopted the horse and became quintessential mounted bison hunters. During the first half of the nineteenth century, the Lakota entered into treaties with the United States intended to guarantee their territory and to establish relationships between sovereign nations. As settlement pressure from the east intensified, the 1868 Fort Laramie treaty was signed, guaranteeing the Sioux their Great Reservation and ensuring safe passage for Euro-American settlers through Sioux lands to the west. Within a few years, however, the treaty was abrogated, and reservation lands were reduced when gold was discovered in the Black Hills in 1874 by George Armstrong Custer. Shortly thereafter, in 1877, the Black Hills were seized by the United States government and opened up for gold mining and settlement. The Lakota consider the Black Hills to be sacred land, called *Paha Sapa*, and their ownership remains contested to this day. Additional lands were removed from tribal control, and reservations were established through various congressional acts in retaliation for the Indian Wars of the 1870s. Acts such as these, continuing into the early twentieth century and supported by numerous court decisions (Biolsi 2001), opened up reservation land to white settlement, removed whole counties from within the original reservation boundaries, and created checkerboard patterns of ownership of relatively affluent white-owned ranches and mostly unproductive Indian lands within the reservation boundaries of today.

In addition to establishing reservations, treaties and congressional actions from the mid-nineteenth century forward had provisions for "civilizing" and "acculturating" Indians through conversions not only in faith, but also in subsistence, with the near annihilation of the bison. Civilizing included sending missionaries from various denominations, primarily Jesuits and Episcopalians, to provide "moral religious agents to care for Indians on the reservations" (Sneve 1977, 5). At first, the Lakota recognized the benefits (e.g., access to resources) of having missionaries attached to their reservation. For example, Spotted Tail, leader of the Sicangu in the 1870s, went so far as to request both Catholic *and* Episcopalian missions for his agency, which became the Rosebud reservation (Sneve 1977; Cerney 2005). The Catholic Church and its priests and nuns at the St. Francis Mission School constituted a dominant acculturation force throughout the nineteenth and twentieth centuries. While some of their strategies were benevolent, others were negative and harsh; for example, contemporary Lakota affirm that some priests and other officials withheld food from government distribution if individuals did not attend church regularly. Episcopal and Catholic priests played active roles in preserving language, material culture, and oral tradition, while at the same time attempting to undermine traditional religious practices which were thought to be pagan and un-Christian (Cerney 2005; Stebinger [interview]). Other denominations sending missions in the past, many of which continue to have a presence on the reservation, include Methodists, Dutch Reformed, Congregationalists, Unitarians, Baptists, Presbyterians, Friends, and a variety of unaffiliated evangelical groups.

More long-lasting acculturation efforts involved boarding schools for children run by the Catholic Church (Sneve 1977; Cerney 2005). On the Rosebud, St. Francis Mission School was established in 1886 and was staffed by Jesuits and Sisters of St. Francis until 1972, when control was transferred to a local group (Marquette Library Collections Archives n.d.). During the late nineteenth through the mid-twentieth century children were the targets of civilizing in boarding schools, where they were required to have their hair cut (an act of domination) and to dress in western clothes, and forbidden to speak Lakota. Children were taught skills as an effort to civilize/modernize/develop them, including sewing, cooking and other skills for girls and farming for boys. In other words, women's roles remained essentially the same (cooking and sewing) but with new materials and technology. Farming, however, was an alien subsistence practice to people who prior to the reservation era had subsisted largely on buffalo and collected wild foodstuffs.

Still other attempts to civilize continued into the mid-twentieth century with the federal government's Urban Relocation Program, administered by the Bureau of Indian Affairs, which sought to move Native Americans from the reservation to urban areas. Many of these individuals exchanged rural poverty for urban poverty and were separated from traditional practices, family, and belief. Others found employment with the federal government, either short-term with the military or longer-term with other branches of government. Eventually, many returned to the reservation because of family and other ties.

Today, the people of Rosebud live in the context of nineteenth- and twentieth-century actions resulting in acculturation, domination, and loss. While the buffalo are recovering from near extinction, the Sicangu people occupy a remote area in South Dakota on lands much reduced from their nineteenth-century territory. They experience rates of unemployment as high as 82 percent (Rosebud Sioux Tribe 2009), teen suicide, teen pregnancy, low graduation rates from high school (about 30 percent), homelessness, alcohol and drug addiction, discrimination, and other diseases of poverty as they struggle to regain full sovereignty and self-determination in an economic climate that was desperate even before the recent economic downturn. Much of their economy is informal, or is vested in microenterprise efforts including jewelry and star quilt making, as there is little industry. The few attempts to bring various kinds of industry and other business to the reservation have failed due to a variety of social, political, and economic factors (Pickering 2000). Today, the main employers on the Rosebud reservation are federal, state, and tribal governments. Most businesses such as grocery stores and gas stations are owned by non-natives, though as of this writing (2009) there is a tribally owned gas station and a half built tribally owned grocery store. Unlike some tribes, gambling profits have passed the Sicangu by, as their casino is located far from population centers and expressways, and income from this venture provides only limited winter heating assistance to elderly members of the tribe. Some Lakota who have completed high school or college leave the reservation in search of jobs, but many eventually return to family still living on the reservation (Pickering 2000).

After a decline during the mid-twentieth century, church attendance has reportedly increased somewhat (Marquette Library Collections Archives n.d.). However, many of the Lakota who maintain an affiliation with the Christian church also participate in traditional ceremonies, including the Sundance, Sweat Lodge, *Yuwipi* (healing) and others currently undergoing revitalization on the reservation. Other Lakota describe themselves as strictly "traditional," and some are not affiliated with any tradition. One Lakota informant noted there are probably hundreds of sweat lodges on the reservation. Several informants suggested that the church is great for crises, but the traditional religion is what sustains people on a daily basis.

Family ties, organized around a large extended family structure called the *tiyóspaye,* are strong, providing a series of mutual rights and obligations that permeate everyday life. Oral tradition is also strong, and boarding school experiences are still fresh in people's memories. For the most part, one hears English spoken in public in most contexts on the reservation. Lakota is used for prayers at pow wows and the Rosebud fair, and interspersed with English at other ceremonies. When I first heard a sixty-something woman speak Lakota to another elder in a non-ceremonial setting (at a store), she said with some embarrassment, "Oh, we were told to never talk it at [boarding] school, we only talked Indian at home." However, many Lakota, especially those under forty or so, do not appear to speak more than a few words of the language. Nevertheless, the tribal college, Sinte Gleska University, actively works to promote Lakota culture and language, offering classes and degree programs in Lakota language and culture in addition to a variety of two-year technical programs.

In sum, the Sicangu Lakota of the twenty-first century have experienced considerable trauma, loss, and acculturation, but have maintained traditional beliefs and practices while being integrated into the U.S. and global economy through microenterprise (Pickering 2000) and other networks, including the church.

Methods

Data were collected over several years, beginning with a one week visit to Tree of Life in 2001 as a Volunteer in Mission adult chaperone for a group of youth from a United Methodist Church in Grand Rapids, Michigan. A second week-long trip with youth from the same church in 2007 led me to a more lengthy stay during the summer of 2008, when I served as a long-term mission volunteer working with groups in a variety of different programs sponsored by Tree of Life. In 2007 I was fascinated by the changes that had occurred since my previous visit, including expanded services, increased collaboration with the tribe, and, most obviously, the movements of considerable quantities of material (food, construction supplies, and clothing) through the operation. In observing both inter- and intra-group dynamics, I became very aware that volunteers brought many different expectations, needs, and beliefs to a mission experience.

Although this was originally conceived as a project to explore the attitudes and motivations of volunteers working on the reservation, the question of how Lakota culture and historical experience impacted volunteer efforts and the success of the organization emerged as additional foci of my inquiry. Qualitative data collected through participant observation and through informal and formal interviews with volunteers and staff were supplemented by research on the Internet, examination of files pertaining to the history of Tree of Life, and copies of Tree of Life Newsletters sent to volunteers. A number of interviews were conducted in the field, and several more were conducted after volunteers had returned from their experience at Tree of Life.

Tree of Life

Defining itself as a faith-based relief agency, Tree of Life is relatively new to the religious landscape of the reservation when compared to the long-term presence of Catholic and Episcopalian missions. Beginning very modestly in the mid 1980s with a part-time missionary and limited funding, the organization now is a full-time, year-round, substantial presence in Mission, South Dakota, providing a variety of services. Supported in part by the Dakotas Conference and General Board of Global Ministries of the United Methodist Church (UMC GBGM), Tree of Life has grown from a modest organization serving ten families per week to one serving 350 families through a variety of programs (General Board of Global Ministries 2009). According to the Board of Global Ministries, Tree of Life's mission is:

Tacan ki awankiglakapi
Lakol woicun yuwas akapo
Nagi ki yuwas akapo
Nurture the body, Strengthen the culture, Enhance the spirit
(Translation by Chief Duane Hollow Horn Bear)

1. Provide groceries and meals to the hungry, with a goal of 600 families per week. Provide repairs to substandard homes, with a goal of 90 per year.
2. Support local teachers in their efforts to reclaim their culture and language, by providing buildings for classes and opportunities to teach both the Lakota youth and visitors from off the reservations.
3. Recognize the traditional faith of the Lakota and engage in dialog [sic] where the principles of Christianity can be shared in a different way from the historical methods of forced enculturation.

(General Board of Global Ministries 2009)

Information provided to volunteers during the summer of 2008 summarized these objectives in the following way:

- To build a bridge of friendship and mutual respect and trust with the people of the Rosebud (and Crow Creek) Reservations
- To provide support to meet poverty needs
- To help reclaim language and culture
- To assist in building a sustainable economy

The permanent year round presence maintained by Tree of Life is unusual on the reservation, as other short-term mission groups such as Youth Works operate only during the summer months. Current permanent full-time staff includes a director (a Methodist pastor) and mission director (his wife). This couple has been at Tree of Life for about four years (as of 2009), replacing another pastor/wife couple that served for several years until 2004, and two individuals who had short-term appointments that did not work out. In addition, TOL employs a construction manager who is Lakota, and from four to sixteen part-time and seasonal workers, most of whom are Lakota. Tree of Life also operates a smaller, but growing, operation on the Crow Creek (also Lakota) Reservation to the northeast.

During the summer, and to a much less frequent extent during the year, approximately seventy groups (about 1500 individual volunteers in 2008) participate in short term pilgrimage-like mission trips to Tree of Life, where volunteers work in the home repair/construction program and the Warm Welcome, a food pantry/clothing closet and hot meal program. Until recently, the operations have been centered at a complex that included the directors' residence and office, a dorm for volunteers, and a building which housed both the Warm Welcome and the staging area for home repair projects. This is normally a highly gendered workspace in which men dominate home repair and women mostly work in food and clothing areas, reflecting gender roles present in both Euro-American and Lakota societies. Among volunteers there are exceptions to the gender role differentiation, with some men preferring to work in the kitchen and some women preferring to work construction, but among the staff, men work construction and women work in the Warm Welcome. In general, when women and youth work construction they are relegated to painting, primarily because they lack necessary skills. During late 2008 a new building to house the construction side of the program was added, to some extent separating the two major parts of the program and relieving some of the gender conflict that existed in the combined workspace.

Additional housing for volunteers is at two former parsonages located within a few blocks of the office and Warm Welcome. Occasionally extra housing is rented from another organization some distance away from the TOL office and other residences. This occurs most often during the peak of the volunteer season in July, when the requests for reservations from the mission groups for particular time slots is highest and Tree of Life is stretched to its capacity. Under these circumstances, the experience of some volunteer groups is diminished by their perception of having been placed in housing that was not what they expected.

Volunteers perform charitable acts, paying $250 apiece for a week at TOL to work in Warm Welcome or the home repair program. In addition, volunteers have opportunities to serve as tutors, to help at a nursing home and other venues on the reservation, and to attend evening cultural education activities. One-week cross-cultural health services are also being developed for some skilled volunteer groups. For example, a group of nurses provided foot care to people for one week during 2008, and dental care is provided for one week each year through the Delta Dental-Ronald McDonald partnership hosted at Tree of Life. These ventures are somewhat like medical mission trips common in Central America and the Caribbean, in that they are short-term and unsustained. They differ, however, in that the Lakota do have ongoing access to health care through the federal government (Indian Health), although services are limited and individuals frequently must seek specialized health care in hospitals almost two hundred miles from the reservation in Rapid City or Sioux Falls.

The vast majority of volunteer time is spent meeting the first two goals of the organization, namely, fostering mutual respect through cultural awareness and helping to meet the needs of the poor through home repair and the food/clothing programs. According to the director, cultural awareness education is almost as important to the mission of TOL and to the experiences of the volunteers as is the help that they provide.

Additional goals and objectives of TOL include providing the opportunity for volunteers to feel a call to ministry due to their experiences, and to build "a foundation for having a Native American congregation join the U[nited] M[ethodist] Conference" (General Board of Global Ministries 2009). However, TOL does not see itself as a charitable organization, since "charity . . . is seen by the Lakota as a negative respect-robbing act. . . . We design our programs to be cooperative efforts, demanding the participation of those receiving of our help" (General Board of Global Ministries 2009). One example of this is the expectation that adults participating in the food or clothing pantry contribute a dollar, in exchange for which they receive a hot meal and sacks that they can fill with food and clothing. The required contribution has the purpose of making the transaction seem less like charity and more like a cooperative, maintaining a degree of respect for people participating in the program. Another indicator that Tree of Life is attempting to move beyond charity is the close attention paid to what kinds of clothes are put out in the clothing area of the Warm Welcome. Clothing which is stained, damaged, or dated (polyester, for example) is not put out and is disposed of, literally the last stop on a cycle of recycling clothing through garage sales, clothing banks and other institutions in the communities of the relatively affluent. In a nod to cultural preferences and dislikes, corduroy and turtlenecks also end up in the garbage bag.

When volunteers were asked to describe the most important aspect of their coming to the Rosebud reservation and Tree of Life, they gave the following answers, listed here in order from the most frequently expressed to the least:

- wanting to take part in cultural tourism and help at the same time
- wanting to do good to Native American people who were treated badly historically (white guilt); we have an obligation to repair the wrongs
- having a good feeling in return for some work
- work with the youth from their church so that they can understand social issues like poverty
- working with the mission group as a way to bond within themselves and with their church
- getting away from home and family
- witnessing Christian love through helping others
- having to be a chaperone
- learning about Native American culture
- confronting personal fears about people who are different
- wanting to bring the Christian message to people perceived to be pagan

Few of the volunteers I spoke with articulated development or justice reasons for participating in the mission trip or as important motivating forces. The two who did were engaged in social work professions at home. Most often, adult volunteers expressed their commitment to help others because they expect it of themselves—to act on their faith to help other people less fortunate. A few volunteers assert that it has nothing to do with their faith; rather, they come to TOL because they feel they have much and should share their good fortune with others. One wonders, however, whether this is an unintended or unconscious reference to Luke 12:48, which calls believers to give because they have been blessed by having much.

Other activities of TOL during the "off season" when there are few or no volunteers include maintaining the Warm Welcome food and clothing operation, providing school supplies to children, prom dresses for girls, sleeping bags for the homeless, a Thanksgiving community dinner, Christmas presents for kids, and a community Easter Egg hunt.

The last Tree of Life goal, that of assisting in building a sustainable economy (i.e., development), is less visible, and volunteers play only a minor role in its implementation. For the Lakota, a sustainable tribally controlled economy would be one that can be maintained without the infusion of massive amounts of outside aid from the federal government and/or faith-based and other non-governmental organizations. Tree of Life engages in some activities that could lead to sustainability, but as yet very little sustainable development has occurred through their work. Following are a few examples that have emerged over the last several years, primarily under the current leadership. As part of its effort to build sustainability, and to cooperate with the tribe, TOL has begun working collaboratively with the tribal government on home repair and other projects. Previously, a person could request help from TOL and the tribe independently, with the result that some families got more help than others. TOL was reportedly more efficient (i.e., had access to more and better resources) in home repair efforts than the tribe, repairing more than one-third again as many homes as the tribe did. Now, a person requesting home repair from TOL must have a tribal council or community representative sign the application. This represents collaboration but perhaps not sustainable development, since the net effect is that TOL is repairing fewer homes than previously. There are a number of other ways that TOL cooperates with the tribe through resource sharing and participation in assisting at various community events. During 2008, one volunteer group helped construct picnic tables for the tribe at the Rosebud fair grounds. Again, however, this seems more like charitable collaboration rather than sustainable development.

Another effort involves the operation of a small gift store by TOL in their office/dorm, where handmade crafts made by Lakota people—including drums, beaded jewelry, star quilts and other items—are sold with no profit for TOL. For many Lakota, making and selling these items in as many venues as possible is their primary source of income, given the high unemployment rates and lack of available jobs. Tree of Life is one of several outlets on the reservation for crafts-people. In addition, there is informal door to door selling and bartering with visitors to the Reservation, as well as organizations that purchase items for resale. For example, during 2007, I was approached by a shy ten- to twelve-year-old boy who was selling inexpensive ballpoint pens with beaded sleeves for about $3 per pen. The income from these microenterprise efforts seems hardly sufficient to earn a decent living, but it may be the only available income for some community members. Another attempt at sustainability planned for fall 2008 was an "Internet café," where it was hoped that people would be able to use computers to market crafts through an Internet link to the outside world. This effort has not been successful as of yet, given space and equipment limitations.

Pickering (2000, 38-43) describes how Lakota values of egalitarianism, family relations, and redistribution (generosity) conflict with development efforts and implementation of wage driven market economy models. In essence, anyone who becomes successful at some enterprise, whether beading, getting resources from helping agencies such as Tree of Life, or developing some kind of small business, is expected to be generous to those with whom he/she has obligations through their *tiyóspaye* or other relationships. The profit from beaded pen, jewelry, star quilt sales, and small businesses is not enough to support the *tiyóspaye* and trigger the kind of change that is needed to bring the Lakota into even "decent poverty" (Tropman 1998). The Lakota commitment to egalitarianism, generosity, and family demands a large scale change, one that will enable many, not just the few who cannot easily afford to be generous because they have been the focus of TOL's current short term mission/ development orientation. Short term missioners identify individuals they want to help, often singling out individuals such as promising artists or home repair clients with whom they connected, but their well meaning acts of support and charity fail to address underlying causes of inequality, which are structural and deeply embedded in the histories and cultures of both the Lakota and those who want to help.

Still another aspect of the TOL program that has potential for sustainability is paid employment of Lakota people in the home repair program and the clothing and food bank, and as speakers at cultural presentations. At present, however, Lakota people working in these positions are employed fewer than forty hours per week, and earn minimum wage with no benefits provided. They are employed by TOL and its board of directors, which is composed of active and retired Euro-American clergypersons, a majority of whom live off the reservation. When I asked the director what other development efforts might be implemented through Tree of Life, he indicated that there were so many factors precluding development (many of which Pickering discusses; see above), he was not sure how it could happen. When I raised the idea of development with a Lakota woman, she thought community gardening would be a good thing, but stated that there would have to be twenty gardens from the outset, because there are twenty communities on the reservation, and intra-tribal community jealousy would bring the scheme down if the perception existed that any one community was getting more than another. Barriers to development and sustainability, discussed by Pickering (2000) and reflected above, are rooted in the historical past and present dependency as well as the value systems of the Lakota and those on whom they are dependent.

Turning to the interactions between volunteers, staff, and the Lakota, there are several areas in which relationships between TOL staff, volunteers, and the community hinge on the historical and cultural contexts and themes of acculturation, domination, and loss. Historically, missionaries were charged with "civilizing" the Indian. Part of Tree of Life's discourse as a mission organization is that it seeks to undo past injustice, to "recognize the traditional faith of the Lakota and engage in dialog [sic] where the principles of Christianity can be shared in a different way from the historical methods of forced enculturation" (General Board of Global Ministries 2009). As part of most group orientations, TOL's director states that TOL's goal today is not to try to make converts, but to try to undo past wrongs on the part of missionaries, citing the example of withholding food from those who did not regularly attend church. Rather, Tree of Life serves primarily (and very successfully) as a conduit for an enormous amount of aid, in the form of food and clothing through its food bank, and through home repair assistance. A less overtly stated and infrequently articulated objective is to continue to bring the Christian message to the Lakota with the hope of conversions in the future, while still having respect for their traditions. This perspective is shared only occasionally during some orientation sessions, although it was stated more overtly during a presentation to a group of seminarians visiting the organization. In addition, the TOL directors attempt to work with local, mostly white congregations and volunteers on issues of cultural understanding and acceptance, as the divide between Native and non-Native church communities is quite rigid, with few congregations drawing membership from both groups.

Volunteer cultural education occurs in two settings: during mandatory daily devotions presented by the directors, and in evening cultural activities presented by Lakota people. Volunteers' beliefs about past mistreatment of the Lakota are reinforced during morning "devotions," a time period that contains three elements: a scripture reading, cultural information, and prayer concerns. The scripture reading frequently attempts to link Christian belief to Lakota tradition. For example, "I will lift up mine eyes to the hills, from whence cometh my help" (Psalm 121:1, KJV) leads to a commentary on the sacred Black Hills and how they were lost due to the discovery of gold. Cultural information imparted in the morning devotions includes a discussion of traditional values, practices such as the Sundance and Sweat Lodge, and the introduction of some Lakota words. One comparison between the Sundance and Christianity was expressed in the phrase "Isn't it wonderful that we do not have to participate in that [piercing, bleeding and flesh offerings in the Sundance ritual] because Jesus already died on the cross for us." Volunteers learn about the Sundance as a ritual from the past that is still practiced. It is a sacred ceremony that continues to be held, but today some notable Lakota Sundance leaders make it possible for curious Europeans as well as Lakota and Euro-Americans to participate. Other Sundances are more restricted to Lakota and occasional visitors.

Another scripture often used in devotions is familiar to Christians who are involved in mission: in Matthew 25:35-46 the disciples ask Jesus when it was that they gave him food, shelter, and clothing, and he replies, "Truly, I say to you, as you did it to one of the least of these my brethren, you did it to me." This passage supports not only the goals of Tree of Life, but also the call to mission that many volunteers cite as their reasons for being engaged in mission activity. But a closer examination of the passage suggests that people are being called to *do for* the least of these, rather than to engage and work *with* the least of these. It calls for people to help by doing charitable work, and implies that the recipients of aid are too weak to change their own circumstances. What is missing from the discussion is a realistic awareness of the historically and culturally grounded structural factors that not only contribute to the current situation but also serve as barriers to sustainable development and justice. This discussion can be grounded in a Christian approach, but it must be one formed through an understanding of theology of liberation (Gutiérrez 1973; Newbigin 1978) rather than the traditional charity or development models. The leadership encourages (*demands*, according to the web page [General Board of Global Ministries 2009]) that volunteers engage the help of people in the homes they are working on, but in many cases the owners are not present or are physically unable. For example, one home that a group worked on belonged to an elderly woman in a wheelchair. Another group, working on a wheelchair ramp for the absent owner, invited her Euro-American husband to help, but he demurred and the volunteers or the part time construction staff person assigned to work with them did not press the matter. Volunteers occasionally expressed the idea that it would be good if there could be more collaboration with homeowners and family members, but I observed little evidence of this kind of collaborative effort where the Lakota control the work being done on their homes. It is difficult for short term volunteers to demand that people work with them as they paint or repair a home, not only because of their relative unfamiliarity with the culture, but also because of their knowledge of past injustices and desire to do something to make amends.

One event that crystallized the significance of the past in the context of Tree of Life's efforts involved the Ronald McDonald dental mobile that came to Mission for a week, sponsored by TOL. After filling out eight pages of paperwork, parents could bring their children in for dental care. There are only two dentists on the reservation for over 25,000 people, and poor dental hygiene is rampant. Lakota children are perhaps even more terrified of visiting the dentist than are Euro-American children. In this context, the dentist can be seen as a metaphor for white domination. Late one day a particularly active and curious four-year-old, the granddaughter of one of the Lakota employees of TOL, was squirming in the dentist's chair, pointing at the equipment, asking "what's that?" The dentist, a white person, attempted to have her put her hands down. Her mother, standing across the room, claimed that he restrained the girl. She went to the grandmother (staff person), who stormed into the makeshift dental office and confronted the dentist. (I later heard the dental assistant claim the dentist did not restrain or harm the child.) The grandmother, seeing the incident as yet another example of white domination, stormed back across the courtyard complaining about "dumb white people" in front of volunteers. When I later asked this same staff member, who is a community activist in addition to her work at Tree of Life, what she thought of the volunteers, she said, "They took our land, now they want our culture too."

A final example illustrates the continued dependency and domination of the Lakota despite the good intentions and assistance provided by Tree of Life. After the rush of the summer volunteer season, and after three years without a break, the directors scheduled a much needed two-week vacation. As the time approached, the three female Lakota staff who worked in the Warm Welcome food and clothing operation became anxious because it was not clear what was going to happen during this period. Without volunteers to help, running a clothing, food, and hot meal program that serves approximately two hundred people a day was/is challenging. After some discussion back and forth among staff, a volunteer, and the directors—beginning with the position that staff would have to take an unpaid vacation—the decision was ultimately made to pay them for most of their time off but to shut the entire operation down while the directors were gone, even though one week before this the three women had successfully operated the Warm Welcome without volunteers. That is, the women who worked at the Warm Welcome appear to have been perceived by the directors as being unable to run a portion of the organization, in spite of evidence to the contrary. In the end, the operation was shut down, and the people normally served by Tree of Life had to go elsewhere for food and clothing for two weeks.

Informal conversations I had with Rosebud people indicate a variety of opinions with regard to the accomplishments of Tree of Life, ranging from the view that TOL does a lot of good for the people, to the view that TOL enables some of the people who rely on their services to be dependent and not work, to the view that TOL is just another organization trying to "save" or "civilize" the Indian. One story related to me by a Euro-American pastor involved a volunteer who was shopping at the local grocery store in early summer, who overheard a Lakota woman say pointedly "here come the Christians again to save us." Another Lakota informant commented on how many of these helping organizations come and go. According to this person, when an organization like TOL fails, those who rely on their services laugh and feel like they have counted *coup* on them. That is, they take them for all the resources they have, then move on to other organizations that take their place—as a kind of get-even justice for past wrongs that never results in equality of any kind (Scott 1985).

There is no evidence that Tree of Life is in danger of failing: volunteers are coming, food is being distributed, homes are being repaired, but the reservation is still poor and people are still suffering after years of good intentions and deeds by volunteers at Tree of Life, the Federal government, and other organizations. TOL does do good work in providing food, clothing, and home repair; and in the education and awareness they provide to volunteers about the desperate conditions on the reservation. But as long as the organization continues to operate within the context created by the legacies of cultural domination, loss, and acculturation, coupled with a top-down charity and development philosophy still grounded largely in a faith based model of doing *to* and *for* rather than doing *with*, their ability to work with the Lakota to effect real structural change will be limited. In this sense, Tree of Life is exemplary of the charity based/top-down development models most typically seen for helping the less advantaged or the "least among us" (Farmer 2003), while at the same time it is conscious of the fact that the past needs to be undone and a new relationship forged. What would a different approach look like, one grounded in social justice informed by a theology of liberation where genuine partnerships and collaborations occur? Tree of Life, in its middle place between the Lakota and a significant body of labor and monetary resources, is positioned to transform its mission to one where the Lakota "become agents of their own destiny" (Farmer 2003, 156) and where volunteers actually do justice.

Acknowledgments

This work was made possible by generous contributions and kindnesses of many people including the following: the directors of Tree of Life for providing the housing and opportunity to do this research; the many volunteer groups who stayed at the guest house and enveloped the "trailer trash" living in their back yard in good food, company, and trust; the Lakota staff and the "guys" and other friends from the Warm Welcome; several colleagues and friends who provided support (Tim, Cindy, Tara, Don and April); and last but not least, Greg, who cared for my four four-leggeds while I was in the field. Thank you all. There are probably mistakes and mis/interpretations that will not seem truthful to some, but this work is from my observations, understanding, and responsibility.

Works Cited

Biolsi, Thomas. 2001. *Deadliest enemies: Law and the making of race relations on and off Rosebud Reservation.* Berkeley: University of California Press.
Cerney, Jan. 2005. *Lakota Sioux missions: South Dakota.* Charleston, SC: Arcadia Publishing.
Farmer, Paul. 2003. *Pathologies of power: Health, human rights and the new war on the poor.* Berkeley: University of California Press.
Freire, Paulo. 1986. *Pedagogy of the oppressed.* New York: Continuum.
General Board of Global Ministries of the United Methodist Church. 2009. Tree of Life Ministry. new.gbgm-umc.org/advance/projects/search/index.cfm?action=details&id=3014837&code=123615&more=1 (last accessed July 23, 2009).
Gutiérrez, Gustavo. 1973. *A theology of liberation: History, politics and salvation.* Maryknoll, NY: Orbis Books.
Marquette Library Collections Archives. n.d. St. Francis Mission Records. www.marquette.edu/library/collections/archives/Mss/SFM/SFMsc.html (last accessed May 30, 2009).
Newbigin, Lesslie. 1978. *The open secret: Sketches for a missionary theology.* Grand Rapids, MI: Wm. B. Eerdmans.
Pickering, Kathleen Ann. 2000. *Lakota culture, world economy.* Lincoln, NE: University of Nebraska Press.
Poppendieck, Janet. 1998. *Sweet charity? Emergency food and the end of entitlement.* New York: Viking Press.
Rosebud Sioux Tribe. 2009. Demographics. www.rosebudsiouxtribe-sn.gov/about/demographics.html (last accessed July 23, 2009).
Sachs, Wolfgang. 1992. Introduction. In *The development dictionary: A guide to knowledge as power,* 1-5. Johannesburg: Witwatersrand University Press.
Scott, James C. 1985. *Weapons of the weak: Everyday forms of peasant resistance.* New Haven, CT: Yale University Press.
Sneve, Virginia Driving Hawk. 1977. *That they may have life: The Episcopal Church in South Dakota 1859-1976.* New York: Seabury Press.
Tropman, John E. 1998. *Does America hate the poor? The other American dilemma: Lessons for the 21st century from the 1960s and the 1970s,* Westport, CT: Praeger.

Chapter 8
What's Islam Got to Do with It? American Pluralism, Ethnographic Sensibilities, and Faith-Based Refugee Resettlement in Hartford, Connecticut

Janet Bauer and Andrea Chivakos

Introduction: Faith-Based NGOs in the "Business" of U.S. Refugee Resettlement

Persons fleeing persecution were admitted to the United States even prior to the adoption of the U.S. Refugee Act in 1980, which belatedly ensured compliance with the 1967 Refugee Protocol for protection of refugees, as therein defined. However, the U.S. approach to resettlement continues to reflect a history of piecemeal responses to the humanitarian needs of refugees rather than thoughtful, proactive approaches to protection of refugee rights. Lacking a coherent or centralized policy, current U.S. refugee resettlement relies upon various national voluntary (mostly faith-based) organizations that partner with the Office of Refugee Resettlement (ORR) in the Department of Health and Human Services to provide resettlement support. These national "partner" organizations include the U.S. Council of Catholic Bishops, Church World Service, the Ethiopian Community Development Council, the Episcopal Migration Ministries, the Hebrew Immigrant Aid Society, Lutheran Family Services, and several others.[1] Through these national umbrella organizations, as well as their local representatives, the U.S. Office of Refugee Resettlement administers a variety of grant programs to offer cash assistance and other services to refugees (Office of Refugee Resettlement n.d.[a]). Local Voluntary Agencies (VOLAGs) are encouraged to provide housing, access to English as a Second Language (ESL) or English Language Learners (ELL) classes, and employment assistance for 30 to 120 days for the refugees they sponsor, irrespective of the refugees' religious affiliation. After this short period of direct support, refugees are expected to become self-sufficient and independent (a hallmark of "becoming American").

Thus, refugees in Greater Hartford, Connecticut, must also depend upon their own networks to navigate the "American system" (cf. Bashi 2007). While the number of refugees officially admitted to Connecticut is relatively small—averaging 537 a year over the last ten years, according to ORR figures (Office of Refugee Resettlement n.d.[b]), which does not include those who arrive through chain migration—the experiences of Connecticut refugees and the changing partnerships between private and public community organizations serving them reflect national trends. With rising numbers of Muslim refugees, increasing refugee assertiveness about inadequate housing and ESL instruction, and pressures faced by refugees to become economically independent, new community organizations and individual cultural brokers with various affiliations have emerged to aid in the post-resettlement process (i.e., taking up where the resettlement agencies leave off). The entrance of Muslim NGOs into the local service arena in Connecticut has pushed the boundaries of pluralism in faith-based co-operation, in addition to raising many questions about the implications of both providing services across faith-based lines and encouraging the use of religious and/or ethnic affiliation as a means of incorporation into the American public sphere. At both the national and the local level, the Bush Administration's Faith-Based Initiative clearly spoke primarily to Christian organizations seeking to provide a variety of community services.[2] In addition, post-9/11 persecution and surveillance of Islamic charities have restricted or diminished (although not technically prohibited) opportunities for Muslim voluntary organizations to receive state mediated resources in their efforts to assist newcomers (cf. Benthall 2007; Carapico 2007).

Religious affiliation is a valuable resource (a kind of social and cultural capital), providing a supportive community and source of identity for Muslim immigrants and refugees and underscoring the efficacy of ethnic/faith-based community organizations in facilitating refugee adaptation (Levitt 2001; Ebaugh and Chafetz 2002; D'Alisera 2004; Stepick 2006; Newland, Tanaka, and Barker 2007). However, organizing around religious and ethnic identities may also contribute to the "segmentation" of the American experience (Williams 2007) or to "alienation" in America (D'Alisera 2004). Among Muslim refugees, the Meskhetian Turks—from a more secular, post-communist society—seem slower to embrace the assistance offered through specifically Muslim initiatives or local mosques than do the Somali Bantu. Some of this variation in the role of faith or faith-based organizations in post-immigration experiences may be explained by emigration from post-communist societies or by the degree of persecution experienced because of religion prior to emigration.

However important faith may or may not be to the adaptation of individual refugees to life in America, refugees do face both pressure and encouragement to identify with and organize around religious heritage, and their own religiously-based organizations can offer assistance. On the other hand, much refugee assistance comes from across the lines of religious faith. Does this complicate the process of refugee adaptation or incorporation? Based on collaborative student/faculty research conducted over a period of six years (2003-2009) in Hartford, Connecticut,[3] this chapter examines the ambiguous and contrasting roles of faith-based organizations and volunteers (working across and within faith lines) and their use of "ethnographic" methods in responding to the needs of refugees in a multicultural society, suggesting personal transitions from faith-based incentives to an ethics grounded in the language of human rights. In particular, we examine the implications of "accentuating" or encouraging religious identities and affiliations for Muslim refugees as it both facilitates social incorporation and increases segmentation of social groups in the public sphere.

Faith-Based NGOs and the Specific Challenges of Refugee Resettlement in Hartford, Connecticut

Faith-based organizations do most of the refugee resettlement work in Connecticut and thus provide valuable services to refugees. Most refugees are resettled in the Greater Hartford area through either Catholic Charities Migration and Refugee Services in Hartford (otherwise known as Catholic Charities), or Jewish Family Services in West Hartford, both of which agree to accept refugees of diverse religious backgrounds who have been vetted through federal agencies before entering the United States. VOLAGs are the intermediaries between refugees and the federal, state, and local benefits for which they qualify. The direct services provided by the VOLAGs are funded through competitive federal grants and state-mediated resources,[4] characterized by Newland, Tanaka, and Barker as a "multiplayer" process (2007, 10).[5] Moreover, these organizations are to a certain extent dependent on volunteers and on the ORR matching funds which are linked to volunteers' hours of service. VOLAGs and volunteers are most likely to act out of faith-based humanitarian motives—a commitment they can share with each other, while stressing their nonsectarian mission to government agencies supporting their work.[6]

Convention refugees—defined as those fleeing persecution because of race/ethnicity, national identity, political opinion, religious affiliation, or social group[7]—often arrive in Hartford with few resources other than their own social and cultural capital (like personal resilience and social networks, including those of a religious nature). In the last twenty years the refugee populations served have changed from those fleeing conflict and persecution in communist or post-communist countries (e.g., Russian Jews, Cambodians, Vietnamese, Cubans, Bosnians and Kosovar Albanians), to Sierra Leoneans, Liberians, Somalis, Iraqis and Afghanis, Meskhetian/Russian Turks, Burundis, and Karins from Burma. This shift is reflected in resettlement statistics, which show that among refugees resettled in Connecticut in 2004, 75 percent were African and 45 percent were Muslim, indicating a departure from Cold War politics.[8] In this same period, mandated federal support for refugees has decreased from thirty-six months to the current 30-120 days, varying by VOLAG and the resources and grants to which they have access.

While there is a patchwork of services and benefits for which refugees can qualify, their immediate challenge is to understand and access that support. Once refugees are processed by the U.S. State Department and assigned to and accepted by local VOLAGs, they receive interest-free loans for their transportation to Hartford, where they are picked up by Catholic Charities caseworkers and delivered to their apartments. Intermediaries like Catholic Charities are responsible for allocating federal grants and implementing state programs for the first several months that refugees are in the United States. Once settled, the refugees wait until caseworkers arrive to begin the process of registering them for benefits like cash assistance, completing health care evaluations, enrolling children in school, and providing information about employment and ESL classes. VOLAG partners of the federal government, like Catholic Charities, are the initial gatekeepers to refugee adjustment in America.

As stated, the length of mandated refugee support provided by VOLAGs currently varies from 30 to 120 days, but the primary goal (and the primary means by which the Federal Government evaluates its partners) is to make families and individuals self-sufficient within four months. Catholic Charities employs caseworkers to help refugees seek medical treatment, and uses their sponsored funding to operate several ESL classes and a youth after-school program in the Hartford area. While VOLAGs are responsible for allocating federal funds at the local level, resources are scarce and refugees often find it difficult to obtain the support they require to continue the process of adapting to American life.

After the initial period of support, refugees may "fall off the radar" of the resettlement agencies, since agencies have no formal responsibility to monitor refugee progress. Some families move in patterns of chain migration to join family and friends in other cities. For example, some Somalis move to Springfield, Massachusetts; Lewiston, Maine; or Minneapolis, Minnesota; while many Bosnians and Meskhetian Turks have come to Hartford/New Britain from St. Louis or elsewhere. This network of family and ethnic-based support becomes extremely important in the post-resettlement process, although some new "actors" have recently begun to fill the gaps in post-resettlement assistance. Even though the VOLAG goal is "self sufficiency"—and the U.S. Conference of Catholic Bishops declared that about 78 percent of the 7,400 government-funded refugees they resettled nationally in 2005 had achieved this within the 180-day period[9]—refugees are usually still paying off their loans for airfare to come to the United States, learning English, and looking for jobs and better housing after four months in the country.

VOLAG partners not only face the challenge of addressing these multiple refugee needs with limited resources, but they must also balance complying with government guidelines while carrying out their own mandates. Nichols maintains that "the idea that private agencies can maintain unfettered independence and also accept material and financial assistance from the U.S. government has proven false in the experience of any number of religious agencies" (1988, 193). In Hartford, for example, Catholic Charities' website indicates that their vision is "Individuals, families and communities will become healthy, self-sufficient and productive, thriving in a just and compassionate society," while their Mission is "Motivated by Christ's social teachings" (Catholic Charities, Archdiocese of Hartford 2008).

We have no supporting evidence that local faith-based NGOs or volunteers in Hartford have pressured refugees to change or compromise their own religious affiliations. On the contrary, many individual volunteers we have encountered working on the ground seem especially inclined to validate the religious faith of "the other." Notably, the most effective NGOs and volunteers employ "ethnographic" techniques of observing, listening, and seeking to understand the needs and backgrounds of specific refugees, regardless of their own religious affiliations. Like ethnographers, they often become immersed (perhaps overly) in the cultures of those they are assisting, participating in their religious (especially Muslim) life cycle ceremonies and rituals. Their commitment, like that of the NGOs (and VOLAGs) themselves, is rooted in an ethic of care—whatever their personal religious faith tradition might be.

The involvement of religious volunteers and voluntary organizations in carrying out the work of the state has caused some tensions at the local level. Despite Catholic Charities' bumpy history (and turnovers in leadership) in Hartford and its philosophy of performing Christian charity, most complaints likely reflect the complexities of the funding calculus (which includes a cash sum per refugee for initial resettlement, from which Catholic Charities can keep some overhead)[10] as well as the gap between refugees' expectations for support and the realities of what they receive. Still, other local groups and individuals have now become active players in post-resettlement in the Greater Hartford area and are often better equipped to listen and respond to individual refugee needs.

A Response to Post-Resettlement Needs: Expanding Local Refugee Services beyond Faith-Based VOLAGs

Observers of international aid organizations serving refugee populations have suggested that refugee rights and needs can be more fully addressed at the local level (Fisher 1997; Loescher 2003).[11] Hartford, Connecticut, is one of the nation's ten poorest cities, presenting enormous challenges to refugees resettling there. Previously traumatized refugees occasionally find themselves placed in marginal neighborhoods wracked by violence, while many of the employment opportunities available to them are located in the suburbs. Often, caseworkers in the mainline resettlement organizations cannot devote individual attention to the breadth of refugee needs. In the late 1990s some of the more independent individual volunteers serving the community, both at ESL classes offered through VOLAGs and at other NGOs like the Jubilee House or the Hartford Public Li-

brary branches, began to respond to the unfilled need for post-resettlement services. They assumed the role of "cultural brokers"—a term developed by Mary
Pipher to describe individuals who mediate the experience of learning and sur-
viving in American culture. "Cultural Brokers," she says, "help ease people into
each other's cultures . . . cultural brokers give newcomers information that directly translates into power" (Pipher 2002, 89).

As a result, a number of new actors (agencies and organizations, both faith-
based and non-faith-based) emerged to offer assistance in "brokering" the refugee experience, mostly out of recognition that the human rights of refugees were
not being fully actualized in the resettlement process. Some were new NGOs;
others, existing organizations creating new programs to respond to the needs of
refugee newcomers: the Refugee Assistance Center, Hartford Areas Rally Together, Hartford Public Library programs, the Joint Refugee Committee, the
city's Youth Services division, as well as churches, mosques, and the Muslim
Coalition of Connecticut. It was clear that attention to human rights and community service, as well as "faith-based" charity, was motivating this expansion
of services.

Individual "brokers" began to stand out as especially important actors in
refugee resettlement. One such broker, having been trained in social work, initially volunteered as an ESL instructor and quickly began to field requests for
assistance in a wide variety of areas—including help with "green card" applications and citizenship tests, assistance in navigating the DSS (Department of Social Services) system, finding an ESL class, or making a doctor's appointment.
She gradually began hosting a once-a-week walk-in center, which finally became formalized and recently funded as the Refugee Assistance Center (RAC).
Although not a sectarian organization, the RAC is based at Jubilee House, an
umbrella facility for a number of social service NGOs staffed mostly by the Sisters of Saint Joseph. While the RAC serves diverse refugee populations, Bosnians and Somalis (Muslims) have been perhaps the greatest beneficiaries of its
services.

In 2006, when Catholic Charities assigned a number of recently arrived
Somali refugees to substandard housing on a street with frequent violence, the
Hartford community responded. Led by the community organization Hartford
Areas Rally Together (H.A.R.T.), refugees and community members rallied in
front of Catholic Charities' offices to request improved resettlement services—
housing, job training and education—with signs reading "Refugee Resettlement
is Your Responsibility." As a result of this public debate, service providers in
Hartford organized the Hartford Refugee Resettlement Joint Committee to ensure greater attention to refugee needs and rights in delivering post-resettlement
services. This joint committee includes representatives from H.A.R.T., Catholic
Charities, the city's Board of Education, the Department of Health and Human
Services, the mayor's office, the City Council, Hartford Hospital, and individual
members of numerous refugee communities. The various member organizations
further enhanced their services. Catholic Charities Migration and Refugee Services expanded its existing classes (like ESL) to include after school tutoring

and drumming classes, as well as therapeutic art classes. The Hartford Public Library (HPL) outreach services also expanded its ESL and citizenship classes, as well as offering workshops on taxes, legal issues, domestic violence prevention, and provider services, and public celebrations like World Refugee Day. In addition, HPL recently created its own umbrella group, the Refugee and Immigrant Gateway Steering Committee. H.A.R.T. also has a refugee committee, and the Somali Bantu (a Somali minority group) have created their own ethnic community-based organizations (ECBO) through which to manage and distribute resources like cash assistance. The Joint Committee became, at least momentarily, a successful example of how state and local partnerships can be fostered through cooperation between the public sector and nonprofit organizations.[12] It has not only broken down the hierarchies of the resettlement process by incorporating local actors into decision-making, but it has also given refugees an opportunity to organize across ethnic divides.

The need for initiatives beyond those offered by traditional providers has generated calls for other faith-based organizations to assist in providing post-resettlement services. Churches, Muslim associations (like the Muslim Coalition of Connecticut), and mosques (like Muhammad Islamic Center of Greater Hartford, on Hungerford Street, and the Islamic Association of Greater Hartford, Berlin) have responded. However, Christian and Jewish faith groups continue to dominate as service providers in the Hartford area. In August 2007, Catholic Charities hosted a meeting with local parishes to generate sponsors for the newest arrivals, Burundi and Burmese refugees, in order to offer support beyond the initial four months provided by the resettlement agencies. Although this meeting was advertised as a community effort to coordinate refugee resettlement in Hartford, many of the non-sectarian and Muslim representatives who had been present at the Joint Refugee meeting the previous June were absent. A church representative who was present underscored the general feeling that the "common denominator of Christ's love" brought these volunteers together to serve the needs of refugees, a sentiment which unfortunately marginalizes the secular and non-Christian volunteers who work on behalf of refugees.

While Muslim caseworkers employed by Catholic Charities Migration and Refugee Services or H.A.R.T. usually attend the monthly meetings of the Joint Refugee Committee (described above), Muslim organizations represented in some of the initial meetings have not continued to participate. We have heard about the general frustrations refugees experience with resettlement organizations—especially those working with organizations outside their own religious traditions. We have no clear indication of bias or proselytizing, even though some individual cultural brokers have at times taken unpopular positions regarding gender and racial equality that some refugees might consider contrary to tradition or to a family's wishes.

There are, of course, misunderstandings that become sources of tension. For example, refugees often assume that organizations like Catholic Charities have access to enormous funds that they do not share with individual refugee families (despite the fact that much of the money they receive comes from competitive or matching grants earmarked for specific programs, not for individual cash assistance). It is hard to calculate whether any implicitly Catholic values (such as the impermissibility of divorce) are subtly promoted through some of Catholic Charities refugee programs (like the "Refugee Families Grow Healthy in Connecticut" program for which Catholic Charities recently received an ORR grant), but it is possible they might contrast with (or be perceived as contrasting with) either Muslim or personal approaches to strengthening the family.[13] Whether as a result of potential conflicts such as these or a growing awareness of the recent increase in Muslim refugees in Hartford, Muslim faith-based organizations (often mosques) have increased their efforts to assist refugees in post-resettlement adjustment, providing one possible source of security for newly arrived refugees.

Bridging the Gap: The Emergence of Muslim NGOs in Refugee Work and the Challenge of Pluralism for Muslims and Muslim Communities

Faith can be an important factor in refugee acculturation in the United States (Warner 2007; Stepick 2006). For example, at the August 2007 meeting of local parishes in Hartford, one Burundi Christian refugee said that there were two things that were most important upon arrival to the United States: the first was finding a job to support his family; the second was finding a church to go to that would support his faith.

With increasing numbers of Muslim refugees in Hartford (45 percent of all refugees who arrived in 2004),[14] local mosques and other Muslim organizations have expanded programs to assist them. However, there were no representatives from mosques or Muslim organizations at either the June 2007 meeting of the Joint Refugee Committee or the August Catholic Charities Migration and Refugee Services"summit" on new refugees. Of course, those organizations, with a long time status as ORR partners (like HIAS and Catholic Conference of Bishops), have greater access to funding for resettlement services, including those mediated through the White House Office of Faith-Based Initiatives.

While the emergence of Muslim faith- or ethnic-based community organizations grows out of the same impetus to serve those in need that motivates other faith-based organizations (cf. Stepick, Ray, and Mahler 2009), these organizations are not part of the network that mediates state and federal resources for refugees. Their lack of representation, in spite of the increasing participation of Muslim organizations and cultural brokers in the sphere of post-resettlement services, raises a set of uneasy questions about the role of Muslim community organizations in bridging the gap in resettlement services. Is their lack of representation a reflection of post-9/11 bias and racism against Muslims and Muslim charities? To what extent do Muslim refugees engage services offered by Muslim organizations, and what is the effectiveness of services provided by refugees' own faith-based and ethnic community organizations in contrast to services offered across sectarian lines? These questions are further complicated by the challenges of pluralism[15] and cultural diversity facing many Muslims and local Muslim mosque associations in America—particularly with some Muslim refugees coming from secularly inclined, post-communist societies (cf. Moore 2007).[16]

For many Muslim refugees, religion is a central part of their identity, and mosque programs—or those of organizations like the Muslim Coalition of Connecticut—can produce therapeutic effects and provide a utilitarian networking resource. Warner suggests there can be advantages for immigrants who affiliate with their coreligionists upon arrival in the United States.[17] Where Muslims have been the scapegoats for the terrorist attacks on the United States, or where they have suffered pre-resettlement traumas, having an institutionalized connection to Muslim-based organizations could help ease their insecurities or offer inclusion and social mobility. Many immigrants and refugees find themselves compromised in the arena of civic engagement or full access to mainstream society. Mosques offer possibilities for social and emotional support; or, as Warner suggests, religious organizations can provide "moral order," "social skills," and a social community that sustains practitioners (Warner 2007, 112).

Hartford's Muslim organizations and volunteers often become aware of specific needs after encountering refugees at Friday prayers. The Masjid Muhammad (Muhammad Islamic Center of Greater Hartford) is located in a Hartford residential area where many refugees are initially placed by Catholic Charities. Over the years, this Islamic center has opened its doors to a diverse set of immigrants, before they move on to other religious centers or towns. The mosque collaborated with the Muslim Coalition of Connecticut in a "backpack project" to provide supplies and clothing to new Muslim refugees, and also initiated an after school tutoring program and weekend religious classes. However, few of the Somali Bantu are regular attendees at these programs. Instead, the tight-knit Somali Bantu community, already discriminated against within the larger Somali Muslim refugee community, has formed its own ECBO, the Somali Bantu Community Association. Through this association, they have successfully coordinated their own resources to establish a "Saturday school," offering these classes at the Jubilee House.[18]

The expansion of Muslim outreach work in the Hartford area follows national trends in the transformation of religious-based social service programs, as well as the challenges of increasing diversity in contemporary mosques, as described by Moore (2007). Immigrants and refugees participate in an ongoing conversation about what the essential core of Islam will be within a context of a pluralistic Muslim American community—a conversation which includes a heightened awareness of broader global events, local racial politics, and cultural differences between generations of "native born" and "foreign-born" Muslims. For example, some newer refugee groups do not feel comfortable in multicultural mosques because of language and cultural differences, preferring instead to hold Ramadan prayers with other Kosovars or Bosnians. As a result, several

Muslim refugee groups have created their own ethnic-national associations or religious communities (as with the Somali Bantu), constituting in effect what Pratt has referred to as safe-houses—finding security in what is culturally familiar. Safe houses are "social and intellectual spaces where groups can constitute themselves as horizontal, homogeneous, sovereign communities with high degrees of trust and shared understandings, temporary protection from legacies of oppression . . . in which to construct shared understandings, knowledge, claims on the world that they can bring into the contact zone" (Pratt 1999, 541).

Religious affiliation has affected the resettlement of various refugee groups in different ways. The Somalis were criticized for carrying on their traditional wedding dances in the mosque—something that others considered "un-Islamic." As D'Alisera points out, new arrivals often struggle with redefining the meaning of Islam and their accustomed ways of observing Islam as they encounter American Muslim communities that de-emphasize cultural values, stress a universalized "authenticity," and conform to some very American (bureaucratized) ways of organizing religious practice. Where religious affiliation was often taken for granted back home, it becomes a (contested) choice for creating new identities in America[19] and provides refugees with both "a sense of belonging and alienation" (2004, 1-2).

The emergence of ethno-religious associations of Muslims from the same ethnic or national group is evidence of a resistance to the paternalism of both the non-Muslim and the Muslim mainstream, as well as a gesture toward self-definition and empowerment. These associations can reduce "dissonant" or dissimilar accommodation across the generations by providing effective instruction for children and youth in the languages and traditions of their parents' home cultures and by placing both parents and children within social networks that provide religious and cultural reinforcement for the messages parents give their children (cf. Warner 2007, 210; Zhou and Bankston 1998). Indeed, in polycultural[20] Hartford, there is clearly a struggle around intergenerational negotiation of cultural tradition.

Potentially, the larger interethnic Muslim community organizations (like mosque associations with many American-born Muslims) may be better placed to engage Islamophobia,[21] interethnic conflict in schools (between African American and Liberian students, for example, or between Puerto Rican and Bosnian or Meskhetian Turkish students), or even racial discrimination among Muslim groups. Indeed, for some Muslim refugees emigrating from postcommunist societies—the Bosnians, Kosovars, and the Meskhetian Turks—there seems to be some discomfort in the creation of American public identities around personal religious practice.[22] When first arriving in Hartford, these refugees engaged in less public display of religiosity. Fewer women wore "modern" styles of extensive hijab (older women wear kerchiefs and younger women no head covering), and men continued to drink at their own Islamic festivities. Tensions between Muslim groups were exacerbated in an adult ESL class when an immigrant teacher tried to separate the class of Africans (mostly Somali and Somali Bantu Muslims) from the mostly European Bosnian and Meskhetian

Turkish Muslims, very likely revealing emerging racial tensions among these groups—which are of course contrary to the spirit of Islam. The outreach from existing American Muslim associations or mosques and the refugees' adjustment to their new religious communities often encourage increasing conformity to certain "standardized" expressions of devout Islamic practice. This presents selected refugee populations with the choice between more secular, cultural forms of practice, or more orthodox religious identities.

So what does Islam have to do with refugee resettlement? Despite the complexities regarding the role of Muslim or any faith-based NGO offering resettlement services, ethnic-based community groups can be important sources of support in accommodating to American society. The need to engage Muslim organization partners seems urgent given the growing percentage of Muslim refugees in Connecticut and the rather negative public opinion directed toward Islam since 9/11, as reflected in a 2003 Pew survey (Pew Research Center 2003). It is important to examine the growing responses of Muslim organizations and volunteers to refugee needs, as religious associations are perhaps the most frequent type of ECBO (Warner 2007). Refugees themselves are encouraged, and soon learn, to organize around their own ethnic or religious affiliations even though not all Muslim refugees are orthodox practitioners. One option might be to encourage Muslim organizations to develop their own resettlement divisions—affiliated organizations through which to develop means of channeling funding—and perhaps expand their mandate to encompass refugees across faith-based lines.

Ethnographic Sensibilities: The Pivotal Role of Cultural Brokers and Women Volunteers Across Faith Traditions

While it is important for the service provider community to work toward developing relationships with the Muslim faith-based and ECB organizations which can model inclusion and offer assistance in engaging the wider society, it is clear that individual "cultural brokers" continue to have a pivotal role in an overworked resettlement system. Although VOLAG caseworkers or agency workers are resourceful liaisons in refugee resettlement, they often denote the "rule of law" for newcomers, working as they do for government-funded organizations. In contrast, individual cultural brokers perform important services for refugee families, going beyond any official roles by providing personal interpretations of some of the nuances of American life. "On the front lines" with their "ears close to the ground," and acting out of a commitment to both humanitarian and human rights interests, these cultural brokers have been able to avoid the kind of essentializing of Muslim refugees that we overheard at the Joint Refugee Committee meetings where, for example, it was suggested that the Somalis and Somali Bantu (African Muslim groups) have more need for help than the Turks or the Bosnians (European Muslims).

Cultural brokers utilize ethnographic techniques of observing, listening, and seeking to understand the needs and backgrounds of specific refugees, in a kind of participant observation. They know what is going on with refugees at home, at school, and on the job. Working through NGOs, schools, city agencies, or faith groups, they go beyond any institutional role, showing a willingness to engage refugees and their communities with what we would call "ethnographic sensibilities." One social worker with whom we worked became aware of the lack of support for immigrant and refugee students in the schools (after the demise of the high school New Arrival Center), and is now one of the petitioners in a lawsuit filed by the Children's Advocacy Center against the Hartford Public Schools. As mediators of American culture, cultural brokers establish the kinds of patron-client relationships that Goodell (1985) suggests are important for reinforcing a reciprocity that transforms paternalism and works against segmentation and exclusion.

The network of Hartford area volunteers who answer the call to be involved as cultural brokers with refugees is ever expanding through the efforts of individuals in existing agencies and faith-based organizations. Not unlike the era of the nineteenth-century evangelical missions movement, those who volunteer for community work with local refugees seem to be disproportionately women (of all faiths). Many of the volunteers we have encountered, although they initially vocalize humanitarian aims, quickly move on to what has been called rights-based discourse in defense of refugee needs.[23] These cultural brokers come to realize that the right to be free of persecution does not simultaneously guarantee other rights of protection: food, shelter, and clothing. In fact, Harris-Curtis (2003) argues that some rights discourse is subsumed in the work of faith-based organizations.

Although many individuals are responding to a religiously inspired ethic of care, most do not proceed from a desire to proselytize "the other." Indeed, many non-Muslim volunteers are particularly conscious of the need to educate themselves about Islam and how to interact with refugees of different faith traditions. This has given rise to groups like the Muslim and Christian Women of Hope and Faith, reading groups, and workshops on "Muslim Immigrant Women" organized by Hartford Public Library's outreach coordinator. Although such efforts tend to have the effect of assuaging the fears of non-Muslims, at the same time they create an essentialized notion of cultural differences.

These committed volunteers sometimes encourage different routes of incorporation for refugees—taking different positions on preserving community "traditions" versus supporting the right to individual choice. In her role as cultural broker, a teacher we worked with supported a young woman in resisting what she claimed was a forced marriage, and helped her seek legal emancipation from her parents; in contrast, the social worker, dressing in Somali garb to attend an arranged marriage ceremony, defended the parents, explaining the daughter's accusations as exaggerations made by a young woman who was practically living with her American boyfriend. It is clear that the reciprocal relationship between cultural brokers and refugees can contribute to what Fisher (1997) observes in the international NGO arena as transformative and empowering for both parties. In part, it is access to relationships outside one's own community (and with different organizations) that destabilizes how we define one another.[24]

Goodell's (1985) observations about the comparative benefits of patron-client relations as opposed to the paternalism of corporate institutions (however benevolent) in aid distribution further contributed to our thinking about the important role of individual cultural brokers in this process. Through their participation in networks of "patronage," cultural brokers establish the kind of reciprocity that can effect some change in the relations of power between immigrants and their host societies and decrease the "oppositional" segmentation of these communities.[25] These relationships sometimes offer the only substantial contact that Hartford area refugees have outside their own communities, creating bridges from more insulated ethnic or religiously-based organizations to inclusion in the American public sphere. One way we have found that voluntary organizations can capitalize on the resources in their surrounding community is to work closely with universities to find and educate student volunteers in the work of the cultural broker.

A New American Pluralism?
The Paradox of Using Religious and Ethnic Identities as an Entrée into American Culture and Civil Society

Faith-based groups continue to be an important means of delivering resettlement services, and it should be recognized that Muslim groups are important partners in this work. Although programs like those of Catholic Charities do not deliberately discriminate based on religion, the cooperation between private, faith-based organizations and public agencies raises questions about the separation of church and state affairs. Increasingly, faith-based work has been infused by the ethics of social justice in a rights framework.[26] This intersection of faith and rights is now discursively framed as post-religious or post-Islamic (depending on the faith tradition)—referring to the increasing acceptance of the infusion of faith-based principles with rights language and pluralism. This moves beyond a commitment to text based, rule bound ethics (Bayat 2007; Moser 2008), just as non-sectarian activist volunteers demonstrate a fusing of moral/religious and rights motivations (Streng, Lloyd, and Allen 1973, 418).

In many ways, the increasing presence of faith-based organizations in resettlement work signals the importance of religious identities in the American cultural landscape. Two adult refugee students at Trinity College (one Kosovar, one Sudanese) remarked that "religion" was not the first identity one claimed in their home countries, but in America (particularly post-9/11) they felt pressured to identify themselves first as "Muslims." These identities become a basis for receiving government grants and services, as well as a means for religious and ethnic groups to maintain some independence from cooptation by the larger society (Fisher 1997, 358)—perhaps preserving their ability to engage in selective accommodation (Portes and Rumbaut 2001) or some combination of assertion and accommodation between home and host societies (Woldemikael 1987). Ethnic and religious identities take on importance both because they are the source of distinction and discrimination, and because they are promoted as a basis for organizing and claiming resources and assistance.[27]

What are the implications of resettlement identity politics for American pluralism? Like Nichols (1988), we could raise questions about the parameters of public/private partnerships in delivering refugee services—particularly the enormous reliance on volunteerism and ethics of care. We cannot help wondering about the paradox of encouraging religious and ethnic identities as a tool of resettlement and adaptation, despite a general understanding that "philanthropy" and volunteerism (secular or faith-based) are undertaken for the common good. Whose sense of common good? The emphasis on ethnic and religious tradition for organizing for resources or engaging one's surroundings raises important questions regarding religious identity in the multicultural public sphere (as well as the relationship between church and state). Does encouraging faith-based identification lead to greater separation in the public sphere, or does it result from racism and discrimination? These questions draw attention to the logic and dynamics of relationships within and between immigrant and nonimmigrant groups and to questions about inter-group dialogue and structural change.

The work of VOLAGs and volunteers in no way replaces the need for government commitment and support for the successful adaptation of new refugee groups or for the development of a clearer conception of American pluralism that includes both multiculturalism and a common cultural repertoire. There should be more explicit guidelines for defining the relationship between federal, state, and local providers of refugee resettlement assistance. There also needs to be more attention to (and less ambivalence about) the type of multiculturalism pursued through these policies. Should differences be celebrated in private or recognized and supported in shared public life? This very question emerged at a meeting of the Hartford Refugee Resettlement Joint Committee: one Somali refugee, Muhammad (who represented a neighborhood agency), argued that youth soccer teams participating in the city refugee soccer tournament should not be organized along the sectarian lines of national or ethnic groups. In America, he said, refugees should be focusing on claiming an American identity, not on creating further divisions within their own communities. Many refugee groups are already divided by religious or ethnic differences (immigrant versus refugee; Muslim versus Christian Albanians; North versus South Sudanese; village versus town among the Bosnians; Somali versus Somali Bantu), yet some of the Somali and Somali Bantu played together when they could not field separate teams.

No community group or agency (even faith-based ones) working with refugees has formulated a policy framework (or programs of support and training) to address the numerous points of conflict between refugees and members of other cultural groups for which refugees have sought resolution—like the physical assaults on Meskhetian Turkish boys and on Somali children, at the hands of other students, for being too respectful of their teachers. Neither has there been recognition that many of the hardships in housing or discrimination faced by the Somali refugees may be linked to larger issues of race relations or race politics in the Hartford area (or globally); instead, Joint Committee members confidently offered that the Somalis were more "needy" and less self-reliant than the Turks.

These instances demonstrate how the dynamics of interactions with the broader community contribute to the creation of identities that may eventually provoke separation and greater reliance on individual cultural brokers or on members of specific ethnic or religious-based community groups. It has largely been Muslim community leaders like the Masjid Muhammad Imam or interfaith groups that have sought to intervene on behalf of groups of Muslim families in the school system or create programs to address community Islamophobia. Such prejudice is reflected in local blog sites where we found the following disparaging comments by user "Time Grease" (2007) about the opening of the Bosnian-American Cultural Association: "I live in Hartford and see these people... They don't dress like us, talk like us, they don't believe what we believe, why should we want them here?" It is important that refugee resettlement agencies become sensitive to this kind of religious and cultural intolerance and its effect on refugees. More importantly, this example demonstrates how the dynamics of engagement and discourse around religious identity have become one of the primary sources of public struggle over diversity and pluralism.[28]

We argue that the inclusion of Muslim NGOs in the resettlement process is constructive; that it can be a means to promote community and interfaith dialogue; and that it will help invite more debate about what kind of plural public sphere we want to create—perhaps leading to what Fisher (1997) describes as a "multicentric" world with respect to American public life. Several faith-based and other organizations are already working to address these issues of coordination and collaboration. For some refugees, however, working with non-denominational, non-governmental organizations could be especially beneficial. College and high school students offer a ready supply of volunteers, eager to participate in internships and volunteer programs while also learning about the cultures they are working with and studying the effects of pluralism in the public sphere.

We reiterate that the work of VOLAGs and NGOs does not relieve the government of the responsibility to coordinate more actively and to provide adequate material support for the successful adaptation of new refugee groups, or for setting the parameters for an inclusive, rights-based pluralism in which minorities have the right to display and enjoy their cultures in public. In the existing context, those cultural brokers who have deployed their "ethnographic sensibilities" with respect to refugee needs have provided excellent examples of how public and private institutions can begin to address the needs of a multicultural citizenry.

Notes

1. Catholic Charities receives funding from the United States Conference of Catholic Bishops (USCCB). In 2005, the USCCB received $14.834 million from the U.S. government, making it one of the top receivers of government grant money for refugee resettlement across the nation. This program originated after World War II and expanded with the formation of Migration and Refugee Services in 1965. Because of this long-established relationship with the government, the Catholic Church has become one of the leaders for refugee resettlement in the United States.

2. For example, the Connecticut branch of the White House Faith-Based and Community Initiatives specifically invited "religious groups (such as *church congregations and synagogues*) to participate in front-line ministry" (emphasis added; online citation no longer available). In February 2009, the Obama administration released its revamping of Bush's program as the "White House Office for Faith-Based and Neighborhood Partnerships," promising "to ensure that services paid for with federal government funds are provided in a manner consistent with fundamental constitutional commitments guaranteeing the equal protection of the laws and the free exercise of religion and prohibiting laws respecting an establishment of religion" (*Los Angeles Times* 2009).

3. Contributors to our collaborative faculty/student research project team over the past six years have also included Alissa Phillips, Jessica Hart, Muhammed Umair, Melissa Pierce, Samilys Roderiquez, Narin Prum, Mary Cavallo, Daniela Santangelo, Katya Yarameyeva, and Jessica Fillion.

4. VOLAGs mediate access to cash assistance through ORR programs such as CMA (Cash and Medical Assistance) or RCA (Refugee Cash Assistance) when refugees do not qualify for state mediated TANF (Temporary Assistance for Needy Families) and state programs (some of which are federally funded). They also compete for federal grants to support refugee services. There is a diverse range of ORR grant programs. For example, under the category of Targeted Assistance Discretionary Grants, Jewish Family Services of Greater Hartford has received grants for citizenship training, and Catholic Charities Migration and Refugee Services, grants for strengthening "healthy families."

5. H.R. 2857 (Generations Invigorating Volunteerism and Education Act) is aimed at community service programs but reflects trends in American public policy that rely on volunteerism.

6. Bruce Nichols examines this ambiguous relationship in his book *The Uneasy Alliance: Religion, Refugee Work, and U.S. Foreign Policy* (1988). Although Nichols draws on the role of faith-based organizations in refugee work abroad, his observations may be relevant to the study of faith-based resettlement agencies in the United States. He finds that, historically, many relief organizations have followed religious mandates like the idea of the "Good Samaritan," a direct reference to the New Testament parable. While most organizations are not assisting others in order to gain religious converts, their underlying mandate is nonetheless religious.

7. As specified by the 1951 United Nations Convention Relating to the Status of Refugees and the 1967 Refugee Protocol.

8. Tabulated from 2000 census data.

9. Office of Refugee Resettlement, Annual Report to Congress 2005.

10. VOLAGs are allowed to keep 25 percent of all transportation loan money they collect from refugees (Refugee Resettlement Watch n.d.).

11. For the most part recent studies have focused on global networks of NGOs (Moghadam 2005; Fisher 1997). While we focus on local NGOs/VOLAGs, many like

Catholic Charities are in fact vertically and horizontally linked to national and international networks.

12. Nevertheless, Muslim associations remain relatively marginalized in this process. Catholic Charities still holds most of the legal responsibility for refugee resettlement (as opposed to post-resettlement) in the Hartford area.

13. For example, the Catholic hierarchy opposes the use of contraception while most forms of birth control are permissible in Islam. We are not sure about the substance of the family program, which is based on a "family wellness model" that teaches communications skills that are said to reduce abuse and divorce. [See it described as "Refugee Families Grow Healthy in Connecticut" at www.acf.hhs.gov/healthymarriage/pdf/Fweb summary_2.pdf and as the "Strengthening Refugee Families and Marriages Program" described at www.usccb.org/mrs/HartfordProgram.pdf].

14. These figures reflect general trends in Muslims as a percentage of total refugees admitted to the United States—increasing from 0 percent in 1988 to a pre-9/11 high of 44.4 percent in 1999 and then rising again to 23.7 percent in 2003, the latest available figures (Maloof and Ross-Sheriff 2003).

15. Pluralism here refers to the recognition or existence of group differences (based on culture, religious affiliation, national origin, or ethnicity), without specifying or modeling how such groups are to engage each other in the public sphere.

16. See Moore (2007) for commentary on Muslim-American community discourse on living as a minority in American society and on the challenges of inclusion of women and diverse Muslim populations.

17. "Regardless of their own human capital, immigrants can be advantaged by joining a preexisting ethnic group already on their way up the ladder of mobility toward homeownership and higher occupational status" (Warner 2007, 146). In a visit to the Berlin Mosque on June 3, 2007, we met with representatives from the mosque who told us how they function as a social network for many resettled refugees. Based on our communications at the mosque and with other organizations in Hartford, it seems as though religious communities offer better social networking for recently resettled refugees than do the service providers.

18. The Somali Bantu Community Organization, currently seeking incorporation as a nonprofit, is a mutual assistance association in which community member volunteers assist each other with cash assistance, translation, and other services.

19. As they adjust to the new Islamic landscape, Sierra Leonean Muslims described themselves as "distant" from Islamic knowledge before coming to Washington, D.C. (D'Alisera 2004).

20. A reference to multiple cultural groups who enjoy horizontal (non-hierarchical) political power vis-à-vis one another.

21. Usually defined as an irrational fear or prejudice toward Islam or Muslims.

22. Many of Connecticut's Muslims arrive with some "post-communist" experience. However, while many Bosnians, Turks, and others come from more urbanized societies with more "secular" practices; the Afghans, Somalis, and Somali Bantu all lived through a period of "fundamentalist" reaction to Marxist governments.

23. See Rimel (2001) on similar transformations in the context of philanthropy and giving.

24. Citing Rajni Kothari, Fisher (1997, 456) establishes that empowerment "emerges through a decentralized self-government. In his view, 'conscientization' and the struggle for new alternatives (and alternative truths) produce a new class of activists." Fisher traces the transformation and liberation of care providers by going beyond themselves: "Changing the self and changing society both require a rejection of the representation of

self imposed by relationships with others. Individuals and groups struggle for the freedom to define themselves and their relationships with others on their own terms" (Fisher 1997, 457).

25. As Goodell argues, "paternalism inspires no loyalty in its beneficiary," making the reciprocal nature of patron-client relations a better mechanism for extending "the gift of aid" in a process of "integration rather than segmentation" (1985, 257). This would perhaps avoid some of the past "mistakes" in aid delivery.

26. Slim calls the shift from basic needs to the rights approach a shift from the "sentimental, paternalistic, and privileged discourse of philanthropy and charity to the more political, empowering and egalitarian ideology of rights and duties" (2002, 4).

27. "While ethnic solidarity—the congregation of individuals around a shared ethnicity—can be perceived by some as a step toward ethnic segregation from the wider community, it can also be an important process that helps refugees and other immigrants actively participate in U.S. civil society via ethnically based interest groups." (Maloof and Ross-Sheriff 2003).

28. Williams articulates how particular groups or "communities of discourse" may become the vehicle through which individuals "articulate their understandings of themselves with salient features of the dominant host society . . . and with other social groups (in this case, other religious groups and traditions). . . .Although forms of discourse may originate within any given group or religious tradition, they often do not remain there—they can become forms of 'public' discourse available to a number of different actors. Thus, I am interested here in how religious diversity—and the extent to which that *diversity* is being transformed into a culturally valued '*pluralism*'—affects the languages and the cultural and institutional logics that are used in the public sphere and to what end, and how effectively they are deployed by the groups that use them" (2007, 43).

Works Cited

Bashi, Vilna. 2007. *Survival of the knitted: Immigrant social networks in a stratified world*. Berkeley: University of California Press.

Bayat, Asef. 2007. *Making Islam democratic: Social movements and the post-Islamist turn*. Stanford, CA: Stanford University Press.

Benthall, Jonathan. 2007. The overreaction against Islamic charities. *ISIM Newsletter* 20:6-7.

Carapico, Sheila. 2007. Muslim NGOs: Sleeping with the devil? *ISIM Newsletter* 20:8-9.

Catholic Charities, Archdiocese of Hartford. 2008. About us. http://www.ccaoh.org/AboutUs.html (last accessed August 28, 2009).

D'Alisera, JoAnn. 2004. *An imagined geography. Sierra Leonean Muslims in America*. Philadelphia: University of Pennsylvania Press.

Ebaugh, Helen Rose, and Janet Saltzman Chafetz. 2002. *Religion across borders: Transnational immigrant networks*. Lanham, MD: Rowman and Littlefield.

Fisher, William F. 1997. Doing good? The politics and antipolitics of NGO practices. *Annual Review of Anthropology* 26:439-64.

Goodell, Grace E. 1985. Paternalism, patronage, and potlatch: The dynamics of giving and being given to. *Current Anthropology* 26(2):247-66.

Harris-Curtis, Emma. 2003. Rights-based approaches: Issues for NGOs. *Development in Practice* 13(5):558-64.

Levitt, Peggy. 2001. *The transnational villagers*. Berkeley: University of California Press.

Loescher, Gil. 2003. UNHCR at fifty: Refugee protection and world politics. In *Problems of protection: The UNHCR, refugees, and human rights*, ed. Niklaus Steiner, Mark Gibney, and Gil Loescher, 3-18. New York: Routledge.

Los Angeles Times. 2009. The new faith-based initiative. February 9. Editorial Section.

Maloof, Patricia, and Fariyal Ross-Sheriff. 2003. *Muslim refugees in the United States. A guide for service providers*. Center for Applied Linguistics, www.culturalorientation.net; and www.cal.org (last accessed November 2007).

Moghadam, Valentine. 2005. *Globalizing women: Transnational feminist networks*. Baltimore: Johns Hopkins University Press.

Moore, Kathleen M. 2007. Muslims in the United States: Pluralism under exceptional circumstances. *The ANNALS of the American Academy of Political and Social Science* 612:116-32.

Moser, Bob. 2008. Who would Jesus vote for? *The Nation*, March 8, 11-16.

Newland, Kathleen, Hiroyuki Tanaka, and Laura Barker. 2007. Bridging divides: The role of community based organizations in immigrant integration. Migration Policy Institute and International Rescue Committee. www.migrationinformation.org/datahub/refugee.cfm (last accessed November 2007).

Nichols, Bruce J. 1988. *The uneasy alliance: Religion, refugee work, and U.S. foreign policy*. New York: Oxford University Press.

Office of Refugee Resettlement, Administration for Children and Families, U.S. Department of Health and Human Services. n.d.(a). Funding Opportunities. www.acf.hhs.gov/programs/orr/funding/funding_opportunities.htm (last accessed August 28, 2009).

———. n.d.(b). Refugee arrival data. www.acf.hhs.gov/programs/orr/data/refugee_arrival_data.htm (last accessed August 28, 2009).

Pew Research Center. 2003. Growing number says Islam encourages violence among followers. *Religion and politics: Contention and consensus,* Washington, DC. people-press.org/reports/display.php3?PageID=722 (last accessed August 31, 2009).

Pipher, Mary. 2002. *In the middle of everywhere. The world's refugees come to our town.* New York: Harcourt, Inc.

Portes, Alejandro, and Rubén Rumbaut. 2001. *Legacies: The story of the immigrant second generation.* Berkeley: University of California Press.

Pratt, Mary Louise. 1999. Arts of the contact zone. In *Ways of reading,* 5th edition, ed. David Bartholomae and Anthony Petroksky, 582-96. New York: Bedford/St. Martin's.

Refugee Resettlement Watch. n.d. Refugee Resettlement Fact Sheets. refugeeresettlementwatch.wordpress.com/refugee-resettlement-fact-sheets/ (last accessed August 31, 2009).

Rimel, Rebecca W. 2001. Charity and strategy: Philanthropy's evolving role. *Proceedings of the American Philosophical Society* 145(4):587-95.

Slim, Hugo. 2002. Not philanthropy but rights: The proper politicization of humanitarian philosophy, *The International Journal of Human Rights* 6(2):1-22.

Stepick, Alex. 2006. God is apparently not dead: The obvious, the emergent and the still unknown in immigration and religion. In *Immigrant faiths: Transforming religious life in America,* ed. Karen L. Leonard, Alex Stepick, Manuel A.Vásquez, and Jennifer Holdaway, 11-38. Walnut Creek, CA: Altamira Press.

Stepick, Alex, Terry Ray, and Sarah Mahler. 2009. Religion, immigration, and civic engagement. In *Churches and charity in the immigrant city: Religion, immigration and civic engagement in Miami,* ed. Alex Stepick, Terry Ray, and Sarah Mahler, 1-18. Fredericksburg, PA: Rutgers University Press.

Streng, Frederick, Charles Lloyd, Jr., and Jay T. Allen. 1973. *Ways of being religious: Readings for a new approach to religion.* New Jersey: Prentice-Hall.

"Time Grease." 2007. Comment on "Bosnian Muslims Find A Spiritual Home In Hartford" from Courant.com, Topix Forums and Posts, comment posted October 29, www.topix.com/forum/health/fasting/T3405JIQNKGKEOK3V (last accessed March 2008).

Warner, R. Stephen. 2007. The role of religion in the process of segmented assimilation. *The ANNALS of the American Academy of Political and Social Science* 612:102-15.

Williams, Rhys H. 2007. Logics, and civil society. The languages of the public sphere: Religious pluralism, institutional logics and civil society. *The ANNALS of the American Academy of Political and Social Science* 612:42-60.

Woldemikael, Tekle. 1987. Assertion versus accommodation: A comparative approach to intergroup relations. *American Behavioral Scientist* 30(4):311-428.

Zhou, Min, and Carl L. Bankston III. 1998. *Growing up American: How Vietnamese youth adapt to life in the United States.* New York: Russell Sage Foundation.

Chapter 9
Translating Religious Traditions into Service: Lessons from the Faith and Organizations Project
Jo Anne Schneider, Laura Polk, and Isaac Morrison

Contrary to assertions that religious involvement in social service is a new development of the neoliberal state, faith communities have always been an integral component of the social welfare system in the United States (Cnaan, Wineburg, and Boddie 1999; Hall 1990; Trattner 1994). The various social welfare, health, and educational institutions translate each religion's theology into practice through system design and day to day agency practice. Over time, these organizations reflect changes in theology, such as the shift from charity to justice after Vatican II for Catholic institutions. Often, change involves ongoing adaptation between various theological traditions, government regulation, and other issues influencing service provision strategies. At other times, agencies can become battlegrounds for arguments about appropriate theology and the use of faith community resources (Schneider, Day, and Anderson 2006).

While most social and political scientists presume that religious symbols and practice indicate religiosity in these organizations (Sider and Unruh 2004), ethnographic analysis shows that each religion's culture and theology is embedded in organizations' systems and practices. This chapter describes how different religious traditions translate their theology into practice by comparing mainline Protestant, Evangelical, and Jewish organizations studied as part of the Faith and Organizations project (Schneider, Day, and Anderson 2006; Schneider et al. 2009). The Faith and Organizations Project is a comparative, multidisciplinary research/practice project designed to assist faith communities and the nonprofits they create in understanding their relationship to their founding faith, the role of religious tradition in agency activities, and faith-based organizations' relationship to the people they serve and wider social welfare, health, and educational systems in the United States (see www.faithandorganizations.umd.edu). In this chapter, we describe how religious tradition, theology, and culture foster

165

social service systems that reflect the religious culture and practical theology of the founding faith. *Religious culture* refers to the current subculture of the religious community that fostered particular nonprofit organizations. *Practical theology* means the formal and informal mechanisms a faith community uses to enact its theological teachings through its religious culture and structures. We conclude with suggestions on strategies for anthropological contributions to understanding faith-based service within its sociopolitical context. The second study, in particular, focused on strategies for *stewardship*, defined as the faith community's efforts to maintain its practical theology of justice and charity in the activities of the nonprofits affiliated with that religion or denomination through a combination of strategies to guide the organization and resources (funding, in-kind donations, space, volunteers) acquired through faith community social capital.

Methods

Data come from two studies by the Faith and Organizations Project. The pilot study, conducted between 2004 and 2006, included eleven organizations in Philadelphia and the Washington D.C. metropolitan area, founded by Mainline Protestants, Catholics, Jews, Evangelicals, Peace churches (Quaker and Mennonite), and African American churches. The subsequent "Maintaining Connections" study (2008-2009) focused on the support and guidance that faith communities provided to organizations, comparing Mainline Protestants, Catholics, Jews, Evangelicals, Quakers, and African American churches. This second study included in-depth work with eighty-one organizations from Philadelphia to Northern Virginia, plus less intensive research in additional organizations in the south and Midwest (see Schneider et al. 2009).

In both studies, research included participant observation in organizations and faith communities, interviews with key staff and faith community leaders, and analysis of agency documents. The pilot study looked at both governance issues and day to day activities, with researchers observing daily agency operations as well as board meetings and faith community events. The Maintaining Connections study focused on governance and stewardship of organizations, with observations focusing on board meetings, volunteer events, and other activities that indicated the connections between the faith community and related nonprofits. Interviews provided some limited data on staff and program participants, but this was not the main focus of the study. Analysis in both cases involved discerning patterns among organizations, identifying both similarities across organizations from different religious traditions and aspects unique to each faith's approach to service.

In contrast to traditional ethnography, comparative multi-methods ethnographic projects like these focus simultaneously on many organizations (see

Schneider 2006b for a discussion of methods used in this project). In each case, a researcher or team of researchers concentrates on a small number of organizations, producing an ethnographic case study similar to a traditional ethnography of an organization or socially defined community. The research used in this chapter involved between three months and two years of data collection in individual agencies and faith communities. Through ongoing conversations among members of the project team and formal analysis of all project data, our analysis develops a comparative portrait for each religion and across the various religions in the study for a particular community or region. Combining results from the pilot and Maintaining Connections studies allows both time depth (diachronic) analysis of several organizations/faith communities that have participated in both studies and further (synchronic) cross-organization comparisons of findings.

Faith Communities and Organizations

This chapter draws from organizations located in Philadelphia, Baltimore, Washington D.C., Annapolis, and the surrounding metropolitan areas of each city. Both the pilot study and the Maintaining Connections study found much in common across communities in the Northeast, but significant differences among general religious traditions. That said, the Baltimore Jewish community profiled here is particularly cohesive and does differ from other U.S. Federations to some degree in the strength of the partnerships among organizations and with their supporting community. While drawing from findings from the wider body of data available from the project, this chapter will focus particularly on specific organizations from Evangelical, Mainline Protestant, and Jewish religious traditions:

We focus on two Evangelical Christian organizations: the Pregnancy Help Center and the Urban Center. The Pregnancy Help Center is a multi-site crisis pregnancy center located outside of Washington, D.C. and Annapolis, and the Urban Center is a community based initiative intended to improve conditions in a particular Washington neighborhood.[1] The purpose of the Pregnancy Help Center is to administer aid to women in "crisis" pregnancies, providing alternative solutions to women they perceive as "at risk" for seeking an abortion. The Urban Center began as a ministry in a distressed neighborhood focused on activities developed in a large residential unit bought by the organization's founders. It consists of three separate entities: a clearinghouse of services that meet the practical needs of the community on a case by case basis, a partnership that reaches out to the youth in the community, and the actual house in which interns and volunteer groups are housed. Although each of these entities has a unique role, there is often overlap in the programs that are offered and the staff and volunteers who are involved.

These two organizations represent a new kind of Evangelical ministry, independent of any particular congregation, founded by college educated Evangelicals in order simultaneously to fulfill a theological mission and to meet a perceived need in the wider community. Both are sophisticated operations with professional outreach staff and ties to all socioeconomic class sectors of their communities. Our general observations about Evangelical practical theology and stewardship strategies will include both these two focus cases and other Evangelical Christian organizations, some of which were grounded in particular congregations, as is more typical of traditional Evangelical initiatives.

Observations regarding Jewish organizations profiled in this chapter come from the wider set of organizations in the study as well, but we will focus on the joint activities of a constellation of organizations in Baltimore as specific examples for this chapter. Baltimore's Jewish community remains very cohesive both geographically and institutionally, despite acknowledged splits among descendants of German and "Russian" Jews, ultra-Orthodox and others. Due to the presence of an ultra-Orthodox seminary, Baltimore has one of the largest percentages of Orthodox Jews (20 percent) of any U.S. city. Baltimore's Federation, a planning and fundraising institution, is one of the strongest in the country, and maintains cohesive partnerships with its member organizations. We have selected examples from Chai, a community development and senior housing organization; the Jewish Community Center (JCC), which provides social services and early childhood education as well as recreational and general educational facilities; and Sinai Hospital. While the hospital is largely independent of the Federation, it is still a member agency and works with other Baltimore Jewish organizations to provide services. For example, these three organizations, along with several Jewish social service and senior services agencies that were not part of this study, have collaborated on holistic supports for the elderly and culturally appropriate services for Baltimore's Orthodox population.

Our Mainline Protestant examples consist of three organizations that provide housing supports, emergency services, and other forms of community enrichment through nonprofits founded by coalitions of Mainline Protestant congregations, sometimes working with Catholic parishes and Quaker Meetings. One of these organizations now also includes Jews and Muslims among its supporters.[2] These organizations are similar to many local Mainline Protestant initiatives, and the strategies we outline here were echoed by other Mainline Protestant affiliated organizations in the study. The Baltimore area Habitat for Humanity chapter was founded independently of a particular denomination, but draws on a specific set of congregations (Lutheran, Disciples of Christ, and other Mainline Protestants). While its general mode of operation is shaped by the international organization, it draws resources, guidance, and volunteers locally. In 2007, Baltimore Habitat developed a program for Muslim and Jewish congregations to contribute to their work independently of the Christian groups that form the bulk of its supporters.

The other two organizations focus on specific communities. GEDCO, "Govens Ecumenical Development Corporation," provides housing and job assistance, operates two food pantries, and provides long-term housing services specifically geared toward the homeless, low-income seniors, and people with mental disabilities in a changing Baltimore neighborhood. Initially the project of a few Protestant congregations and one Catholic church, its stakeholders now include a wide array of area congregations and a few secular organizations as well. Frankford Group Ministries (FGM) served a similar neighborhood in Philadelphia, having been started through a collaboration of four United Methodist congregations in the 1970s. Always located in church properties, with its executive director a minister appointed by the denomination, it offered a variety of programs for youth and emergency services. Unfortunately, with its founding congregations closed or dwindling, and the economic downturn of 2008-2009 cutting supports from government and other sources, FGM closed in late 2009.

Drawing from these case examples and data from the larger studies, we turn now to compare the three religions' unique approaches to providing services in their communities and supporting their nonprofits. We focus first on the impact of U.S. society on these faith-based initiatives before exploring the practical theology behind each religious tradition's work and its governance and stewardship strategies. We also briefly examine the ways that practical theology influences agency structures and activities. Finally, our conclusions suggest ways that anthropologists make a distinctive contribution to a multidisciplinary understanding of the role of faith-based organizations.

Understanding the Confluence of Society-Wide Structures and Religious Traditions in FBOs

Analysis of organizations founded by religious groups necessarily must observe similarities across organizations based on their role as key service providers in the U.S. social welfare system as well as differences based on religious traditions. With the exception of some Evangelical organizations and small congregation-based programs, most nonprofits in our study received some funding from government sources. As a result, their program structures adhered to government regulations relevant to particular types of services, and all programs had some elements in common. For example, all practiced federal government equal opportunity policy regarding equity in who received service, except for religious schools designed specifically to provide faith-based education to people of a particular religion. Most also followed EEOC guidelines that prevented employment discrimination based on race, gender, and religious belief, although the majority expected staff to share the general cultural values of the organization. Best practices shared among organizations also led to a certain degree of similarity among organizations providing the same services, or institutional isomorphism (DiMaggio and Powell 1988). However, contrary to Smith's assertion that government funding forces faith-based or community based organizations toward isomorphism (Smith and Lipsky 1993; Smith and Sosin 2001), our research discovered that faith-based nonprofits simultaneously borrowed strategies from each other and maintained unique characteristics (Schneider, Day, and Anderson 2006).

Despite numerous similarities, we found significant differences among organizations, differences that could be traced back to their founding religion. Community development and emergency services organizations for Mainline Protestants drew their boards, volunteers, and other support through individual congregations. For example, Baltimore Habitat for Humanity depended upon key churches that each developed one house per year. Boards at most of the Mainline Protestant organizations consisted of representatives from founding congregations. Even a recently independent pastoral counseling center still drew its board from among pastors of local congregations. In contrast, Chai, the Jewish community development organization in the study, was supported by the community's central Federation, drawing board members from within the close-knit Jewish community and volunteers from the Federation's volunteer bank. Evangelical organizations relied on networks of people sharing similar beliefs for all types of support, and expressed a strong reliance on divine guidance for resources. Similarly, the expressed motivation for volunteering differed across organizations, with Mainline Protestants volunteering either because of concern over a need or as a practice of individual faith, Jews volunteering to fulfill an expectation of bettering the community through service, and Evangelicals to spread the gospel or to fulfill a gospel-inspired interest such as preserving life through mission activities.

These differences arise out of the practical theology of each religion and its history of nonprofit activity in the United States. We found theology and religious culture embedded in the individual program style of each organization, influencing missions, support strategies, organizational structure, and programming choices. Often, these founding religious values were invisible to most people seeking services from the organization unless they specifically looked for them. However, the overall style of each organization often reflected its founding ethos. Front line service providers at Mainline Protestant and Evangelical organizations were more likely to be volunteers, while Jewish organizations used professional staff. In both cases, staffing choices reflect practical theology, with Mainline Protestants seeing volunteering as opportunities for congregants to minister to those in need while Jews believe that providing the highest quality services through highly trained professionals reflects Talmudic injunctions.

Some differences are best seen through examples. Catholic and Jewish hospitals in the project had few religious symbols or other indicators of their religious tradition visible to the average patient. Below the level of executive directors and other key management staff, few staff came from the founding religion.

Except for abortion,[3] both provided a similar range of services and had good reputations in the local community. However, in the Catholic hospital, front line professional staff (nurses, lab technicians, aftercare counselors) had limited authority and information, turning to their supervisors to handle situations requiring any deviation from standard practices. One Jewish professional, now a leader in a Jewish healthcare institution, recalled being told that she would not fit into a more hierarchically based Catholic institution. In contrast, even the lab techs at the Jewish organization were able to explain agency policy and make suggestions to address a patient's unique needs. These differences arose from the Jewish emphasis on shared decision making and professionals at all levels having authority for their work, in contrast to the ingrained Catholic sense of hierarchy which limited the amount of information given to front line workers, emphasized established procedure, and granted only to supervisors the authority to permit deviation from the norm.

Differences in Practical Theology

Mainline Protestant organizations emerged from a theology of individual faith, with congregations as the central organizing structures for both worship and nonprofit activities. As Hall (2005) describes, Mainline Protestants have made a conscientious effort to spread their founding values throughout U.S. society, and much of the Mainline Protestant religious ethos is similar to that found in secular organizations. At some point, the majority of nonprofits in the study were started by key individuals affiliated with a particular congregation or by an interfaith initiative. While some of the emergency services initiatives like soup kitchens and homeless shelters were operated by a single congregation, most Mainline Protestants tended to incorporate their nonprofits separately, with governing board members appointed from among the participating congregations. Our study included a number of these interdenominational collaborations. Pastors of the participating congregations sometimes served on these boards, but appointments were just as likely to come from among church lay leaders, chosen by congregational committees to represent the congregation. Individual religious calls to help the needy through participating congregations were used to garner donations and volunteers for the organizations, and most relied heavily on volunteers in various capacities.

Based on concepts of practicing faith through works, Mainline Protestants also underplay outward signs of religion in service provision in an effort to welcome people from all backgrounds to their organizations. The same is true of their partnering with neighboring congregations, as Mainline Protestant organizations often included Catholic parishes, and sometimes Jewish congregations, in their support networks. GEDCO, for example, was founded by a coalition of six Mainline Protestant churches and one Catholic church. Together, the congregations started a food pantry and other neighborhood-based emergency services initiatives, drawing in-kind goods and volunteers to run the initiative from the founding congregations. Over time, the congregations collaborated to provide housing services for local seniors and other low- to moderate-income people, with congregational representatives serving as the board for the organization. Funding for the housing initiatives came from a mix of federal, state, and local government sources, with significant supplemental money coming from the member congregations. While the religious background is an important part of the organization for its board and volunteers, it is not visible in service provision. The organization's name reflects its ecumenical nature and its neighborhood focus. Likewise, FGM was founded by a visionary pastor in Philadelphia who brought together a coalition of four United Methodist churches. As with many faith based organizations, it provided non-sectarian programs to its neighborhood but was housed in church property and drew on its founding congregations for board members, volunteers, and other resources.

Like Mainline Protestant organizations, Evangelical organizations in this study grow from the personal vision of their founder(s) to provide a particular ministry, but these organizations generally lack the formal congregational support systems seen in Mainline Protestant organizations. Instead, organizations rely on networks of people who share similar beliefs and want to support a given ministry. All of these organizations represented in our study had a core leader who carried the organization's vision forward and served as the center of the network that supported it. This leader may be the pastor of a core congregation or an individual lay leader with a calling to perform a particular service. The Evangelical organizations profiled here are reflective of the diverse ways that such organizations form: one was founded by two individuals who were active in their own faith communities and held many social ties within the city; the other was started by a single evangelical church but is now supported by multiple churches in the area that share a common belief in the organizational goal. Both organizations claim to have no prior denominational criteria for those who wish to join them to move the work of the ministry forward; however, closer examination finds that many of those who are active as staff, volunteers, or supporters with them hold beliefs that are generally congruent with those of the organizations.

Evangelical organizations frequently make reference to concepts such as divine "appointment" and "intervention," reflecting a belief that much of their work occurs through the hand of a higher power. The success of these organizations is rarely measured in quantifiable terms. Traditional metrics of self-evaluation such as charts and graphs are often rejected; rather, emphasis is placed on the relationships that are formed and the effect that the work has on the lives of the clients served. Individual interactions between volunteer and paid staff and people in need are the primary form that service provision takes, with programs openly sharing Evangelical approaches to scripture in a belief that sharing the gospel is an important part of healing both individuals and communities. Both the Pregnancy Help Center and the Urban Center seek to live out their Christian witness through actions; whether it is through advocating for the poor, leading a Bible study, mentoring young women in crisis pregnancies, or other ways to meet the needs of the community.

For Evangelicals, theology inflects the work that they do, but it is not often emphasized, or even called "theology." Personal and individual stories of hope and of lives being transformed are often used as tools to raise funds and to recruit congregations and churchgoers to a particular cause. Scripture is most often cited as the basis for an evangelical organization's beliefs, but it is sometimes unclear how specific Bible verses relate to the work of the organization because the theological concepts run background to its work.

For example, the Urban Center was founded as a place where people from the community could go to experience hospitality. The vision for the house was to be a "presence for Jesus in the community," as well as be "in fellowship with the people in the community." Founders sought to establish a relationship with residents in the surrounding neighborhoods and, through those relationships, to begin to meet the needs that arose. The Center's programs evolved as individuals came to the house with ideas and as volunteers from various Evangelical networks brought resources and ideas. The Urban Center engages in fundraising primarily through telling a series of what they term "miracle stories." These are composed of accounts of ways the center has obtained items for the house, donations of labor, staff and volunteers; as well as individual stories of lives that have been affected through the programs that the center offers.

Jewish communities and their organizations present a notable contrast to mainline Protestant and Evangelical strategies of maintaining relationships with their nonprofits, in large part because education and social supports are seen as the responsibility of the entire community, with a heavy emphasis on community wide planning and collaboration across agencies through Federations, umbrella organizations responsible for community-wide fundraising, planning, and other supports for community organizations. The Jewish support system also differs from that of other religions because the Federation system of support for Jewish nonprofits was not formed by synagogues or temples, and is in fact considered a neutral entity where Jews from various branches of Judaism and secular Jews can work together. While most Federations today have some form of outreach to synagogues/temples, the worship communities remain separate from the Federations.

The Jewish theology of charity, justice, and support for those in need comes from a combination of the Torah and the Talmud (the Hebrew scriptures and commentary on them), and is regularly reinterpreted in Jewish communities and their institutions. It starts with a moral sense of responsibility for the community and each other, taught through a combination of family practices and religious education. Carp (2002, 182) comments that "the responsibility for those in need is a Jewish requirement that is rooted at the very foundation of our communal processes. . . . Jewish people have always understood that caring for the poor and sick was too important to be a matter of individual conscience alone." This sense of community responsibility also influences the nature of service, with Jewish organizations relying heavily on trained professionals in order to provide the highest quality of care. Jewish community service programs provide graduate training to Jewish professionals, and people from other religions with similar values also work at these organizations. While some organizations involve volunteers, direct service is more likely to be provided by professionals.

Three key concepts embody Jewish philosophy on social welfare: *tikkun olam* (to heal the world), *chesed* (loving-kindness), and *tzedakah.* While the Hebrew tzedakah roughly translates as charity, the concept more accurately combines charity, justice, and righteous duty. English translations cannot encompass the full theological or cultural meanings of these words. Tzedakah, chesed and tikkun olam are all *mitzvot,* which literally means commandments, but often is translated as "good deeds." Jewish law obliges community members to provide for others, whether through regular financial donations, volunteering, or professional work. One organizational staff member stated, "I feel that in a way I'm doing God's work through this organization and there is some scripture that says, 'Working for the Jewish community or working for the good of humanity is equivalent to being in prayer.'"

Justice and charity are also merged in Jewish thinking. Supporting and improving the community is meant to heal the world: tikkun olam. Thus, Jewish organizations participated in policy change initiatives early in U.S. history and continue a tradition of best practices and involvement in policymaking. "Justice" and "charity" are often used interchangeably to describe activities. For example, a rabbi associated with a Jewish day school commented to us: "We have a full department of what we call a *gemilut hasadim* (social justice) work. We send about 700 volunteers a year out into the field and soup kitchens, Habitat builds, any variety of local efforts that we partner with." However, school recruitment literature translates similar activities (gemilut hasadim) as "acts of loving kindness."[4] These two translations are two sides of the same concept: through acts of loving kindness, one improves the world, thus promoting social justice.

These values and strategies were integral to the organizations studied here. Most were members of their local Federation or received some support from it. As such, they received a small portion of their budgets from the combined United Jewish Appeal campaign, similar to a United Way campaign but only for Jewish organizations (Bernstein 1983). Most worked together collaboratively with other Jewish organizations in joint initiatives encouraged by the Federations. For example, Chai is involved in a joint program with the local Jewish social service agency, JCC, and the hospital to provide supports for seniors. Similarly, the Washington, D.C. senior services organization has worked with several synagogues and other Jewish senior services organizations to provide social programs for senior adults in various parts of the DC metropolitan area.

The contrasts between Mainline Protestant, Evangelical, and Jewish practical theology indicate that each has different core beliefs that influence the way they develop nonprofits to address issues of common concern such as poverty, health, community development, housing, and senior services. These differences also appeared in their initiatives to solve a full range of social issues, improve society, and advocate for social change. It is relevant to point out here that Evangelical organizations included both organizations on the political right and organizations stemming from Evangelicals with leftist politics like Jim Wallis's initiatives or organizations following Ron Sider's approaches (Sider 1999; Sider, Olson, and Unruh 2002). While the two organizations profiled here were more politically center-right, the Urban Center in particular reflected a strong goal of fostering equality and uplift that would appeal to left-of-center Evangelicals. We next briefly describe ways that practical theology plays out in the support structures for organizations and organizational systems.

Practical Theology in Governance and Resource Acquisition

All incorporated nonprofits in the United States outline their mission and governance structures in their bylaws. Bylaws may be written by the founder and those s/he gathers to form the first board, or they may be written by representatives of founding institutions through a process unique to those communities. Governance structures described in organizational bylaws reflect potential sources for support and guidance for the organization over time. For faith-based organizations, founding practical theology influences what stakeholders are named in these bylaws and how the organization's guidance systems are structured. As an organization grows and matures, its major constituencies may change, and the organization may change its bylaws to reflect this by altering its mission statement or requiring board representation from newer constituencies. But often these changes occur more informally, through new vision statements, name changes, outreach to new stakeholders, and in response to requirements from funders. For example, many organizations receiving government funds are required to include on their boards a representative from the target group or community being served. If those served come from a different religious tradition, this requirement may alter the nature of boards. Organizations that reach beyond their original faith base and/or shift their focus to the community served may change to the point that they are no longer effectively connected to their founding faith and/or no longer reflect the founding ethos. These changes may be positive or negative, but do reflect shifts from the original founding community's networks or ideals (Cnaan, Wineburg, and Boddie 1999; Smith and Sosin 2001; Jeavons 1994; Powell 1988; 1996; Schneider 1999).

These governance and guidance systems also can serve as key sources for the support organizations need to fulfill their goals. Resources take several forms: funding; in-kind resources like office space, furniture, equipment, or goods to be given away to people served; or human resources in the form of volunteers or networks to find appropriate paid staff. Faith communities often play an active role in providing these supports to the organizations they sponsor. For example, almost every organization in this study started out in buildings provided by the faith community—often churches or synagogues—or land donated by faith community members. Many still are housed in space owned by the faith community. For example, GEDCO and FGM are located in churches, while the Baltimore Federation owns the real estate for all its member organizations.

Social capital from the founding faith community is often an even more important resource than direct financial support. In our work, *social capital* refers to networks based on reciprocal, reinforcable trust that provide access to resources (Schneider 2006a; 2009; Portes 1998). People and organizations gain access to a network through cultural cues, described by Bourdieu and others as cultural capital (Schneider 2006a; 2009).[5] Access to religious network resources for organizations is powerfully tied to their ability to maintain the culture of their founding community (Schneider 2009; Schneider, Day, and Anderson 2006). In the case of faith-based organizations this may include board members who know people with money or how to obtain government grants; the ability to solicit donations through member congregations or the Jewish federation campaign; or a volunteer pool available through faith community networks (Schneider 2009; Schneider and Morrison 2010). Faith community networks often serve as a key resource for strong faith-based organizations, while weak ties to the founding community and/or ties only to communities with limited resources often contribute to organizational struggles. For example, Chai and the other Jewish organizations in this study depended on strong networks within the Jewish community to find board members who were able to identify resources and guide the institutions. GEDCO also benefited from similar supports—initially from its founding congregations, and then from the others it drew into its expanding network. FGM, on the other hand, failed after thriving for nearly thirty years because two of its founding congregations closed and the remaining two dwindling congregations had aging members who lacked the connections or knowledge to support the organization.

As indicated in the previous section, the organizations founded by Mainline Protestants, Evangelicals, and Jews developed different governance and resource development systems based on their practical theology. Mainline Protestants anchored their board and resource development strategies in founding congregations. In most cases, organizations were founded by an individual who felt a calling to develop a particular service, but that individual was either a pastor or an influential congregation member able to reach out to other congregations for support. For example, FGM and GEDCO were founded by pastors who sought colleagues in like-minded congregations as their partners. Their bylaws call for board members to be appointed by these founding congregations. While the Baltimore Habitat chapter was not founded by a specific congregation, its long-term support network has come from congregations that were known to its founders. Most of the houses built by Baltimore Habitat are constructed by members and funds from those churches, with each church building one house per year.

These governance structures, often through the board members, also provide a key mechanism for maintaining ties to the founding faith. For example, when a few members of GEDCO's leadership attempted to change the organization's mission statement to de-emphasize the faith-based nature of the organization, board members from the original churches objected, halting the proposal (Schneider and Morrison 2010). In addition, as we have seen, for many Mainline Protestant organizations volunteers are a key source of staff. These established volunteers also play a significant role in maintaining the faith culture of the organization. As happened with FGM, when volunteers age or die and the supporting congregations fail to generate new volunteers for either board or staff, organizations may close. In the United Methodist Mainline Protestant culture, the denomination sees congregations as the key source for nonprofits, and thus did not step in to save the organization (Schneider and Morrison 2010).

Analyzing Mainline Protestant strategies suggests that organizations rely on a combination of bonding social capital among members within supporting congregations and bridging social capital among like-minded Mainline Protestant congregations or within an interfaith coalition to maintain the nonprofit organizations. Bonding social capital refers to networks among homogeneous groups that share similar cultural traits, while bridging social capital crosses group boundaries but fosters a common cultural or value centered ethos among people from diverse backgrounds (Putnam and Feldstein 2003; Schneider 2009). Cultural capital is particularly important in maintaining all faith-based organizations, and this study found several elements that Mainline Protestants expected to see. Organizations were expected not only to reach out to member congregations for support, but also to provide opportunities for the faithful to practice justice and charity work through volunteering. The creation of such opportunities for volunteers to support those in need themselves through donating to food pantries, serving soup, or building houses, simultaneously allowed Mainline Protestant organizations to obtain personnel to carry out their missions and fulfilled the cultural mandate that nonprofits provide an outlet for individuals to provide faith-inspired service. This reciprocal relationship further strengthened the ties between nonprofits and their supporting congregations or other stakeholders.

Organizations like GEDCO thrive when they are able to meet the cultural expectations of their supporters through improving the lives of people in their neighborhood in a manner consonant with the beliefs and practices of members of the founding churches. Success bred success as other congregations beyond the founding churches learned of the organization's work and began to contribute to GEDCO themselves. The organizational leadership's strategy of both fostering bonding social capital among its initial congregational base and actively bridging by bringing other congregations or like-minded nonprofits into its operations through expanding board appointments or collaborations is an example of Mainline Protestant stewardship strategy at its best.

The Habitat for Humanity chapter tried to use a similar strategy with less success. In this case, key members from the contributing congregations each relied exclusively on their personal networks to support the organization. As a result, financial and human resources came from limited networks. The organization's leadership did little to make connections across these groups, and effectively reinforced this strategy by having each church build its own house. Instead of expanding bridging social capital through network strategies, organizational leadership used standard marketing techniques such as web appeals and fundraising letters to raise money, and continued to create additional bonding systems by reaching out to specific churches and synagogues. At the end of our research project, the organization was continuing to struggle, although its work went on. As discussed above, Frankford Group Ministry lost social capital as key leadership retired and the membership of churches that formed its base aged, died, or moved away. Older volunteers were less able to support the organization's full range of programs, and fewer new volunteers came from the surrounding neighborhood. Without additional bridging social capital, FGM's initial resources dwindled to the point that it could no longer survive.

Governance and resource acquisition for Evangelical organizations had some similarities to Mainline Protestant strategies. Both drew resources and volunteers from among individual believers and congregations with similar religious outlooks. Both relied heavily on volunteers to carry out the mission of the organizations. However, Evangelical organizations differed in that support systems drew exclusively on the networks of their founders, with supporters even more closely sharing the values represented in the organization than for Mainline Protestants. For example, volunteers serving through Habitat for Humanity could subscribe to a Mainline Protestant theology of providing for the stranger (Good Samaritan) without any expectation that they were witnessing for Jesus, or they could bring to their work the belief that they were being a witness who would actively contribute to the salvation of the family in need, beliefs reflecting Evangelical practical theology. The organization's leadership would be comfortable with either motivation for service. However, volunteers and supporters of the two Evangelical organizations all shared similar approaches to the Bible and to their ministries, with the Pregnancy Help Center drawing from Evangelicals active in the right-to-life movement and the Urban Center from people interested in sharing its ministry of witness.

While Evangelical organizations drew on both congregations and individuals, they relied exclusively on informal network ties rather than institutionalized congregational relationships. Thus, Evangelical organizations depended largely on bonding social capital. Both of the example organizations had small boards drawn from the close networks of the founders. The Urban Center, shunning traditional hierarchical structures, relies on a core group of individuals who serve as accountability partners for the organization. Members of this group are usually community and church leaders, who advise the Urban Center founders. The Pregnancy Clinic relies on a traditional board that is made up of church leaders, local businesspeople, and community members. The board is generally in charge of decision-making regarding the overall goals and strategies of the clinic for reaching out to the community. Although there is no denominational requirement for members, they all hold the same theological and social views. Clinic staff consists of a few paid staff, and several volunteers who carry out both administrative and medical services.

While resource strategies for these sophisticated Evangelical organizations looked similar to those of other nonprofits, organizational leaders reported that they were grounded in their faith. Some strategies rely on Evangelical belief systems; for example, the Pregnancy Help Center distributes baby bottles with slots for coins throughout their networks as a fundraising strategy, drawing on Evangelical beliefs that every fetus is a baby from the moment of conception. Key resources are attributed to divine intervention; for example, the pregnancy help center director reported that an Evangelical architect and builder contacted the organization to ask how he could help just when they had acquired a new building in need of renovation. Founders of the Urban Center similarly describe the ways in which they acquired furnishings for their building—through the kindness of staff, volunteers, and friends of the Center. In fact, much of their fundraising strategy consists of sharing "miracle" stories of lives that have been transformed by the work of the Center, and/or of items and services that have become available just when needed. One specific example: due to limited funds, the Center once had difficulty paying its electric bill. The founders came in contact with an artist who was looking for loft space to rent. They reached a kind of barter agreement: the artist paid the electric bill in exchange for space. Center leaders point to occurrences such as this as signs that their work must continue.

Jewish strategies differ from these two Christian styles in their reliance on communal structures and differing practical theology to carry out their work. As mentioned earlier, social supports within the Jewish community are organized through community wide structures, which in the United States are institutionalized through the Federations, independent nonprofits that bridge among the various groups in a local Jewish community (Bernstein 1983). Federations rely on the religious cultural belief in a responsibility to support community members and others: tikkun olam, gemilut hasadim through monetary or in-kind donations (tzedakah), and providing leadership for community organizations. As such, the Federation is an important fundraising and leadership development center for organizations in its community. Both Chai and JCC receive annual allocations from the Federation from United Jewish Appeal funds, limiting their need to run individual fundraising campaigns. JCC hosts a fundraising event, the Jewish Hall of Fame, with the blessing and support of the Federation. Sinai, as a community hospital which is part of a larger hospital system, does hold independent fundraising campaigns, but receives annual legacy contributions from family foundations held in trust at the Federation. The Federation owns the land for all three organizations and is responsible for building and maintenance for Chai and JCC. The Federation's Leadership Development program and religious education activities for board members ensure that these Jewish organizations' boards follow the ethos of the religion, distributing talent through Federation member organizations.

Volunteer and board recruitment style reflects the strong bonding social capital among Jews in this community. Organizations draw from a known pool of individuals affiliated with either the Federation, synagogues and temples, or Jewish business communities to find appropriate board members. While none of the boards required that its members be Jewish, all were either exclusively or almost entirely Jewish because of the strong bonds within the community. The project found significant movement of individuals among boards of the various Jewish organizations and Federation committees, often by design, as the Federation encouraged individuals to contribute to organizations where they felt their talents would be most useful.

Volunteer networks showed a combination of reliance on bonding social capital through Federation and other sources, and limited bridging social capital based on other collaborations. Each of these organizations drew some volunteers through the Federation's centralized volunteer bank as well as relying on their own networks, which drew a combination of program participants and other volunteers through synagogues and the wider Jewish community. Chai also drew a limited pool of volunteers from Christian congregations or secular businesses, but these volunteers were secondary to the Jewish networks. For example, our fieldworker who volunteered at a Chai weatherization event found himself placed with a small group of "unaffiliated" volunteers because most others were in large groups from synagogues, the Federation, or Jewish day schools. This unaffiliated group included some non-Jews drawn to the event through Jewish friends.

Taken together, comparisons show faith traditions shaping the way that organizations from different faiths accomplish the same goals of governance and resource acquisition. Each strategy has varying strengths and weaknesses. While religious practical theology is less obvious in organizational program strategies, it also influences agency structure and approach to service provision. We briefly examine this issue next.

Practical Theology in Agency Structures and Activities

Practical theology was far less obvious in direct services than in governance structures. The small to mid-sized Mainline Protestant organizations in the study resembled similar secular organizations, with a few exceptions. First, those that maintained active ties with their faith traditions tended to have clergy or active members of one of the supporting denominations in the role of executive director. Second, organizations relied heavily on volunteers, drawing them primarily from congregations. This strategy is congruent with a practical theology which sees nonprofits as incorporated ministry arms of congregations that provide opportunities for church members to practice their faith through service. However, this strategy was little different from secular organizations, which also tended to network with faith communities as a key source for volunteers (Schneider 2006a). Our study suggests that Mainline Protestant organizations, regardless of their size, tend to design programs explicitly so that they involve opportunities for denominational or interfaith volunteers. For instance, the large Lutheran multi-service organization in our pilot study and the national Lutheran organization that serves refugees, analyzed in the Connections Study, both designed their refugee services and senior services programs to engage individual congregations to resettle refugees, support at-risk seniors and provide other direct services (Schneider, Day, and Anderson 2006; Schneider et al. 2009). However, reliance on staff or volunteers from the faith community did not generally translate into proselytizing or programs that actively used faith elements. More often, staff or volunteers had worship activities or prayed for clients among themselves, but did not openly include faith elements in their direct relationship with program participants. (See also Bauer and Chivakos in this volume.)

Evangelical organizations most clearly fit the model of faith-based organizations portrayed in the media as institutions that incorporate faith actively into all aspects of the organization. For example, The Pregnancy Clinic's stated mission is: "To impact our community for Christ by addressing the needs of women unprepared for pregnancy, encouraging life-affirming decisions, healing lives traumatized by abortion, and challenging them to embrace a biblical view of sexuality." The clinic operates with the assumption that abortion is emotionally and physically damaging, and that clients can come to them for "healing." When expectant mothers arrive for a consultation, staff and volunteers usually have a checklist of items to ask along with the regular clinical intake, including questions about the client's religious background and a presentation of the Christian message. According to staff and volunteers, they seek to serve people regardless of their beliefs. The clinic offers all services free of charge, and when clients question their motives for this, they use the opportunity to share their Christian faith. However, they insist that this is not emphasized at the beginning, nor is the religious background of their clients a determining factor in whether or not they receive services.

The clinic has recently expanded to a second location, the site of a former abortion clinic. To the staff, this location takes on a whole new meaning to their work of seeking to dissuade expectant mothers from seeking abortions. Of particular note is the symbolism of a room formerly used for late-term abortions. It was ultimately converted into a "prayer room," serving as type of memorial. This room contains a candle, chairs, and a table covered with a tablecloth. Located in the middle, in place of the procedure table, is a rug covering up an old bloodstain. The walls contain handwritten scripture, as well as a professionally framed old yellow post-it note, left over from the previous clinic, with procedures for closing the room. The staff often shares with pride the stories of numerous clients who have come to the clinic seeking abortion services who have instead become "success stories," i.e., women who subsequently chose to carry their pregnancies to term.

Jewish organizations tend to be highly professionalized, a strategy that at first appears as secularization. However, this emphasis on trained professionals connects to Talmudic lessons describing the provision of high quality service in order to help someone become a contributing member of society. As with most larger Mainline Protestant organizations, leadership staff tend to be Jewish, but most organizations hire non-Jews with appropriate professional credentials in mid-level and front line positions. In this context, professionalism is seen as a religious value.

The second difference in Jewish organizations is the level of collaboration with other Jewish organizations to provide holistic services. Chai, JCC, Sinai Hospital, and the Jewish social service organization have collaborated on several projects together, including an initiative to provide social, health, and recreational supports to frail seniors in their own homes. Chai, through its subsidiaries, provided both elderly housing complexes and home repair to seniors remaining in their own homes. The social service organization provided case management and various social service supports. JCC provided programs for seniors and some other social supports. Sinai provided health screenings and other senior services through part of its larger hospital network.

While collaborations such as these are not unique, the ease with which they developed stems from the centralized planning in the Jewish community. This particular idea came from a board member at one organization who shared it among his social network and key staff and lay leaders at the Federation. Other initiatives come from the Federation itself, through formal planning processes or discussions among lay leaders about future directions. This strategy comes out of the practical theology of centralized community supports for all those in need.

Conclusion: Anthropological Approaches to Understanding Faith-Based Organizations

This brief analysis of nonprofits affiliated with three distinct religious traditions suggests that organizations simultaneously follow the structures and strategies for nonprofits in the United States while still relying on their founding traditions for guidance, organization, program design, and resource acquisition strategies. Since many of the religious aspects of an organization are embedded in its structures and practices, practical theology may not be evident through research strategies that rely exclusively either on quantitative measures or on the superficial case studies performed in many of the management and policy sciences. Anthropology's contribution to understanding faith-based organizations and their supporting context comes from our ability to recognize the interplay between culture, ideology, and practice through both listening to what people affiliated with faith-based organizations say and watching what they do. The discipline's preference for using theory actively in interpretation, as this chapter uses social capital, is another asset that ethnographic analysis can contribute to research on faith-based organizations.

However, our research will not serve as a catalyst to change policy or practice if we simply produce rich case studies using academic language of interest only to scholars within the discipline. Comparative ethnography focused on practical issues can provide these insights. As such, effective anthropological contributions to the discussion of faith-based organizations depend on our ability to cross disciplines and bring our rich, ethnographic examples into the framework of practical or policy concerns.

Notes

1. These two organization names are pseudonyms. Organizations had the choice of using their own names or choosing pseudonyms. In general, most of the Evangelical organizations used pseudonyms but most of the Mainline Protestant and Jewish organizations used their own names. The other organizations profiled here are actual names.

2. While data on Jews, Evangelicals, and one Mainline Protestant case were gathered by the authors, the other Mainline Protestant cases draw on ethnographies by team members Kevin Robinson and Jill Sinha.

3. Catholic health care organizations are forbidden to perform abortions or offer certain kinds of family planning, based on decisions by U.S. bishops and the Pope.

4. Hasadim is a different transliteration of the plural for chesed (loving kindness).

5. For those interested in the definitions of social capital used in our work, please see Schneider 2006a; 2009.

Works Cited

Bernstein, Philip. 1983. *To dwell in unity: The Jewish Federation movement in America since 1960*. Philadelphia: Jewish Publication Society.

Carp, Joel M. 2002. The Jewish social welfare lobby in the United States. In *Jewish Policy and American Civil Society*, ed. Alan Mittelman, 181-234. Lanham, MD: Rowman and Littlefield.

Cnaan, Ram. 1999. *The newer deal: Social work and religion in partnership*. New York: Columbia University Press.

DiMaggio, Paul, and Walter Powell. 1988. The iron cage revisited: Institutional isomorphism and collective rationality in organizational fields. In *Community organization: Studies in resource mobilization and exchange*, ed. Carl Milofsky, 77-99. New York: Oxford University Press.

Hall, Peter Dobkin. 1990. The history of religious philanthropy in America. In *Faith and Philanthropy in America*, ed. Robert Wuthnow, Virginia Hodgkinson, and Associates, 38-62. San Francisco: Jossey-Bass.

———. 2005. The rise of civic engagement tradition. In *Taking faith seriously*, ed. Mary Jo Bane, Brent Coffin, and Richard Higgins, 21-60. Cambridge, MA: Harvard University Press.

Jeavons, Thomas. 1994. *When the bottom line is faithfulness: Management of Christian service organizations*. Bloomington, IN: Indiana University Press.

Portes, Alejandro. 1998. Social capital: Its origins and applications in modern sociology. *Annual Review of Sociology* 24:1–24.

Powell, Walter. 1988. Institutional effects on organizational structure and performance. In *Institutional Patterns and Organizations: Culture and Environment*, ed. Lynne Zucker, 115-38. Cambridge, MA: Ballinger Publishing Company.

———. 1996. Trust based forms of governance. In *Trust in organizations: Frontiers of theory and research*, ed. Roderick M. Kramer and Tom R. Tyler, 51-67. Thousand Oaks, CA: Sage Publications.

Putnam, Robert D., and Lewis M. Feldstein. 2003. *Better together: Restoring the American community*. New York: Simon and Schuster.

Schneider, Jo Anne. 1999. Trusting that of God in everyone: Three examples of Quaker based social service in disadvantaged communities. *Nonprofit and Voluntary Sector Quarterly*, 28(3):269-95.

———. 2006a. *Social capital and welfare reform: Organizations, congregations, and communities*. New York: Columbia University Press.

———. 2006b. Using multi-methods ethnography to promote quality service and understand interactions among organizations: Examples from the Kenosha Social Capital Study and Neighborhood Settlement House Needs Assessment and Evaluation. *Nonprofit Management and Leadership* 16(4):411-28.

———. 2009. Organizational social capital and nonprofits. *Nonprofit and Voluntary Sector Quarterly*, 38(4):643-62.

Schneider, Jo Anne, Katie Day, and Gwynneth Anderson. 2006. Connections between faith communities and their non-profits: Findings from the Faith and Organizations Project Pilot Study on the Role of Religious Culture and Theology on Social and Health Services. Washington, DC: George Washington University.

Schneider, Jo Anne, Isaac Morrison, John Belcher, Patricia Wittberg, Wolfgang Bielfield, and Jill Sinha. 2009. Maintaining vital connections between faith communities and their nonprofits, Education Report: Phase I Project overview. College Park, MD: University of Maryland College Park. Available at www.faithandorganizations. umd.edu.

Schneider, Jo Anne, and Isaac Morrison, ed. 2010. *Comparing strategies to maintain connections between faith communities and organizations across religions.* Washington, D.C. University of Maryland College Park. Available at www.faithand organizations.umd.edu/.

Sider, Ronald J. 1999. *Just generosity: A new vision for overcoming poverty in America.* Grand Rapids, MI: Baker Books.

Sider, Ronald J., and Heidi Rolland Unruh. 2004. Typology of religious characteristics of social service and educational organizations and programs. *Nonprofit and Voluntary Sector Quarterly* 33(1):109-34.

Sider, Ronald J., Philip N. Olson, and Heidi Rolland Unruh. 2002. *Churches that make a difference: Reaching your community with good news and good works.* Grand Rapids, MI: Baker Books.

Smith, Stephen, and Michael Lipsky. 1993. *Nonprofits for hire: The welfare state in the age of contracting.* Cambridge, MA: Harvard University Press.

Smith, Stephen, and Michael Sosin. 2001. The varieties of faith related agencies. *Public Administration Review* 61(6):651-70.

Trattner, Walter. 1994. *From poor law to welfare state.* New York: The Free Press.

Chapter 10
Religious Organizational Identity and Environmental Demands
Scott T. Fitzgerald

Religious organizations play a key role in the provision of social services in the United States. It is estimated that the number of people served by "religion-sponsored social service organizations" exceeds 60 million (McCarthy and Castelli 1997), and an estimated $21.1 billion of non-religious programs are provided by religious organizations (Hodgkinson and Weitzman 1993).

The scale and scope of these activities vary widely. Congregational activity is at one end of the spectrum. There are over 300,000 congregations in the United States; the majority of these congregations provide some form of social service, although typically it is limited to providing short-term relief such as emergency food, clothing, and/or shelter. Most do not receive government funding for such programs (Chaves 2004). At the other end of the spectrum, large, national nonprofit organizations, such as Catholic Charities and Lutheran Social Services, provide extensive long-term services and more closely resemble government social service agencies than religious organizations (Vidal 2001). Adding to the diversity of religious social service provision, a particular organizational form has becoming increasingly common: faith-based community development organizations[1] (McCarthy and Castelli 1997; Scott 2002; Vidal 2001; Wuthnow 2004). While many FBCDOs existed prior to the Charitable Choice Provision of the 1996 federal welfare reform and the 2001 executive orders connected to President Bush's "faith-based initiatives," these public policy developments have raised important questions regarding organizational and program effectiveness, the constitutionality of government sponsorship of religious social service provision, and the effects of government funding on religious identity and autonomy (Bane, Coffin, and Thiemann 2000; Black, Koopman, and Ryden 2004; Davis and Hankins 1999; Dionne and DiIulio 2000; Jeavons 1994; Monsma 1996; Wuthnow 2004).

Collaboration with the state (whether through formal working relationships or funding) both enables and constrains FBCDO activity (Jeavons 1994; Vanderwoerd 2004). Applying insights from organizational theory and the sociology of religion, this chapter advances the study of religion, organizations, and the state by examining organizational responses to environmental demands. Specifically, I focus on a particular organizational form, the FBCDO, and the mechanisms through which organizational religious values are enacted and maintained. Empirically, the enactment of religious identity within this specific organizational form (local, nonprofit corporations that were established by, but are separate from, a specific congregation) and set of relationships (collaborations between these organizations and the state) takes place through several mechanisms including prayer, informal religious discussions, and volunteer opportunities. Theoretically, these findings demonstrate how organizations respond to competing environmental demands through organizational structures and processes.

The growth in faith-based community development has taken place within the context of new environmental demands created by the changing American welfare state. The FBCDOs in this study are a part of a larger national movement toward collaboration between sectarian civil society and the state in the provision of social services and community development. This shift can be characterized by changes in both "supply" and "demand." Religious leaders have increased the supply of non-governmental, community-based responses to social and economic inequalities by entering into the nonprofit sphere through the establishment of 501(c)(3) organizations. During the same period, increased "demand" is the result of changes in the American welfare state that have reduced the size and scope of the federal government and encouraged outsourcing of social service and community development functions once performed by the state (Cnaan, Wineburg, and Boddie 1999). This has created greater need for organizational partners located outside the bureaucratic state willing to take on these tasks. This change in supply and demand is an intriguing and important development in the evolution of the American welfare state and the role of sectarian organizations in the public sphere.

The public goods created by collaborations between this component of the religious sector and the state are neither purely sectarian nor purely secular in character. Specifically, while the public goods produced are secular and market-focused (e.g., affordable housing, job training), for the FBCDOs involved both the motivation and meanings attached to these projects are indelibly religious. Conceptually, faith-based community development organizations are not simply organizations—rather, they represent an organizational form through which both religious and civic values and beliefs are enacted. The story of Zion Development and the Grand Hotel, in Rockford, Illinois, illustrates this point.

During the late 1990s, Zion Development (ZDC) created the city's first permanent supportive housing facility for the homeless by remodeling and transforming a historic downtown building. Built in the 1920s, the 83-unit Grand Hotel was, for decades, part of a thriving working-class neighborhood in Rockford. Yet as the 1970s drew to a close, the Grand began its slide into destitution and infamy. Drugs, prostitution, and violence became identified with the hotel. In 1992 members of ZDC met with members of the "Mayor's Task Force on Homelessness" to discuss the feasibility of creating permanent housing for the area's homeless population. After a year of deliberation the Mayor's task force, the City of Rockford, and the Police Department agreed that ZDC should purchase and renovate the Grand Hotel. As evidenced in the following excerpt, the organization emphasized the benefits of this endeavor not only for its future residents but for the government, taxpayers, and wider community:

> Statistics for Rockford indicate we need 135 permanent "beds" for people who would otherwise be homeless. Without permanent supportive housing, the homeless are caught in an unending cycle from crisis or transitional housing to the streets, to emergency rooms, to mental institutions, to crisis housing again—or death. The costs to the State of Illinois are between $9,600 and $31,200 annually for each homeless person. At the Grand Apartments our per-unit housing cost will be about $3,500 per year. Creating permanent supportive housing is not only the right thing to do, it's the financially smart thing to do [ZDC external document circa 1998].

Once the project was underway, and following changes made by the new management team from Zion Development, the number of 9-1-1 calls to the building dropped from 1200 in 1995 to 28 in 2000. The final project involved a plethora of nonprofit agencies, for-profit businesses, and government agencies, and cost over $5.3 million. The transformation of the Grand Hotel was spearheaded by ZDC, but, as leaders emphasized at the ribbon cutting ceremony in 2000, it was a collaborative effort. The message was clear: without active backing from local and state government officials, ZDC would not have been able to finance the project.

The benefits of public goods, or positive externalities, are widely dispersed and are not limited only to those who create the good (Oliver 1984; Olson 1965). The housing described above (and the other services provided by the organizations in this study) meet this definition of public goods. First, the housing is available to anyone who meets the income requirements; it is not limited only to members of the church or to "believers." Second, the positive impact of permanent supportive housing extends well beyond those who now reside at the Grand Hotel. As evidenced by the attendees at the ribbon cutting ceremony (members of ZDC, neighborhood residents, local business owners, both the current and former Mayor of Rockford, a state senator, the Chief of Police, the Fire Marshal, and local religious leaders), the transformation of the Grand Hotel into a permanent supportive housing facility affected many stakeholders. For example, in addition to addressing the needs of previously homeless men and women, this project helped city officials and neighborhood residents reduce crime in the area and encouraged future economic development. Zion Development collaborates with the state (and the various other for-profit and nonprofit organizations involved in these projects) to create a secular, public good: safe, affordable housing.

But this is not the complete story—the creation of secular, affordable housing by ZDC is also indelibly religious. Zion Development originated with a congregation of believers, is guided by a mission statement affirming their commitment to God, and is motivated by notions of Christian service. Thus, for example, according to Zion Development, a safe and affordable house is not simply a safe and affordable house—it is the manifestation of God's love. This multidimensionality illustrates that creation of public goods (e.g., affordable housing, job skills, and educational improvement) by FBCDOs and secular actors (e.g., government) is neither purely sectarian nor secular.

Data and Methods

The data used in this analysis come from a comparative case study of three local FBCDOs. To gain greater explanatory power, the organizations were selected following the logic of John Stuart Mill's indirect method of difference (Ragin 1987). This method necessitates selecting cases that have many organizational and environmental similarities and a few key organizational differences. The organizational similarities include (1) nonprofit status, (2) organizational connections to a specific congregation, (3) provision of social service and community development programs, and (4) partial government funding. The key environmental similarities include (5) neighborhood size, (6) neighborhood socioeconomic composition, and (7) region. My choice of differences was driven by both substantive interest and theoretical concerns. The key differences are (1) religious tradition and (2) organizational programming.

Data Collection and Analysis Techniques

Over a seven month period beginning in November 2001 data on three organizations were collected. For each organization, *organizational histories* were created by triangulating data collected through multiple sources, including semi-structured interviews with directors, staff, and board members (n=22); internal documents (e.g., mission statements, incorporation statements, memoranda, minutes of meetings, budget records and grant applications) and external documents (e.g., promotional materials, press releases, publications, and newspaper articles); and infrequent direct observation of meetings, day-to-day activities, public events and associated religious services.[2] All interviews were recorded and transcribed. The research questions guiding the larger study were directed at uncovering how religious values influence the collective action frames and programming of faith-based community development organizations, and specifying how funding relationships with state agencies affect FBCDO structures and strategies. With the goal of answering these initial questions, I employed a theoretically motivated flexible note taking system (guided by organizational and social movement theory) to facilitate data reduction when examining nearly 3,000 pages of internal and external organizational documents. The resulting field notes comprised 350 single-spaced pages representing organizational histories (from founding date) detailing information on staff and board membership, organizational projects and milestones, descriptions of religious activities and symbols, and verbatim reproductions of all religious language used within the documents.

The Cases

All three organizations are 501(c)(3) corporations located in economically distressed urban neighborhoods, and are engaged in producing public goods. Each organization was created by, and continues to be connected to, a local congregation. In addition to private donations and grants, each organization receives funding from the state (i.e., local, county, state, or federal governments) through grants and contracts.

Established in 1982 by members of a local Lutheran church, Zion Development Corporation (ZDC) has produced an estimated $13.7 million in renovation and construction in Rockford, Illinois. Since its founding, ZDC has maintained its focus on the Midtown district, and has developed single-family homes and townhouses; a 45-unit assisted living single room occupancy (SRO) complex for the homeless; a low-income housing complex and health program for seniors; property management for local businesses; and a small-scale manufacturing workshop that provides employment and job training. During the data collection period, Zion Development employed twelve paid office staff plus additional employees at three different locations within the neighborhood. The mission statement of ZDC reads: "In response to God's command, working together as neighbors building stronger, healthier neighborhoods where people are proud to live, work and worship."

Table 10.1 Organizational Comparison

	Zion Development Corporation (ZDC)	Rockford New Hope (RNH)	Urban Hope Ministries (UHM)
Founded	1982	1995	1995
Location	Rockford, IL	Rockford, IL	Minneapolis, MN
Religious Tradition	Mainline Protestant	Mainline Protestant	Black Protestant
Programs	Primary: Housing	Primary: Housing	Primary: Referrals
Interviews	12	5	5

Rockford New Hope, Inc. (RNH), located less than a mile from ZDC, serves an adjacent neighborhood. It was founded by members of three local United Methodist congregations in 1995, and has developed a series of small-scale housing projects. The first project, a six-unit apartment complex for low-income families, was begun in 1999 and completed in 2001. In addition, RNH has developed Mother House (a children's crisis nursery center) and Ingersoll Centennial Park Playground. Until the spring of 2000, RNH did not have any paid staff or employees. At the time of data collection there was one paid staff member (the executive director) and a volunteer executive board. The mission statement of RNH reads: "Strive to improve the quality of life in stagnant, declining or low-income neighborhoods of the greater Rockford area by improving residential and/or commercial properties so that they may become affordable, decent, and safe."

Located in the Hawthorne-Jordan neighborhood of Minneapolis, Minnesota, Urban Hope Ministries (UHM) was founded in 1995 by the co-pastors of Faith Tabernacle Gospel Church, a nondenominational evangelical black Protestant church. Urban Hope Ministries is a network organization that links individuals with existing services by developing a database of social service agencies and creating individualized "action plans" for clients. Although UHM does very little direct service, they have contracted with the county government and the Minneapolis school district to provide truancy prevention programming, and previously provided computer training classes as part of a job skills development program. During the data collection period Urban Hope had five paid staff members, including the executive director. During the course of the study the organization was in the process of recruiting a new board of directors. The mission statement of UHM reads: "Urban Hope's mission is to provide spiritually based resources for empowerment of others; to restore hope in our city; to break the cycle of poverty, abuse and violence in the ever changing environment of our cities."

Findings

Organizational Responses to Environmental Demands

A growing body of research has demonstrated that robust explanations of the practices, relationships, and structures of religious organizations conceptualize these organizations as both *religious* and as *organizations* (Jeavons 1994; Vanderwoerd 2004; see also Demerath, Hall, Schmitt, and Williams 1998). Although a comprehensive organizational analysis of FBCDOs is beyond the scope of this chapter, there are three organizational theories that can be usefully applied to this case study: new institutionalism, resource dependence, and "inhabited institutions." New institutional and resource dependence theories of organizations direct attention to the ways that internal and external pressures influence organizations (Zucker 1987). New institutionalism's prediction (DiMaggio and Powell 1983; Meyer and Rowan 1991) that, under certain conditions, organizations incorporate the practices and procedures (or structural differentiation) of proximate institutions is evidenced in the development of the organizational form analyzed below. According to this perspective, the practice of establishing separate 501(c)(3) organizations, complete with standardized operating procedures, accounting practices and bureaucracies, has developed and spread within the field of religious social service provision because doing so confers legitimacy. In other words, congregations and others engaged in religious social service providers adopt this organizational form primarily to appear more legitimate to outside actors—particularly funding agencies.

Resource dependence theory, on the other hand, stresses that organizational activities are often attempts to manage external dependencies and ensure survival of the organization, and to gain more autonomy and freedom from external constraint (Leicht and Fenell 2001; Milofsky 1988; Pfeffer 1982). From this perspective, the decision of congregations to establish separate 501(c)(3) organizations represents an attempt to provide congregations with greater autonomy by creating a "firewall" between the social service nonprofit and the congregation. Government oversight of funds and practices is then limited to the actions of the social service nonprofit, allowing congregations to pursue their sectarian goals unencumbered by the state.

Binder (2007) develops a theoretical account of organizational responses to environmental demands by eschewing the rational actor assumptions of resource dependency and new institutionalism's focus on culturally legitimated action. Beginning with symbolic interactionist assumptions and applying the "inhabited institutions" perspective (Hallett and Ventresca 2006) to the study of a transitional housing organization, Binder posits, "organizational actors viewed in this light neither purely rationalize their action nor seamlessly follow institutional scripts. Rather, they combine and generate practices that are intended to satisfy multiple demands, and they do so in interaction with others" (Binder 2007, 549).

Each of these perspectives provides leverage in understanding the creation of organizational structures and organizational processes. The organizational histories of these three FBCDOs reveal that establishing 501(c)(3) organizations was in part an attempt to gain legitimacy and also to gain greater autonomy by separating secular and sectarian goals. However, the quest for legitimacy and autonomy does not adequately explain the processes by which these organizations maintain religious identity while engaging in the production of secular, public goods—this is the result of the interactive process described by the "inhabited institutions" perspective.

Organizational Structure

State policies and institutional factors influence the origins and behavior of nonprofit organizations (DiMaggio and Anheier 1990; Chaves, Stephens, and Galaskiewicz 2004; Marwell 2004; Salamon 1995; Smith and Lipsky 1993). In the past few decades a relationship of mutual dependence between government and nonprofit organizations has emerged in the United States. In a process described as "third-party governance" local, state, and federal government officials have become increasingly dependent on nonprofits to produce goods and services that heretofore have been the domain of governmental agencies. As a result, many nonprofit organizations rely heavily on government subcontracts and grants. FBCDOs that engage in cooperative relationships with the state to create public goods are both enabled and constrained by government funding (cf. Vanderwoerd 2004).

The emergence of third-party governance has affected the structure of many nonprofit organizations. For example, as government spending on nonprofit organizations has increased, so too have demands for accountability (Smith and Lipsky 1993). The Charitable Choice Provision of the 1996 federal welfare reform legislation allows religious and non-religious organizations to pursue and accept federal money. Yet in order to maintain adequate separation between church and state as defined in the establishment clause of the Constitution, there are provisions that constrain how the money is used (Black, Koopman, and Ryden 2004; Queen 2000; Vanderwoerd 2004).

An organizational strategy adopted by some congregations has been to establish a separate faith-based community development nonprofit corporation in order to engage in community development. Establishing a 501(c)(3) organization that is separate from, but remains connected to, a specific congregation prevents government oversight into the financial records of the congregation. This separation provides religious organizations an opportunity to cooperatively engage in social service and community development activities with the state while minimizing state oversight into the sectarian activities of the congregation. Interestingly, there appears to be little resistance or resentment toward the bureaucratic expectations of government agencies. Zion Development and Rockford New Hope both treat the paperwork, certification, and other requirements of government much as they view the existence of complex building codes—these things simply "come with the territory." This view is largely echoed by Urban Hope, with one member of the organization stating that the accounting standards required by government agencies actually benefit the organization in the long run by forcing them to develop good business practices.[3]

As discussed above, this particular organizational form is located at the confluence of state, market, and voluntary sectors. As a result, FBCDOs are affected by multiple environmental logics and demands. Organizational actors must respond to market conditions and inefficiencies as well as governmental bureaucracies and regulations, while simultaneously navigating the demands and expectations of private donors and volunteers. It is within this context and confluence of pressures that FBCDOs publicly enact religious identities.

Organizational Processes: The Enactment of Religious Organizational Identity

Following Marty (1998), I define public religion as the expression of religious beliefs or behavior, either by individuals or groups, which affects the public realm. For example, while the act of praying is considered a private act, when it is led by the director of a nonprofit organization at the start of a board meeting, it becomes public.[4] The appropriateness of public expression of religious beliefs has long been debated. Some have argued that religion is a private (i.e., personal) matter and should not be brought into the public (i.e., political) realm. From this perspective, organizations that represent the state (either directly or indirectly) should refrain from all expressions of religiosity. Others, such as Neuhaus (1984), have bemoaned the rise of the "naked public square," one that is stripped of all meaning and sustenance by disallowing religious expression in the public/political realm. Within this larger debate, disagreement exists as to what *types* of religious expressions are culturally appropriate and legally acceptable. As others have noted (cf. Chaves 2004; Unruh and Sider 2005; Wuthnow 2004; Monsma 2007) what is often missing in debates on church and state issues is a nuanced understanding of *how* religion animates organizations and individuals, and precisely *what* religious organizations do when they are acting in the public realm.

Similar to Vanderwoerd (2004), I found that faith-based social service organizations have a variety of techniques and processes that maintain religiousness even when faced with secular pressures associated with government funding and the creation of public goods. The organizations in the present study publicly enact their religious identities while engaging in the creation of secular, public goods, in two key ways: (1) by *publicly pronouncing* how their religious beliefs *motivate* the organization to engage in the creation of public goods, and (2) through the use of prayer, informal religious discussions, and volunteer opportunities within the organization. Taken together, these processes serve to *create* and *maintain* a religious organizational identity in organizations that, on a day-to-day basis, are primarily engaged in secular work.

First, each of the organizations in this study publicly pronounces the religious motivation of its work in organizational documents and promotional material. Throughout the organizational documents of Zion Development a variety of biblical passages is invoked to support the call for service. Citing Deuteronomy 14:22 - 15:1, one external organizational document states, "The Bible powerfully and repeatedly makes the point that the poor in your community are not to be ignored." Another document references Psalms 41:1 and Romans 15:26 to implore, "God says, 'provide for the poor.'" Yet another states:

> We seek to live out Christ's commandment: "You shall love your neighbor as yourself" (Matthew 12:31) by fulfilling our mission, "In response to God's command, working together as neighbors building stronger, healthier neighborhoods where people are proud to live, work and worship." Furthermore, service to the materially poor and building up the body of Christ are themes at the absolute core of our understanding of the gospel. The Christian context in which we do our ministry is stressed with all staff and volunteers. We live and breathe it daily [ZDC external document circa 1997].

Organizational documents from Urban Hope also present the religious motivation of the organization to the public, quoting Matthew 5, "Let your light shine before men so they may see your good deeds and praise your father in heaven" [UHM external document circa 1999]. This biblical calling to "let your light shine" is premised on the notion that by doing good deeds, one is making others aware of the bounty of Christ and thereby creating an opportunity for others to learn of Christ. Rockford New Hope also provides biblical justification for its work. As one Rockford New Hope respondent put it, "Most of us put our faith together [with] 'if you do unto the least of these.' We provide housing, and we are doing a ministry Christ would expect us to be doing" [RNH interview 03].

Second, consistent with prior research on other organizational forms which has shown that religious identities can be maintained through organizational procedures and processes (Baggett 2001; Sider and Unruh 2004; Vanderwoerd 2004), I found that prayer, informal religious discussions, and volunteer opportunities maintain organizational religious identities at organizations that are engaging in producing secular, public goods. Prayer is used to open and close board and staff meetings at all three organizations. This practice reaffirms the religious identity of the organization and expresses the individual religiosity of participating members. Prayers are led by different members of the organization, and prayer leadership is not limited to ordained clergy at any of the three organizations. Prayers offered at these meetings are often brief invocations asking for the Lord's guidance and blessing for the work that is being done. In addition, Zion Development holds weekly prayer meetings at the organization's offices. The date and time (Monday noon) of these prayer meetings are posted on the outside door of the building, and advertised as "open to the public." Despite the attempt to create a space for community members and staff to pray together, frequently the meetings are attended by only a few staff members.

All three of the organizations include nondiscrimination clauses in organizational documents, stating that neither religious participation nor conversion is required to qualify for services. At first glance, this may appear to be the "naked public square" feared by Neuhaus (and championed by others)—one where religious organizations are forced to remove and/or minimize their particularistic claims. However, while there are no religious requirements, informal religious conversations do take place within the organizations between co-workers and with clients. My fieldwork and interviews revealed that all three organizations discuss questions of faith and religion with clients "if the clients initiate it." Interestingly, this precise phrase was used by members within each organization. Although this phrase does not come directly from federal funding guidelines, the sentiment is consistent with regulations allowing voluntary religious participation and suggests a common "on the ground" understanding of the issues surrounding the separation of church and state.

Urban Hope's documents contain explicit religious content and strong hope for explicitly religious experience or change, while allowing participants the option to participate in religious programming—what Sider and Unruh (2004) classify as *faith-centered* programming. Most organizational documents contain a version of the following: "While participating in religious activities is not a requirement for any of our services, we do assess and address each client's spiritual needs in our services. Our services are available to all people regardless of religious belief of affiliation. We respect the rights of our clients to deny this aspect of our service" [UHM internal document circa 1999]. These statements deliberately create a space for religious discussion to take place.

In contrast, Zion Development and Rockford New Hope offer *faith-affiliated* programming—representing "invitational, relational, or implicit" religious engagement (Sider and Unruh 2004, 115), where programming contains little or no explicit religious content and little hope or expectation for an explicitly religious experience or change. However, given the visible connections between the 501(c)(3) organizations and the founding congregations, it is not surprising that some tenants approach staff members with questions of faith and religion—which may lead to further informal religious discussions.

For all three organizations, the use of volunteers serves two important functions. First, as is the case for all nonprofits, it allows the organization to keep project costs down by reducing labor costs. Rockford New Hope's small size and limited economic resources makes the extensive use of volunteer labor (both manual and managerial) a fiscally necessary strategy. Similarly, during the early years of its existence, Zion Development also relied on volunteer labor in order to complete specific projects. As the organization has grown in size and resources it is no longer driven by necessity to use volunteer labor, yet projects are still structured to facilitate volunteerism. Why? Because doing so serves a second function of volunteers: it provides a space for predominantly Christian volunteers to grow in their faith through service. As one promotional document from Zion Development states, ". . . volunteers came with hearts, hands, hammers, nails and a great spirit of caring." The language of having "heart" is consistent across all three organizations and connotes being charitable and gracious and committed to helping others. This theme is also developed in the narrative of Urban Hope's promotional video. "We talk about how we have a heart for the inner city. But unless we invest our finances, our time, our energy and throw our self into it, we really aren't—we don't have a heart for the inner city."

In sum, the organizations in this study employ a variety of practices that produce and maintain religiosity while engaged in predominantly secular tasks. Taken together, these practices (e.g., prayer at organizational meetings and gatherings, religious language in organizational documents, occasional discussions of faith with co-workers and clients, and volunteerism as a space for religious growth) actively respond to and preserve the religious concerns of organizational members (Baggett 2001; Jeavons 1994; Vanderwoerd 2004).

Religious Tradition and Organizational Programming

The import of religious tradition is brought to light by comparing the nondenominational evangelical black Protestant organization (Urban Hope) and the two mainline Protestant organizations (Zion Development and Rockford New Hope).[5] Urban Hope differs from the two other organizations both in the *amount* and the *content* of religious language employed. As discussed in greater detail below, while all three organizations include biblical quotes in most organizational documents, at Urban Hope the daily interactions and conversations are routinely laced with religious phrases—much more so than at Zion Development or Rockford New Hope. Additionally, Urban Hope's programming focus (e.g., individual needs assessment and counseling) also differs from the focus of the other two organizations. The differences in religious language and organizational programming can be traced to Urban Hope's black church culture[6] and to its evangelical orientation.

Pattillo-McCoy (1998) demonstrates that black church culture can shape how politicians and other government officials pursue secular goals. For example, the extensive use of religious language and particular rhetorical styles at political gatherings in an African American neighborhood in Chicago made it "difficult to distinguish the political figures who spoke in support of the candidate from the ministers who delivered the blessings" (Pattillo-McCoy 1998, 781). Similarly, Urban Hope's leadership and staff routinely engaged in "God-talk"—conversations heavily infused with religious themes and references—and did so to a much greater extent than the leadership and staff at either Zion Development or Rockford New Hope. It is important to note that differing levels of religious language reflect differences across religious traditions rather than different levels of religiosity (Ammerman 1997; Lichterman 2005). Christian evangelicalism is premised on letting the world know about Jesus (Smith 1998). To be vocal about the Lord is understood as a natural and celebratory part of being Christian. As one organizational member vividly states,

> That is what makes me. I can't go around and not say anything about the Lord, because He blesses me, He [does] things for me. You don't need people to do things for you, the Lord will do it for you. He will just put it on somebody

else's heart to do it, but He does it. How can I not just . . . how can I live on this earth and not say nothing about him? That's impossible. It's impossible for me [UHM interview 03].

While meetings at Zion Development and Rockford New Hope are opened with prayer, and the religious connections of the organizations are known in the community, the majority of organizational documents and public actions of these organizations are not overtly religious in nature. Despite this fact, religious values and beliefs are central to each organization's identity. Despite many historical differences, the denominations that Zion Development and Rockford New Hope are connected to—the Evangelical Lutheran Church in America and the United Methodist Church, respectively—share an interest in social action and the pursuit of social justice (Mead, Hill, and Atwood 2001). Organization members can refer to historical and contemporary denominational statements of faith and action that stress works over words: "It has always been what we do. It has never been what we talk about. It is not a showy thing to Lutherans but it is the core of what we [do]" [ZDC interview 12]. This quote explains the modicum of religious language present in the public face of the organization. Like other mainline Protestants many Lutherans are uncomfortable *talking* much about faith (Lichterman 2005; Wuthnow and Evans 2002). For members of Zion Development, service to others is "what we do"—it is religiously motivated and rooted within the Lutheran tradition, but it is not something that is talked about. Similar to the findings of Baggett's (2001) study of Habitat for Humanity, volunteer recruiting pools are easily expanded to incorporate a wide range of theological or religious beliefs—including "lay liberals" (Hoge, Johnson, and Luidens 1994) or "Golden Rule Christians" (Ammerman 1997).

There is also an important connection between religious tradition and organizational programming that becomes apparent by contrasting the mainline Protestant Zion Development and Rockford New Hope with the black Protestant Urban Hope. The organizations involved primarily in housing focus on the material needs of neighborhood residents and clients. By definition, "people programs," like the ones offered by Urban Hope Ministries, focus on individuals— these programs involve individual intake, assessment, and counseling. They are focused on providing individualized treatment to individuals in crisis. The central tenet of Urban Hope's approach is identifying the underlying cause of individuals' problems. At Urban Hope, it is assumed that most often the root cause is spiritual (at least in terms of "a loss of hope"). This individualized approach is consistent with what Smith (1998) labels the "personal influence strategy" of American evangelicals: "Evangelicals thus often render themselves, through their personal influence strategy, largely incapable of seeing how supraindividual social structures, collective processes, and institutional systems profoundly pattern and influence consciousness, experience, and life-chances" (Smith 1998, 189). It is worth noting that American evangelicals are not dramatically different in this approach from other Christians (or, for that matter, secular Americans), but that this tendency is exaggerated within evangelical communities (Smith 1998).

In sum, religious traditions and organizational programming are closely related and combine to influence the enactment of religious identities by FBCDOs. Religious traditions influence the amount and content of religious language, which affects the "mapping" (Lichterman 2008) done by the organizations to maintain religious identities. Religious traditions and identities, in turn, influence the choice of organizational programming.

Conclusion

Faith-based community development organizations are analytically located at the confluence of the three primary structures of American society: the state, market, and voluntary sectors. As a result, these organizations are faced with competing demands. The FBCDOs in this study respond to the demands of the state and market primarily through organizational structures (e.g., establishing a 501(c)(3), adopting formal accounting standards, developing "bureaucracies"). The mechanisms for maintaining religious identities, on the other hand, are primarily a response to demands from certain segments of the voluntary sector (i.e., congregations). Multiple organizational processes (e.g., prayer, informal religious discussions, and volunteer opportunities) allow FBCDOs to maintain a religious identity while engaging in otherwise secular work. Further, differences in religious tradition and organizational programming shape the public expression of religious identity.

The organizational form represented by the faith-based community development organizations studied in this project can also shed light on the complex and dynamic relationship between the state, voluntary, and market sectors of society. Drawing from previous research (Baggett 2001; Wuthnow 1994), the decision by congregations to establish separate 501(c)(3) organizations to provide community and social services can be interpreted as an organizational response to the rationalizing forces of society. Yet acknowledging this tells only part of the story. The organizations examined in this analysis demonstrate that in addition to reflecting the structures and processes of secular organizations, faith-based community development organizations can also maintain a distinct space for religious expression. In fact, it is precisely by creating separate 501(c)(3) organizations that religious groups can distinguish between the purely sectarian work that continues to take place in congregations and the religiously inspired creation of public goods produced by the separate nonprofit organization.

Future research can build on these findings. In particular, some religious leaders claim that any funding relationships with the state categorically hurt religious organizations. For example, Richard Land of the Southern Baptist Convention has argued that collaboration with government will corrode religion, and vowed to "not touch the money with the proverbial ten-foot pole" (Laconte 2001, A26). Is this pronouncement applicable to all religious traditions or organizational forms? As shown above, it appears that at least some organizations are able to partner with the state and other secular organizations without severing their religious roots. While the results of this case study should not be interpreted as representative, they do provide evidence for theorizing that religious traditions and local environmental demands play an important role in specifying the conditions under which this is likely to be the case.

Notes

I would like to thank Kevin Leicht, Lisa Troyer, Jennifer Glass, Lisa Rashotte, Yang Cao, Rebecca Matthews, and Salome Raheim for valuable comments on previous drafts. This research was supported in part by the National Science Foundation (SES-01171143).

1. Faith-based community development organizations are what John Orr and colleagues categorize as *freestanding public benefit nonprofit corporations* and are the most diverse type of religiously based social service providers (Orr 2000). The unifying characteristic is the provision of nonprofit social services by locally based organizations that originate from and to varying degrees continue to be linked to congregations. Some organizations within this category are members of interfaith organizations offering a range of social services; some engage in specialized service provision focused on a single target population; while others are engaged in "community development" (Orr 2000; Vidal 2001). All three organizations in the present study describe their work in terms of community development rather than simply as social service provision. In addition to providing assistance to clients and community members, each organization attempts to develop grassroots leadership and community empowerment. Of the three, Zion Development Corporation has been the most successful in meeting this goal.

This organizational form can be compared to other forms of religious social service provision: congregations, denominations, faith-based national networks and faith-based for profit organizations. *Congregations*, defined as local community-based groups organized around regular religious worship, provide a wide range of social services. There are approximately 350,000 religious congregations in the United States and most provide some form of social service. Among the most common are meal programs, alcohol/drug counseling, parenting classes, and temporary shelter (McCarthy and Castelli 1997). National and regional *denominations* (e.g., the United Methodist Church, the Roman Catholic Church, the Presbyterian Church) often have offices within the denominational structure that advance their social justice and social service agendas (Orr 2000, 25). *Faith-based national networks* represent the social service arm of denominations and networks of organizations. Examples of national network organizations are The Salvation Army, Catholic Charities USA, Lutheran Social Services, and Jewish Federations. Many of these organizations meet the same accreditation as secular social services and also are the most likely to contract with government to deliver social services (McCarthy and Castelli 1997; Orr 2000). *Faith-based for profit corporations* largely resemble the previous category except that the services offered are by organizations that have not registered as nonprofit corporations with the Internal Revenue Service (Orr 2000).

2. I identify the source of quotes by identifying whether it comes from (1) internal documents, (2) external documents, or (3) interviews. In accordance with the IRB protocol followed in this study, the confidentiality of *individuals* (not organizations) was maintained. Therefore, the citations for interviews contain only a code number. Data that are not specifically cited in this manner were drawn from direct observation.

3. In terms of Scott's (1991) typology of organizational responses to environmental demands, each of these organizations exhibits elements of authorization, inducement, imprinting, and incorporation. Given the political rhetoric surrounding FBCDOs at the time, it is somewhat surprising that there was little evidence of either "imposition" or "bypassing."

4. The key distinction here is between personal, private expressions and public expressions that are visible to and/or involve others. There are, of course, different degrees of "public" that this distinction conflates. That is, prayer at a board meeting of a nonprofit corporation is less "public" than at a political rally or city council meeting.

5. The "black church" has emerged in the United States as distinct from other Protestant traditions (Roof and McKinney 1987); yet it is, of course, not monolithic (Smith 1998; Fowler, Hertzke, and Olson 1999). Black congregations can, and do, differ quite strongly on a host of theological, social, and political issues (e.g., the Civil Rights Movement). Thus, I also include UHM's evangelical orientation. Regarding contemporary evangelicalism in the United States, Christian Smith writes, "through the institutionalization of their own cultural codes and discursive strategies, these traditions continue to retain much about their distinctive historical subcultures (although this continuity varies between them), which significantly influences those who locate themselves within them. Thus, to identify oneself as evangelical, for example, means one's religious orientation and actions are shaped by a tradition and subculture which makes them significantly different from someone who self-identifies as, say, a mainline Protestant" (Smith 1998, 234).

6. "The power of prayer, Christian imagery, and call-and-response interaction lie not only in the possibility of realizing concrete results from particular supplications, but also in the *cultural* familiarity of these tools among African Americans as media for interacting, conducting a meeting, holding a rally, or getting out the vote. Black church culture constitutes a common language that motivates social action" (Pattillo-McCoy 1998, 768).

Works Cited

Ammerman, Nancy. 1997. Golden rule Christianity: Lived religion in the American mainstream. In *Lived religion in America*, ed. David D. Hall, 196-216. Princeton, NJ: Princeton University Press.

Baggett, Jerome P. 2001. *Habitat for Humanity: Building private homes, building public religion.* Philadelphia: Temple University Press.

Bane, Mary Jo, Brent Coffin, and Ronald F. Thiemann. 2000. *Who will provide? The changing role of religion in American social welfare.* Boulder, CO: Westview Press.

Black, Amy E., Douglas L. Koopman, and David K. Ryden. 2004. *Of little faith: The politics of George W. Bush's faith-based proposals.* Washington, D.C.: Georgetown University Press.

Binder, Amy. 2007. For love and money: Organizations' creative responses to multiple environmental logics. *Theory and Society* 36:547-71.

Chaves, Mark. 2004. *Congregations in America.* Cambridge, MA: Harvard University Press.

Chaves, Mark, Laura Stephens, and Joseph Galaskiewicz. 2004. Does government funding suppress nonprofits' political activity?" *American Sociological Review* 69:292-316.

Cnaan, Ram A., Robert J. Wineburg, and Stephanie C. Boddie. 1999. *The newer deal: Social work and religion in partnership.* New York: Columbia University Press.

Davis, Derek, and Barry Hankins. 1999. *Welfare reform and faith-based organizations.* Waco, TX: J. M. Dawson Institute of Church-State Studies, Baylor University.

Demerath, N.J. III, Peter Dobkin Hall, Terry Schmitt, and Rhys H. Williams, eds. 1998. *Sacred companies: Organizational aspects of religion and religious aspects of organizations.* New York: Oxford University Press.

DiMaggio, Paul J., and Helmut K. Anheier. 1990. The sociology of nonprofit organizations and sectors. *Annual Review of Sociology* 16:137-59.

DiMaggio, Paul J., and Walter W. Powell. 1983. The iron cage revisited: Institutional isomorphism and collective rationality in organizational fields. *American Sociological Review* 48:147-60.

Dionne, E. J., and John J. DiIulio. 2000. *What's God got to do with the American experiment?* Washington, D.C: Brookings Institution Press.

Fowler, Robert Booth, Allen D. Hertzke, and Laura R. Olson. 1999. *Religion and politics in America: Faith, culture, and strategic choices.* Boulder, CO: Westview Press.

Hallet, Tim, and Marc J. Ventresca. 2006. Inhabited institutions: Social interactions and organizational forms in Gouldner's patterns of industrial bureaucracy." *Theory and Society* 35:213-36.

Hodgkinson, Virginia, and Murray Weitzman, eds. 1993. *From belief to commitment: The community service activities and finances of religious congregations in the United States.* Washington, DC: Independent Sector.

Hoge, Dean R., Benton Johnson, and Donald A. Luidens. 1994. *Vanishing boundaries: The religion of mainline baby boomers.* Louisville, KY: Westminster/John Knox Press.

Jeavons, Thomas. 1994. *When the bottom line is faithfulness: Management of Christian service organizations.* Bloomington: Indiana University Press.

Laconte, Joseph. 2001. The Right's doubting Thomases are wrong. *The Wall Street Journal*, May 22:A26.

Leicht, Kevin T., and Mary L. Fennell. 2001. *Professional work: A sociological approach.* Malden, MA: Blackwell Publishers.

Lichterman, Paul. 2005. *Elusive togetherness: Church groups trying to bridge America's divisions.* Princeton, NJ: Princeton University Press.

———. 2008. Religion and the construction of civic identity. *American Sociological Review* 73(1):83-104.

Marty, Martin. 1998. Public religion. In *Encyclopedia of religion and society,* ed. William H. Swatos. Walnut Creek, CA: AltaMira Press. Available online at hirr.hartsem.edu/ency/PublicR.htm (last accessed January 28, 2010).

Marwell, Nicole P. 2004. Privatizing the welfare state: Nonprofit community-based organizations as political actors. *American Sociological Review* 69:265-91.

McCarthy, John, and Jim Castelli. 1997. *Religion-sponsored social service providers: The not-so-independent sector.* Washington, D.C.: Nonprofit Sector Research Fund, The Aspen Institute.

Mead, Frank, Samuel S. Hill, and Craig Atwood. 2001. *Handbook of denominations in the United States.* Nashville, TN: Abingdon Press.

Meyer, John W., and Brian Rowan. 1991. Institutionalized organizations: Formal structure as myth and ceremony. In *The new institutionalism in organizational analysis,* ed. Walter W. Powell and Paul J. DiMaggio, 41-62. Chicago: The University of Chicago Press.

Milofsky, Carl. 1988. Scarcity and community: A resource allocation theory of community and mass society organizations. In *Community organizations: Studies in resource mobilization and exchange,* ed. Carl Milofsky, 16-41. Oxford: Oxford University Press.

Monsma, Stephen V. 1996. *When sacred and secular mix: Religious nonprofit organizations and public money.* Lanham, MD: Rowman & Littlefield.

———. 2007. *Putting faith in partnerships: Welfare to work in four cities.* Ann Arbor: The University of Michigan Press.

Neuhaus, Richard John. 1984. *The naked public square: Religion and democracy in America.* Grand Rapids, MI: William B. Eerdmans Publishing Company.

Oliver, Pamela. 1984. If you don't do it, nobody else will: Active and token contributors to local collective action. *American Sociological Review* 62:779-99.

Olson, Mancur. 1965. *The logic of collective action: Public goods and the theory of groups.* Cambridge, MA: Harvard University Press.

Orr, John. 2000. Faith-based organizations and welfare reform. *California religious community capacity study: Qualitative findings and conclusions.* Los Angeles: Center for Religion and Civic Culture, University of Southern California.

Pattillo-McCoy, Mary. 1998. Church culture as a strategy of action in the black community. *American Sociological Review* 63:767-84.

Pfeffer, Jeffrey. 1982. *Organizations and organization theory.* Boston: Pitman.

Queen, Edward L. 2000. *Serving those in need: A handbook for managing faith-based human services organization.* San Francisco: Jossey-Bass.

Ragin, Charles C. 1987. *The comparative method: Moving beyond qualitative and quantitative strategies.* Berkeley: University of California Press.

Roof, Wade Clark, and William McKinney. 1987. *American mainline religion: Its changing shape and future.* New Brunswick, NJ: Rutgers University Press.

Salamon, Lester. 1995. *Partners in public service: Government relations in the modern welfare state.* Baltimore: John Hopkins University.

Scott, Jason D. 2002. *The scope and scale of faith-based social services.* Washington, D.C.: The Roundtable on Religion and Social Welfare Policy.

Scott, W. R. 1991. Unpacking institutional arguments. In *The new institutionalism and organizational analysis,* ed. Walter W. Powell and Paul J. DiMaggio, 164-82. Chicago: The University of Chicago Press.

Sider, Ronald, and Heidi Unruh. 2004. Typology of religious characteristics of social service and educational organizations and programs. *Nonprofit and Voluntary Sector Quarterly* 33(1):109-34.

Smith, Christian. 1998. *American evangelicalism: Embattled and thriving.* Chicago: University of Chicago Press.

Smith, Steven Rathgeb, and Michael Lipsky. 1993. *Nonprofits for hire: The welfare state in the age of contracting.* Cambridge, MA: Harvard University Press.

Unruh, Heidi R., and Ronald J. Sider. 2005. *Saving souls, serving society: Understanding the faith factor in church-based social ministry.* New York: Oxford University Press.

Vanderwoerd, James R. 2004. How faith-based social service organizations manage secular pressures associated with government funding. *Nonprofit Management and Leadership* 14(3):239-62.

Vidal, Avis C. 2001. *Faith-based organizations in community development.* Washington, D.C.: U.S. Department of Housing and Community Development, Office of Policy Development and Research.

Wuthnow, Robert. 1994. *Producing the sacred: An essay on public religion.* Urbana, IL: University of Illinois Press.

———. 2004. *Saving America? Faith-based services and the future of civil society.* Princeton, NJ: Princeton University Press.

Wuthnow, Robert, and John H. Evans, eds. 2002. *The quiet hand of God: Faith-based activism and the public role of mainline Protestantism.* Berkeley, CA: University of California Press.

Zucker, Lynne G. 1987. Institutional theories of organizations. *Annual Review of Sociology* 13:443-64.

Chapter 11
"Bio-pistis": Conversion of Heroin Addicts in Prisons, on Medicine, and with God
Timoteo Rodriguez

I started using heroin when I was sixteen years old. I was living with my grandma when some family members came back from Vietnam addicted to heroin. It was 1968 . . . I kept buggin' them, then they finally shot me up. . . . After years in and out of prison . . . and nine months on methadone, I was still a dope fiend . . . 'til 2005. That's when I came to the Home and God saved me.
—Bill[1]

Awaiting Sentencing

A young adult drug offender waits before a California judge for his prison sentencing. In the courtroom he is comforted by the presence of a local minister. This evangelical pastor represents the "Home," a faith-based drug recovery program. The pastor asks the judge to give the young addict a day-for-day credit in his faith-healing program in lieu of prison time. The pastor knows he's a good kid, and petitions the judge "to give the addict a real chance to heal." The drug offender looks down.

As they wait for the judge's reply, another interested party speaks: a representative of Proposition 36, the Substance Abuse and Crime Prevention Act of 2000. This act initiates a decriminalization of nonviolent drug offenders by diverting them into substance abuse programs. The representative says, "Your Honor, their recovery home is not state licensed . . . you cannot allow this defendant to go to their facility."

With over one hundred Homes throughout California and over six hundred across the globe, this particular church organization has maintained cooperative relations with the criminal justice system for the past forty years. Even though drug offenders have been referred to and placed in this recovery program, Proposition 36 has changed the treatment and recovery scene since 2000.

The judge, without taking his eyes off the paperwork, replies, "This church had a history of success long before Prop. 36." He then turns to the pastor and asks, "Is your recovery Home state licensed?"

The pastor responds, "No, Your Honor. We are not because we opt not to be licensed. We do what works and we have success . . . and we don't want the state regulating how we run our programs."

The Art of Governing

In California the problem of substance abuse is worked upon through a continuum of institutional sites and discursive practices ranging from carceral punishment to medical treatment to faith healing (see Bourgois and Schonberg 2009, 15-19 for a theoretical framing of "substance abuse"). The above courtroom episode illustrates the conceptual interconnections of approaches to a common problem—where the individual substance abuser is understood and acted upon as part of a deviant population, an addicted body, or a hurting soul. By proposing a modality of power, knowledge, and care that I term "bio-pistis," this study conceptualizes how government policies and evangelical faith communities are jointly yet distinctly equipped to reckon with the relational object of the "soul" as a unit of analysis in discourse and practice.

Focusing on the interface between faith healing and public policy, this chapter reveals how heroin abusers move between competing and complementary institutional sites of prisons, medical clinics, and faith-based organizations. As exemplified above with the young man awaiting sentencing, a complex of moral effects and pragmatic reasoning emerges through these institutional apparatuses. The discursive practices of incarceration, medical treatment, and faith healing together form a philosophical nexus—an assemblage of linkages between the individual and the collective, the legal and the ethical, the technical and the political, the secular and the faithful. As the drug abuser stands before the judge, he is produced in a categorical distinction as an *object* of *relations* through competing truth claims, intersecting modes of subjectification, and a range of strategies of intervention (Rabinow and Rose 2006). Although penal, medical, and faith institutional distinctions are designed to accomplish both pragmatic and moral goals, in order to attempt both, their discursive practices engage ways of thinking about, experimenting with, and organizing "knowledge and care" through managerial solutions. Moreover, these solutions are actually working on a common problem through different modalities of power that combine, delineate, and act upon drug users alternately as "populations," "bodies," or "souls."

This chapter emerges as part of a larger project on formerly incarcerated men who have converted to evangelical Pentecostal Christianity and are recovering from long-term heroin addiction. I have conducted participant-observation at a number of faith recovery Homes in California metropolitan areas. I research the spiritual, physical, and social practices of recovery in these faith Homes, of which there are more than four hundred in the United States. They are supported by an international evangelical organization, referred to here as "the Church." In the mid-1960s, the Church started faith Homes *by* and *for* addicts in the barrios[2] of Southern California. This inquiry studies a faith community, its bureaucratic dealings with state policies, and how, in the conversion of a heroin addict, the Church pursues bio-political methods of faith healing, thus opening significantly new points of view and different conditions of possibility—one that I describe as a "bio-pistis" mode of power.

A Conceptual Frame of Power

Following Michel Foucault's understandings of power, I will start with a few premises of power in terms of its relation to *knowledge* and *care*. In the Tanner Lectures on Human Value, Foucault (1979) articulated characteristic features of power not as exchange, production, or communication, even as power relations combine with these elements. Instead, power is how some individuals or groups can, more or less entirely, determine the conduct of other individuals or groups. Crucial here is that the power to determine the conduct of others is not accomplished by exhaustive or coercive means. Given this, power is not a *substance*, but simply a type of relation between individuals. Another point Foucault makes is that "there is no power relation without the correlative constitution of a field of knowledge, nor any knowledge that does not presuppose and constitute at the same time power relations" (Foucault 1977, 27). This leads to the third premise that "if there are relations of power throughout every social field, it is because there is freedom everywhere" (Foucault 1987, 123). Even though *freedom* is always coupled with *power*, and *power* with *knowledge*, Foucault (2005) makes the point that "salvation" is not acquired by knowledge alone; a deliberate practice of liberty rests on the imperative: "taking care of yourself." The matrix of power, knowledge, and "care for the self" sets the conceptual scene for this chapter as I arrive at the emergence of *bio-pistis* power by considering the modalities of carceral power, biopower, and pistis power ethnographically. Further, these modes of power lead toward a relationship between the *body*, the *population*, and the *soul*.

In situations such as the above courtroom setting, *pastoral* power and *carceral* power become two initial modes that influence the capacity and condition to "know and care for the self." Briefly, *pastoral power* is a Christian adaptation of the Hebraic metaphor of the shepherd as guardian to the flock of the faithful (Foucault 1979). In this mode of power the local pastor petitions for the release of the drug offender, but at stake, more than just the soul of the lost sheep, is the pastor's salvation that emerges as a "rebound effect" (Foucault 2005, 16) in guiding the individuated souls of the flock. *Carceral power* is a punitive disciplinary mechanism that produces docile bodies, but, unlike other forms of discipline (Foucault 1977), carceral power does not increase individual (and/or collective) capacities through reward. Thus, the young man handcuffed in the courtroom is subjected to force exerted over his docile body. Yet he is not exactly subjected to power. Force is not power. In fact, the amount of force used can be thought to measure the lack of power, at least in the way that I intend to problematize its interactions with carceral power. I will expand on this in the next section, but the point here is that the courtroom scene samples the homogenizing dealings between the politics of carceral power that works within the State of California as a legal framework of accord, and the politics of pastoral power as the pastor's duties of constantly ensuring, sustaining, and improving individual lives—in particular that of the lost sheep. In this situation, the problem of governmental rationale is interlinked with pastoral concern for an individual's salvation. Thus, in California the problem of substance abuse is not just how public policies socially weigh in on faith-based programs (Hansen 2005), but also how the *art of governing* puts into question the rationalization of power modalities. These modes of power facilitate a movement of one's potential toward living it. This movement becomes a question of *freedom*—that is not about the *right to be*—but rather, *freedom* as a capacity of flourishing[3] and the *right to do*.

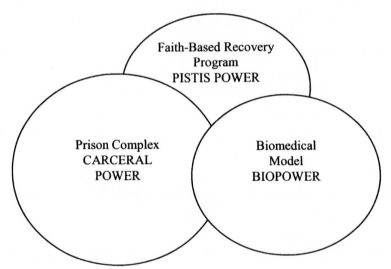

Figure 11.1. The above schema depicts the common space of convergence for the three primary loci of this inquiry.

Punishment and the Body

Carceral power operates upon groups and individuals by criminalizing them and effectively taking their bodies out of the public sphere, seized in the apparatus of prison through a discourse of penality. Far beyond the prison walls, carceral power also punishes those living in the enclaves that feed the prison system. If punishment in general and the prison in particular are about a political technology of the body (Foucault 1977, 30), then how I appropriate the term "carceral power" extends and slightly alters Foucault's idea of "carceral network."

First, the purpose of the contemporary prison system is not so much perpetual "social discipline" or even "security" as it is "punitive warehousing" (Simon 2000; Irwin 2004) through a carceral symbiosis (Wacquant 2001), where—for Latinos in urban enclaves—prison is like the *barrio*, in that it augments the status of an incarcerated individual. The barrio becomes more like a prison through peculiar surveillance coupled with "advanced marginality" (Wacquant 2008). The practice of augmenting status through prison is illustrated in a conversation I had with a recovering heroin addict and ex-convict. This Latino man in his forties, Rene, sits with me in a small prayer room of the Church. On this summer midday, he wears a tank top. Solidly built and sleeved with tattoos that look like iconic Chicano murals mixed with barrio gang tags, Rene tells me: "I first went to prison years ago. I wanted to go. I thought I would be around people of respect, killers. It was a way to come up [in gang life]." For many like Rene, prison is a rite of passage (Van Gennep 1960) that earns individuals street respect upon returning to the barrio. He behaves in accordance with particular norms and ethical standards. But the status acquired in this prison-barrio rite often has the effect of "liminality" (Turner 1969) that becomes *perpetual* through prison recidivism.

The status of perpetual liminality forms a relationship "betwixt and between" (Turner 1969) the prison and the urban enclave. A carceral network allows recruitment that creates a normative system of docility and delinquency from the barrio to the prison and back to the barrio. The peculiarity of this surveillance becomes not only police patrols, but also an internal barrio rationale where *veteranos* or *shot callers* keep *peewees* in check.

Secondly, Foucault (1977) shows that the modern soul emerged as a historically specific correlative to a technology of power over the body, a means of governing individuals through the regulation of time and space, and surveillance. In today's carceral power the relational anchor point, its object, is not about a correlate of *body* to *soul*, but instead a relationship between *body* and *status*. From the early inceptions of the penitentiary system, its founders set out to discipline not merely the body but, more important, the soul of an inmate—and by extension to work to individualize and contain those remaining outside or at the limits of the bourgeois public sphere of the eighteenth century (Meranze 1996). Through this progression toward social disciplining, the soul was emphasized as an object in its relation to the body. "The soul is the effect and instrument of a political anatomy; the soul is the prison of the body" (Foucault 1977, 30). This penal "soul," then, was not a substance extracted through violent force over the body, but instead an element that articulated the effects of the power of normalization and referenced a formation of knowledge, a site of a "power-knowledge" relation (Foucault 1977, 29). Thus, for the founding visionaries of penitentiary discipline (Magnani and Wray 2006), the consolidating connection, the anchor point in a series of regulation, surveillance and re-composition, was intended to have as its object relation of "body-soul."

Third, carceral power, through its *mode of composition* (Rabinow and Bennett 2007), interfaces apparently heterogeneous elements that function in an integrated way and effectively regulate a criminalization of bodies-statuses. The carceral network in *Discipline and Punish* is an ensemble of three elements: *police-prison-delinquency*. Each supports the other, forming a circuit. On this Foucault writes, "Police surveillance provides the prison with offenders, which the prison transforms into delinquents, the target and auxiliaries of police supervisions, which regularly send back a certain number of them to prison" (1977, 282). For those living in an urban enclave like East L.A., police work the "beat" with an ethos and gaze that measure individuals and groups as potential criminals. Similarly, those living in a place like East L.A. return a collective gaze toward the police with the attitude that cops are just another gang to avoid. Further heterogeneous elements such as employment, education, sexual heath, and parenting, join a relationship between one's body and status and in effect normalize conditions of possibility that function to regulate a composition of the modality of carceral power.

An example of this comes from a conversation I had with Marcus, a husky black man in his early twenties, with thin dreads draping a warm smile. We sit in a church office, and I switch on the recorder. My first question is, "Tell me about how you and your partner met." He says to me: "We met at the candle light ceremony. Her sister's boyfriend had got murdered. . . . My lady was fourteen, and I was sixteen years. A few months after the funeral, I was picked up by the police for not wearing a helmet on my bicycle. I had a case pending so I got locked up for ninety days."

As carceral power extends far beyond the so-called delinquent, it is composed of a symbiotic relationship between the prison and prison feeder enclaves. In places like Marcus's neighborhood, or like Manhattan's East Harlem (Bourgois 2002), Chicago's South Side (Wacquant 2008), or East Los Angeles (Rodriguez 1993), a vital capacity permeates a paradox of power that Loïc Wacquant best characterized as a "deadly symbiosis" (2001). This paradox unfolds with Marcus's narrative:

After my ninety-day stay . . . unless I was runnin' the street or in jail, I was always with my lady . . . Then, in 2005 she got pregnant with my son. This was right before I got sent to San Quentin. That was stressful, 'cus she had to move in with my mom, and it was my first time in the penitentiary.

During the first four months in San Quentin, you go through in reception, which means I was locked up twenty-three hours a day, and the room was hella li'l. But, I kept it together by writing her. I came out after eleven months, and my son was already born. It felt good to have him 'cus everybody be telling me how he looks like me, so that made me feel good but at the same time, deep down inside I didn't feel good, cus I didn't have nothing.

Thaaatt's what made me be back on the streets!

So I didn't have to ask nobody for nothing.

I made my own money. But, that's what got me locked up again.

Not only is the lack of employment skills and opportunities part of the symbiotic relationship between the prison and ghetto, but, as Foucault put it, "prison indirectly produces delinquents by throwing the inmate's family into destitution" (1977, 268). So for Marcus's partner and son, who are not in prison but still inhabit and maneuver within the social, spatial, and embodied parameters of a carceral symbiosis, what occurs is a "secondary prisonization" in that a domestic partner—or a parent, sibling, child, or loved one—of an imprisoned individual is "at once captive and free, and [a domestic partner] thus is a status marked by profound ambivalence" (Comfort 2008, 16).

As a context and product, this status of ambivalence radiates through a relational field of at least two poles: one coordinate is a barrio, a ghetto, an urban enclave, a place that feeds the other extremity, the prison itself. In *Doing Time Together*, Megan Comfort (2008) coins the term "secondary prisonization" to refer specifically to women with a husband, boyfriend, or fiancé in the penitentiary. Following Comfort, secondary prisonization is extended to other meaningful relationships of inmates, as the composition of penalty for the inmate's family functions in accord with a criminalized relational field of the prison system. Thus, criminalization as a metric is not only relevant to the inmate's status, but also measures the condition of punishment for people who are emotionally and economically dependent on or invested in the life of the inmate (Gilmore 2007).

Foucault (1977) shows that the body as a site of political power shifts with the nineteenth-century displacement of the eighteenth-century sovereign state. As the "social contract" legitimates the rise of the governmental state, the power to punish becomes a responsibility of "society"—not a regal "right to take a life or let live" (Foucault 2003a, 241). Society mourns the loss of the citizen who breaks the law. The re-establishment of order is no longer a concern of punishment; instead, preventing crime becomes a problem for social accountability. Punishment, as an act of mourning, assumes responsibility over the convict's body by attempting to reclaim the soul through timetables and a prison cell (Foucault 1977). This idealized approach draws on practices of monastic piety and a pastoral modality of power in a circuit of surveillance, examination, and confession of the individual. Further, since prison sentencing makes impossible the spectacle of public punishment, a peculiar relation of the convict to the punisher establishes a diluted and perverted modality of pastorship; i.e., the prison guard is vigilant over a convict's soul via the punitive non-public disciplining of the body (Rhodes 2004).

At stake here are several issues. First, the contemporary prison system functions with the purpose of punitive warehousing (Irwin 2004), and, thus, the relational anchor point of carceral power—its object—is a correlation between the *body* and *status*. How status relates to the body is understood as one's *habitus*— an embodied generative disposition—in a social *field* accumulating *symbolic capital* (Bourdieu 1990; Bourdieu and Wacquant 1992). Still another critical consideration is the context of "perpetual liminality," in which an ex-convict's status is always in danger of penal relapse. Further, a social topography of prison recidivism binds criminal status with an ethno-racialized identification, vis-à-vis a criminalized body as a "race" in a place, in an "ethnoscape" (Appadurai 1990; 1996) of a carceral symbiosis. Moreover, as both a context and product, status is about one's perceived bodily presences, but also has a *disembodied affect* of moving between places. This affect—a spatialized diffusion of identity formation—shapes an individual's perceptive opinion of experiencing a place (Castillo Cocom and Rodriguez n.d.), i.e., a neighborhood or a prison cell. Moving in between these places normalizes an embodied paradox of presence through a disembodied emotional disposition of everyday violence (Scheper-Hughes 1996) and symbolic violence (Bourdieu 2000) that gnaws at one's status. So, if the barrio is like the prison and the prison like the barrio, then what secondary prisonization results in is an individuated pathos caught in the collectivity of a carceral symbiosis (Clear 2007; Braman 2004). This collective form of the status-body object is structurally homogenized into an ethno-racialized carceral underclass (Simon 2001; Garland 2001), and the modality of carceral power results in a docile affect in groups of individuals.

Instead of increased capacity through reward, a punitive discipline exerts punishment with little or no reward. What emerges is the prison warehouse (Irwin 2004) with a carceral imperative of "concentration in space and containment" (Simon 2000), and the displacement of the ideal type of soul-body object by a normalized status-body. Accentuating this yet operating on a non-mutually exclusive level, the object of population emerges with the modality of biopower. As Foucault clarifies, "After a first seizure of power over the body in an individualizing mode [of discipline] . . . a second seizure of power that is not individualizing, but . . . *massifying*, that is directed not at the [hu]man-as-body but [hu]man-as-species . . . a 'biopolitics' of the human race" (2003a, 243; emphasis added).

This specific and extended attention to a conceptual framing of carceral power is critical in part because in 2008 the United States had over 7.3 million people on probation, in jail or prison, or on parole—one in every thirty-one adults (U.S. Bureau of Justice Statistics, http://bjs.ojp.usdoj.gov)—and in California today about 170,000 are in correctional facilities (http://www.cdcr.ca.gov/). Prison is too often the institutional solution for the problem of drug offenders. Below, I will concisely characterize the modes of biopower and pistis power in order to move toward an ethnographic framing of the notion of bio-pistis.

A Politics of Population

The term *biopower* is used by Foucault to frame the emergence of modern nation-state governance in conjunction with the eighteenth- and nineteenth-century domains of health and illness, census, epidemiology, demography, a science of race, and eugenics. The exercise of biopower is the politics of *massifying human-as-species* in a regularizing pole of discipline over the body to the collectivizing pole of a quantifiable mass—a *population*. Unlike carceral power, biopolitics operates openly in society by establishing "the right to make live and to let die" (Foucault 2003a, 241).

In the matrix of power, knowledge, and care, the notion *to make live* (or to foster life) becomes the condition of possibility, which uses probabilistic series to forecast, statistically estimate, and measure overall the power of *making live* by a ratio to *letting die*. Thus, the ontological mode in the figure of biopower is a regulatory relationship *not* between life and death, but a technology of power of "a new body, multiple bodies . . . [a] Biopolitics [that] deals with the population . . . as a problem that is at once scientific and political, as a biological problem and as power's problem" (Foucault 2003a, 245). Biopower has as its object a relationship between *populations* and *bodies*. Its method and purpose are clearly defined in the following passage:

> Centered upon life: a technology which brings together the massing effects characteristic of a population, which tries to control the series of random events that can occur in a living mass, a technology which tries to predict the probability of those events (by modifying it if necessary), or at least to compensate for their effects . . . [and] aims to establish a sort of homeostasis, not by training individuals, but by achieving an overall equilibrium that protects the security of the whole from internal danger (Foucault 2003a, 249).

Heroin abusers on Methadone Maintenance Treatment (MMT) exemplify a contemporary and concrete example of biopower at work. In Philippe Bourgois's ethnographic analysis of MMT, he writes, "the methadone clinic is an unhappy compromise between competing discourses: a criminalizing morality versus a medicalizing model of addiction as disease"(2000, 165). This unhappy compromise is revealed in a conversation I had with Bill, a former heroin addict who eventually gained sobriety through faith healing. He shared with me: "I wanted to keep my kids, so we went to court. They were going to give them to me, but then my wife told the court that I used dope [heroin]. So in order to keep my kids I had to go on Methadone. For nine months I was at 75 milligrams."

The psychopharmacological truth discourse of MMT seeks to regulate the addict's body, and thus normalize the user's mood, cognition, and social behavior. Governmental neurological vigilance of daily methadone doses statistically estimate the probability of narcotic withdrawal in order to maintain docile opioid users. Bill continued: "What bothered me about it [MMT] was when I had to sign a paper stated that the 'clinic is not responsible for the "side effects" that I will have.' I thought 'Side effects?' Anyway it was like cheap heroin but lasted longer. You don't get as high, so I would chip with other stuff, too."

Paul Rabinow and Nicolas Rose clarify that biopower combines at a minimum three dimensions: (1) a truth discourse, with authorities to speak those "true knowledges"; (2) strategies for intervention upon collective existence in the name of life and health; and (3) modes of subjectification in which individuals can be brought to work on themselves in the name of individual or collective life or health (Rabinow and Rose 2006, 197). Given these three criteria, Bill's situation samples the modality of biopower in that: (1) the authority of the courts establish and hybridize biological and demographic truth claims about the vital character of the human condition through MMT; (2) within the moral economies of the court's intervention and clinic's policy on "side effects," Bill's "biolegitimacy" (Fassin 2009) as a parent is reconstituted in the form of "biological citizenship" (Petryna 2002) inasmuch as a collective existence of life and health has a specific anatomo-politics of status that officially recognizes assistance in "making lives"; and, thus, (3) Bill is brought to work on himself in the name of his own health, for his family, and—from a governmental point of view—for the population as a whole.

Pistis Power and the Soul

> I was in and out of jail because of my addiction, then at my first chapel services, the Pastor spoke on faith . . . I opened up my heart to the Lord and accepted Christ in my life. At that altar call, I felt this deep wave or like a rush through my body and instantly my obsession for drugs left my body. It was really instant. I have never used drugs again.   —Abel

The Christian notion of *pistis* emerges out of the Apostle Paul's writings on faith some two thousand years ago. Drawing on research by David M. Hay (1989), a Pauline understanding of pistis is the "objective ground of faith." Hay shows that Plato used the term pistis as an argument or proof for the immortality of the soul. Aristotle used the term in relation to *ethos*, the moral character of the speaker, but further developed the concept of pistis as a means of rhetorical persuasion that depends on proofs, classifying some pistis as items of evidence available to lawyers such as witnesses, contracts, laws, and oaths. After Aristotle, the common use of pistis continued to mean "evidence" or "pledge." Thus, in the Apostle Paul's contemporaneous context when writing the books of the

New Testament (in Greek), pistis meant "pledge" or "evidence" (Hay 1989). Foucault (2009, 1979) makes the point that Christian identity appropriated two essential instruments at work in the Hellenistic world: self-examination and the guidance of conscience. Thus, crucial to the concept of pistis as a faith practice is how *evidence* is related to *knowledge*, and *pledge* to *guidance*.

In Paul's writing, the patriarch Abraham is the great prototype of faith, yet the movement of thought in the New Testament pivots on pistis not as a general pledge of guidance or evidence of knowledge. Rather, Paul's pistis is faith as an *objective* salvation for *subjective* faith in Jesus of Nazareth (Hay 1989). Hence, the mode of "pistis power" is not a general spiritual possibility, but distinctly Christian. As such, faith power in Paul's pistis entails a commitment to the missionary truth discourse that the God of Abraham has acted for human salvation through Jesus Christ. A contemporary mode of pistis as particular evidence of salvation, for a specific pledge of faith in Christ, is conveyed by the testimony of Abel, an assistant pastor in the Church: "God delivered me from my addiction, but other areas of my life needed work. So as a convert, prayer became more natural. The word of God became more alive. The rules of Home became easier to comply with. I was given more responsibility as I grew in my faith through the Home. And now it's been twenty years."

For Foucault (1979), Christianity shaped the idea of a pastoral influence continuously exerting itself on individuals and the demonstration of their particular truth through a continuous circulation of individuated knowledge and confession, pastoral guidance and correction. Pistis power is not a term Foucault ever discussed, but it is related to the concept of pastoral power in that the "soul" is the pivotal relational object for both. They are two sides of the same coin, so to speak, in that pistis is both the pledge and the evidence of salvation, and pastorship is the guidance and knowledge for perpetual salvation. In Abel's case, he opened his heart to faith that God heals, and then worked on himself through this pledge of guidance of the Home and the Church. The objective truth is that he never used drugs again, which becomes the evidence of subjective faith.

The Church and its Mission

I started to notice a common trend that as we work with addicts and they would convert and be clean . . . well, once they left our program, the churches that we sent them to, didn't know how to deal with heroin addicts. The congregation and the [former] users would feel uncomfortable. . . . The guys we helped "save" would go back to using [heroin].　　　—The Church Founder

In 1967 the Church and the first Home started in East Los Angeles in the house of its founder, a man who himself was a former heroin addict and who gained sobriety through a faith program. Over the past forty years the Church has de-

veloped its ministry and successfully replicated its methods of a faith drug recovery program. The basis of its accomplishment is conveyed most clearly in
the Church's mission statement:

> . . . an international, church-oriented Christian ministry called to the task of
> evangelizing and discipling the hurting people of the world, with the message
> of hope and plan of Jesus Christ. This call involves a commitment to plant and
> develop churches, rehabilitation homes and training centers, in strategic cities
> of the world. [The Church] inspires and instills within people the desire to ful-
> fill their potential in life with a sense of dignity, belonging, and destiny.

I met with the founder of the Church in a San Francisco hotel lobby. This
charismatic, compassionate man greeted me with a hug. As we sat on the lobby
sofa, his mobile phone rang. He talked for a few minutes to confirm his travel
dates to visit Homes first in El Salvador, then in Germany, and ending in South
Africa. I started our conversation by asking him how the Church, which started
in a marginal inner-city Chicano neighborhood, had grown to be an international
faith community with the focus of helping drug addicts. He told me:

> I saw a need for a church for addicts, so I approached the youth organization
> that I worked with at the time [mid-1960s]. I requested that we start our own
> church where former users could feel comfortable. The leadership conveyed to
> me that this organization was a "para-church," not a church. So, a core group of
> us started an indigenous church for addicts by addicts. People thought I was
> crazy to build a church just for drug addicts.

In the early 1970s, members of the Church started Homes and satellite
churches in barrios and inner cities across California, and by the 1980s the
Church had emerged at the forefront of mission-focused ministries by planting
nodes across the United States and Latin America. The founder continued:

> My vision started very local—just East L.A. because that's where the need was.
> . . . A place where the Home was connected with Church, and the Church con-
> nected to the neighborhoods. So our ministry grew out of my house into a small
> church, then to an auditorium. . . . Other churches invited me to different cities
> to speak, and as I traveled, I realized that the same problem of drug addiction
> was in all the inner cities throughout the world. The vision expanded.

As some of these satellite churches grew to over a thousand members, this
success spurred the next move: a trans-Atlantic, cross-cultural Church that first
planted a Home in Amsterdam, The Netherlands. From the 1990s onward, there
has been exponential growth both in the United States and abroad. The founder
also makes the point that "[t]here was a real need to help people who weren't
getting the care to heal—to transform their lives with dignity. So I spoke the
vision, and congregation members caught the vision and acted upon it."

The Home and the Politics of Faith

In the 1970s, with heroin use on the rise, government agencies experimented with various methods to approach the problem of heroin addiction; e.g., the expansion of the prison system and the introduction of Methadone Maintenance Treatment. States and counties also offered funds for faith organizations to provide social services. In 1975, the Home in East Los Angeles accepted government funding to bolster its drug recovery program. In that year the Home staff grew from a handful to about two dozen. But at the end of that year, the Church let go of its government funding. A staff member who had worked at the Home in 1975 explained:

> We made good money that year. I went from making $5.00 a week and having faith, to almost $200.00 per week. I had so much money I did not know what to do with it.
>
> But that money came with so many stipulations. The bureaucratic guidelines were too adamant about keeping church and state separate. We weren't even allowed to say "God bless you" to people who called on the telephone.
>
> The government gave us money but told us how to run the program. They tried to change our structure and the way we did things. So after the first year ended, we did not renew our funding.
>
> Without that funding we went back to walking by faith and out of about twenty staff, only six or seven of us stayed on.

This particular staff member eventually became a pastor and established satellite churches and Homes in Northern California, the Philippines, Indonesia, and South Africa. When I asked the founder about the 1975 funding, he shared:

> We let that money go after one year because we can't be dependent on the government. Our purpose is to build the person's mentality to be a winner—from an addict to somebody that can do anything. We help change the way addicts think.
>
> Our churches are in the barrio and inner city, but we want people to get out of a poverty mentality and think of themselves as winners with dignity.
>
> In 1975 we let go of the government funds because I wanted to make sure that we were not depending on welfare kind of mentality, or becoming another social program working from grant to grant. If we would have kept the government funding, then we would not have been able to grow as we have today. Now our newest churches and rehabs are in Germany and La Havana, Cuba.

The institutional structure of the Church as an international faith organization is that each satellite church and its recovery Home are semi-autonomous, but adhere to the guidelines established by the mother Church in Los Angeles. Further, there are yearly international conferences, as well as bimonthly regional meetings. A person may enter the Home by simply walking in off the street, through referrals from the courts, or, most commonly, by outreach of Church members who conduct street evangelism. The Church locations are always in the same community as their respective Homes. Typically there are both men's and women's Homes in the same community, ranging in size from five to thirty people. Homes and churches are established most often in communities that are economically underserved and socially marginalized. Most people who enter the Home make a commitment to stay for twelve months, with the understanding that they are free to drop out earlier if they wish. There is no cost to the person, but he or she must adhere to the rules of the Home, which are sobriety, prayer three times per day, an overtly Christian adaptation of Alcoholics Anonymous and Narcotics Anonymous meetings, Bible studies (Bielo 2009), Church attendance, vocational workshops, and education programs (such as anger management, grieving classes, parenting, marriage and couples classes, GED courses). An intake interview includes a personal assessment to gauge psychological wellness, medical and criminal issues, and drug addiction history. A Home director explained to me: "I open up a file on the men when they arrive and do a case management with their medical and legal issues . . . that is, if they are on probation, parole, or have warrants. We keep a dialogue open with the social workers, probation officers, or other referring agencies."

In 2001 President George W. Bush invited the leaders of the Church (as well as other faith organization leaders) to the White House to help launch the Faith Based and Community Initiative. While between fiscal years 2003 and 2005 the total dollar amount of all grants awarded to FBOs increased by 21 percent, and more than $2.2 billion in competitive social service grants were awarded to faith-based organizations during the fiscal year 2005 (USGAO 2006, 43), the Church never accepted any FBCI funding.

In 2006 the founder was again invited to Washington, D.C. by the Office of the FBCI; there, he was offered a multimillion-dollar federal grant to support the organization's recovery Homes. He rejected this opportunity, not wanting to repeat the 1975 governmental imposition. In this regard, he shared with me:

> Other secular programs replace one drug for another [methadone maintenance] . . . spend a lot of money on very expensive facilities, and in the end they don't heal or save the addicts. . . . Our Homes are not well funded, but we have faith, and we continue to grow and save addicts . . . and this is where our faith that God will provide comes through as evidence to our mission.

This passage exemplifies what the Apostle Paul meant by pistis. Furthermore, this passage conveys the idea of pistis-power at work by considering the Church's continuous growth as both objective ground *for* subjective faith and objective ground *of* subjective faith.

An addict's "pledge" to faith healing through the method of "conversion" results in a "dope fiend" changing his or her life. For the Church, this started in 1967 with a handful of "saved" former addicts helping to heal other addicts through salvation in Christ Jesus. The growth of the Church over the past forty years has become "evidence" for other users for the possibility of objective healing through subjective faith. For example, in Church services, a common practice is for former users to give testimonies of conversion. Moreover, there is a tremendous intermixing of international Church members as they visit one another's churches across the globe. In the years that I have attended Sunday worship services, I have listened to testimonies of members from South Africa, Europe, Southeast Asia, Latin America, and all over the United States (Robbins 2009; Coleman 2003). These testimonies provide a glimpse of life outside the urban enclave of the barrio. As Gabriel shared with me:

> So, the fifth time I was in, I had a case pending for dealing. That is how I supported my habit. Anyway I ended up picking up another case inside for a fight. I busted this guy's face wide open. I hurt him bad. I was looking at over three years in prison. I said "whatever." I'll do it.
> But as I was fighting the case, I realized that I was going to end up like my dad. Or, like these tore up shot callers. They were fifty-year-old men who acted like they were sixteen. I started to feel disgusted at what I would become if I continued on this path in prison.

The Home attempts to move an addict like Gabriel away from a "perpetual liminality" of prison recidivism and drug relapse by way of habituated practices of pistis power. This equipping of faith is described as "spiritual technologies" (Jeavons 1998)—works of mercy in redemptive salvation in the deliverance of God. Further, they permit individuals, with the help of others, to effect their own means of transformation by a number of operations on their bodies, thoughts, conduct, or ways of being (Foucault 2003b). These technologies are also acts of service in the practice of caring for the soul that transform the self. A consequence of this spiritual approach can be a "rebound effect," allowing the saved not only tranquility of the soul (Foucault 2005, 16), but the faculties to help others to take care of themselves. Rene, a recovering addict in the Home, conveys this point:

> I didn't know a way out [of my heroin addiction and prison recidivism] until the Church.
> They [church members] would pray for us on the streets, and when I really started losing everything and hurting my family and myself, I remember their prayers, that there was hope for me, whereas other people told me that you are going to die in prison—a dope fiend.
> And it was eating me up inside and at a point I didn't want that life.
> They told me that there is something better, and I never forgot that. So when I had the opportunity to go in [to the Home], I did, and I have never been the same, and the feeling is like no other feeling through drugs or relationships.
> I had fallin' out of the Home a few times, but I knew that I had to get back, I knew that is where the answer is.
> This is my third time back in the Home, and I have been here over eleven months, and I just want to tell other people that there is a way.

There is no denying the biochemical conditioning of chronic drug use or the structural factors and medical consequences of heroin addiction (Ciccarone et al. 2001; Ciccarone 2009). For those dope fiends falling in and out of chronic drug relapse, and for those achieving long term sobriety, a "regime of the self" through habitual drug use or struggles with daily soberness is shaped by a knowledge of, relating to, and affecting the body, entangled in an often prudent yet always enterprising life course of a "somatic individuality" (Rose 2006; Novas and Rose 2000). Further, opioid abuse and recovery foster the formation of a "biosociality" in a collectivity (Rabinow 1996). A conversation I had with Gabriel conveys this point, as he talks about the trust he had for Julian, his "running partner" (Bourgois and Schonberg 2009, 215), who eventually helped him in his faith recovery from addiction:

> So I remembered that my old running partner, Julian. We were homies ever since we were li'l kids riding bikes. Julian was a staff member at the Home.
> So a year prior, I was runnin' the streets. I used to love being in the street, in the hood—where all the action was! Anyway Julian had gotten clean through the Home and he "witnessed" to me and let know whenever I want to change, there is a bed for me at the Home.
> When he prayed for me, I really didn't think nothing of it. He was still my homeboy, and my old running partner, so I trusted him.
> Anyway a year later I am in jail trying to fight this case and feeling nauseated by all people that surrounded me. These older guys that I had respected before as veteranos, now just made me sick. Then I thought about my dad.
> So I got ahold of Julian and the Home people. I was going to court twice a month, and the Home staff would show up to plead my case, so that I could not go to prison but rather do my time in the Home.
> I was arrested on Feb. 13 and on the May 13 of that same year, the judge suspended my sentence and released me to the Home.
> I never ever went to church in my entire life. I didn't know anything about God or religion. I went into the Home with the mentality of changing my life, I didn't think that it would be through God. When I first got there I thought it was pretty weird 'cus of all the spirituality. I thought that worship songs sounded childish, like for li'l kids.
> But my running partner was there, so I thought at least my homeboy is here. And he had changed his life—was all clean, was happy and had peace.
> The Home has a very strong spiritual atmosphere, it took me a while to get use to all that. At least I wasn't in an atmosphere that made me nauseous.

Secular, private, and public responses to addiction and recovery operate without necessarily considering the "soul" as part of the equation of healing. How to care for a hurting soul through spirituality is seemingly a different kind of working on one's self in the recovery process. Although there is a growing and rich corpus of literature on substance abuse, spirituality, and religion, primarily in the social psychology discourse (Amaro, Mangual, and Nieves 2004; Dermatis, Guschwan, Galanter, and Bunt 2004; Galanter 1997 and 2006; Gorsuch and Miller 1999; Hatch, Burg, Naberhaus, and Hellmich 1998; Miller 1999), the approach to treating one's soul is ostensibly a less scientific, less medical kind of "technology of the self" (Foucault 2003b). For some, the soul is simply part of the "psyche," and spirituality is a less controlled or less relevant unit of analysis; as Miller and Bogenschutz write: "According to . . . ideology and the testimonials of many individuals who have achieved sobriety . . . spiritual growth is the engine that maintains sobriety, defined as abstinence and increased well-being. To date, scientific study of the recovery process has been unable to verify this claim" (2007, 434).

Emergence of Bio-pistis as a Mode of Power

In the court case that begins this chapter, the Proposition 36 representative tells the judge, "Your Honor, you cannot allow this young man to go to this recovery Home because they are not state licensed."

The judge replies, "This Church had a history of success long before Prop. 36." The judge then asks the minister, "Is your recovery Home state licensed?"

"No, Your Honor," the minister says. "We are not because we don't opt to be licensed. We do what works, and we have had great success, and we don't want the state regulating how we run our programs. . . ."

The minister continues, "I would like to know more about state licensing, and I am not clear on exactly what are all the requirements."

The Proposition 36 representative continues to voice his opinion that the Home could not be allowed to accept this drug offender in their program. Speaking to the representative, the judge says, "What I would like for you to do is to get together with this reverend, and I want you to see what it would take to get their program licensed. They have had great success, and we referred many offenders to their program."

The representative says, "Okay, I will do that. I will call the reverend's office and set up an appointment in a week or so, but as far as this young man today, he cannot go to their program."

The judge responds, "I do not want you to talk with the reverend in a week. I want you to go into the hallway right now and discuss this with him, and we are going to retain this young man until you are done talking."

The pastor and representative go into the hallway, and the representative explains some of the requirements, including the number of hours of education necessary and the provision of twenty-four hour supervision. By the end of their chat, both have discovered that the Home actually supersedes many of the requirements of Proposition 36. When they return to the courtroom, the representative tells the judge, "Well, I just met with the pastor and their program actually surpasses our requirements, and I recommend that this young man be released to their faith-based program."

The Home met the requirements for a Level Four Treatment program, which handles the most severe addicts, and the judge released the young man to the Home that same day. Proposition 36 was a fairly new program, but the judge was aware of the success of the Home, and thus pushed the Church to move toward an emerging mode that I am calling *bio-pistis*.

As a modality of power, bio-pistis is emerging from the ways substance abuse treatment is defined and measured in relation to secular biopolitical governance of pistis or faith programs. This recovery Home did acquire its state license and had to make minor shifts in its lexicon, such as the "ministry" of the Home being referred to instead as the "treatment program." But unlike the Church's 1975 acceptance of state funds that carried strict bureaucratic secular stipulations, today's licensure has created no real impediment to the day to day faith practices of the Home. The major bureaucratic shifts involved following specific state guidelines of intake interviews, charting progress reports, and creating treatment plans with benchmark goals, much of which the Home had already been doing. Now these biopolitical practices must be reported to the State monthly, with rosters documenting the ethnicity of clients, their ages, and other demographics. The director of this Home felt that this electronic tracking system would benefit his ministry by providing statistical measurements of success and recidivism rates as well as demographic data.

Another benefit is that all Home staff members complete Alcohol and Other Drug (AOD) training as a requirement for state licensing. In "traditional" Homes the staff are considered paraprofessionals, with most not having formal biomedical education for the treatment of drug addicts. Rather, most have been former addicts who have become sober and saved through the Home's faith program. AOD training gives the staff a better understanding of the different needs that must be addressed for addicts. In the words of the pastor,

> In the past we have focused primarily on the spiritual needs, but there are other issues too, like health, social, and financial needs. So now we are able to put together a treatment plan addressing all addicts' social and spiritual issues and with the state licensing we can better access to the county social resources. This helps the addicts understand that God knows all their needs, and with the treatment plan we are able to let them know that God cares about all their needs. He cares about their health, about their social problems and all those areas from the faith-based foundation.

In this study, what emerges when considering the conceptual framing of bio-pistis is a different relational "object" in the common problem space of substance abuse managementality. In the composition of biopolitics, the specialist is a social technocrat whose relational object is "population-bodies." And, in pistis-politics, the specialist is a pastor whose object is "soul-community." In bio-pistis the specialist is an augmented faith leader/social technocrat, and the relational object becomes population-body-soul.

In the milieu of drug dependency is a continuum of institutional sites and discursive practices ranging from incarceration to medical treatment to faith healing, each working on the drug abuser in competing and complementary modes of power. For the problem of substance abuse, the modalities of power (carceral, bio, or pistis) are linked to knowledge and "care for the self," and thus work upon addicts through the notions of the body, the population, and the soul. The integration of government bureaucratic, symbolic, and economic support into faith healing practices is an emerging modality of power that I describe as bio-pistis. In this chapter's conceptual and ethnographic framing of power, knowledge, and care of the substance abuser, the contemporary effectiveness of "faith healing" (Cnaan and Boddie 2006) is considered as a relationship between biopower and pistis power. Thus faith is viewed not as an epiphenomenon but rather as a "social fact" (Durkheim 1982) and a valid component of human practice for substance abuse recovery (Neff 2006; Chen 2006). Further, I consider faith healing through the *method* of "conversion" (Rambo 1993; Buckser and Glazier 2003). Conversion by faith is a perpetual equipping through "spiritual technologies," "works of mercy and acts of service" by way of "caring for the soul." I offer that "bio-pistis" emerges in the collaboration between Church and State as the procedural and philosophical nexus of drug policy and the faith healing (Giordano 2008; Sullivan 2009; Brandes 2002). This interconnectedness may be understood as a vital component of spiritual, physical, and social rehabilitation processes for substance abusers.

Notes

For their intellectual and moral support in this chapter I am indebted to my friends and collegues Anaita Khudonazar, Edoardo Zavarella, Kevin Karpiak, Gaymon Bennett, James Adam Redfield, Madina Regnault, Jose Arias, Jackie Ramos, Malcolm Hoover, Derrick Michael Hensman, Josey Pineda, Sonny Arguinzoni, ISSC Graduates Fellows, BELS Graduates Fellows, the Project RELATE team members; to Professors Patricia Baquedano-López, Paul Rabinow, Megan Comfort, Philippe Bourgois, Daniel H. Ciccarone, Stanley Brandes, William F. Hanks, Cristiana Giordano, Saul Mercado, Jonathan Simon, David Minkus, Susan Suntree; and to the Editors: Tara Hefferan, Julie Adkins, and Laurie Occhipinti.

This research was supported in part by the National Institute of Mental Health (R01MH078743) and the National Institutes of Health grant (DA10164); the RELATE project, the Center for AIDS Prevention Studies (CAPS) at the University of California, San Francisco; a Block Grant from the University of California, Berkeley in the Department of Anthropology; the Center for Latino Policy Research (CLPR); the Institute for the Study of Social Change (ISSC); and the Berkeley Empirical Legal Studies at The Center for the Study of Law and Society, UC Berkeley School of Law.

1. All informant names are pseudonyms.
2. Mexican-American or Latino inner-city neighborhoods.
3. "Flourishing involves more than success in achieving projects; it extends to the kind of human being one is personally, vocationally, and communally. Flourishing is a translation of a classical term (*eudaemonia*): thriving, the good life, happiness, fulfillment, felicity" (Rabinow and Bennett 2007).

Works Cited

Amaro, H., S. Mangual, and R. L. Nieves. 2004. *Spirituality in recovery: An educational group curriculum for women in recovery.* Boston Consortium of Services for Families in Recovery, Public Health Commission, Boston, MA.

Appadurai, Arjun. 1990. Topographies of the self and emotion in Hindu India. In *Language and the politics of emotion,* ed. Catherine A. Lutz and Lila Abu-Lughod, 92-112. Cambridge: Cambridge University Press.

———. 1996. *Modernity at large: Cultural dimensions of globalization.* Minneapolis: University of Minnesota Press.

Bielo, James. 2009. *Words upon the word: An ethnography of Evangelical group Bible study.* New York: New York University Press.

Bourdieu, Pierre. 1990. *The logic of practice.* Trans. Richard Nice. Stanford, CA: Stanford University Press.

———. 2000. *Pascalian meditations.* Trans. Richard Nice. Stanford, CA: Stanford University Press.

Bourdieu, Pierre, and Loïc J. D. Wacquant. 1992. *An invitation to reflexive sociology.* Chicago: The University of Chicago Press.

Bourgois, Phillippe. 2000. Disciplining addictions: The bio-politics of methadone and heroin in the United States. *Culture, Medicine and Psychiatry* 24(2):165-95.

———. 2002 [1995]. *In search of respect: Selling crack in El Barrio.* New York: Cambridge University Press.

Bourgois, Philippe, and Jeff Schonberg. 2009. *Righteous dopefiend.* Berkeley: University of California Press.

Braman, Donald. 2004. *Doing time on the outside: Incarceration and family life in urban America.* Ann Arbor, MI: University of Michigan Press.

Brandes, Stanley. 2002. *Staying sober in Mexico City.* Austin: University of Texas Press.

Buckser, Andrew, and Stephen D. Glazier. 2003. *The anthropology of religious conversion.* Lanham, MD: Rowman and Littlefield.

Castillo Cocom, Juan, and Timoteo Rodriguez. n.d. Ethnoexodus: Maya topographic ruptures. In *The only true people: Linking Mayan identities past and present,* ed. Bethany Myers and Lisa LeCount. Boulder, CO: University Press of Colorado.

Chen, Gila. 2006. Social support, spiritual program, and addiction recovery. *International Journal of Offender Therapy and Comparative Criminology* 50(3):306-23.

Ciccarone, Daniel. 2009. Heroin in brown, black and white: Structural factors and medical consequences in the U.S. heroin market. *International Journal of Drug Policy* 20(3):277-82.

Ciccarone, D., J. D. Bamberger, A. H. Kral, B. R. Edlin, C. J. Hobart, A. Moon, E. L. Murphy, P. Bourgois, H. W. Harris, and D. M. Young. 2001. Soft tissue infections among injection drug users—San Francisco, California, 1996-2000. *Morbidity and Mortality Weekly Report* 50(19):381-84.

Clear, Todd R. 2007. *Imprisoning communities: How mass incarceration makes disadvantaged neighborhoods worse.* New York: Oxford University Press.

Cnaan, Ram A., and Stephanie C. Boddie. 2006. Setting the context: Assessing the effectiveness of faith-based social services. *Journal of Religion and Spirituality in Social Work* 25(3/4):5-18.

Coleman, Simon, ed. 2003. The faith movement: A global religious culture? Special issue of *Culture and Religion* 3(1).

Comfort, Megan. 2008. *Doing time together: Love and family in the shadow of the prison.* Chicago: University of Chicago Press.

Dermatis, H., M. T. Guschwan, M. Galanter, and G. Bunt. 2004. Orientation toward spirituality and self-help approaches in the therapeutic community. *Journal of Addictive Diseases* 23(1):39-54.

Durkheim, Emile. 1982 *The rules of the sociological method.* Ed. Steven Lukes. Trans. W. D. Halls. New York: Free Press.

Fassin, Didier. 2009. Another politics of life is possible. *Theory, Culture and Society* 26(5):44–60.

Foucault, Michel. 1977 [1975]. *Discipline and punish: The birth of the prison.* Trans. Alan Sheridan. New York: Pantheon.

———. 1979. Omnes et singulatim: Towards a criticism of "political reason." The Tanner Lectures on Human Values Delivered at Stanford University, October 10 and 16.

———. 1987. The ethic of care for the self as a practice of freedom. An interview with Michel Foucault on January 20, 1984 conducted by Raúl Fornet-Betancourt, Helmut Becker, Alfredo Gomez-Müller. Trans. J. D. Gauthier. *Philosophy and Social Criticism* 12(2-3):112-31.

———. 2003a. *"Society must be defended": Lectures at the Collège de France 1975–1976.* Trans. David Macey. New York: Picador.

———. 2003b. *The essential Foucault: Selections from essential works of Foucault, 1954-1984.* Ed. Paul Rabinow and Nikolas S. Rose. New York and London: New Press.

———. 2005. *The hermeneutics of the subject: Lectures at the Collège de France 1981–1982.* Ed. Frédéric Gros. Trans. Graham Burchell. New York: Picador.

———. 2009. *Security, territory, population: Lectures at the Collège de France 1977-1978.* Ed. Michel Senellart. Trans. Graham Burchell. New York: Picador.

Galanter, Marc. 1997. Spiritual recovery movements and contemporary medical care. *Psychiatry* 60(3):211-23.

———. 2006. Spirituality and addiction: A research and clinical perspective. *American Journal on Addictions* 15(4):286-92.

Garland, David. 2001. *The culture of control: Crime and social order in contemporary society.* Chicago: University of Chicago Press.

Gilmore, Ruth W. 2007. *Golden gulag: Prisons, surplus, crisis, and opposition in globalizing California.* Berkeley: University of California Press.

Giordano, Cristiana. 2008. Practices of translation and the making of migrant subjectivities in contemporary Italy. *American Ethnologist* 35(4):588-606.

Gorsuch, Richard L., and William R. Miller. 1999. Assessing spirituality. In *Integrating spirituality into treatment: Resources for practitioners,* ed. William R. Miller, 47-64. Washington, DC: American Psychological Association.

Hansen, Helena. 2005. Isla evangelista—A story of church and state: Puerto Rico's faith-based initiatives in drug treatment. *Culture, Medicine and Psychiatry* 29(4):433-56.

Hatch, Robert L., Mary Ann Burg, Debra S. Naberhaus, and Linda K. Hellmich. 1998. The Spiritual Involvement and Beliefs Scale: Development and testing of a new instrument. *Journal of Family Practice* 46(6):476-86.

Hay, David M. 1989. Pistis as "ground for faith" in Hellenized Judaism and Paul. *Journal of Biblical Literature* 108(3):461-76.

Irwin, John. 2004. *The warehouse prison: Disposal of the new dangerous class.* Los Angeles: Roxbury.

Jeavons, Thomas H. 1998. Identifying characteristics of "religious" organizations: An exploratory proposal. In *Sacred companies: Organizational aspects of religion and religious aspects of organizations*, ed. N. J. Demerath III, Peter Dobkin Hall, Terry Schmitt, and Rhys H. Williams, 78-95. New York: Oxford University Press.

Magnani, Laura, and Harmon L. Wray. 2006. *Beyond prisons: A new interfaith paradigm for our failed prison system*. Minneapolis: Fortress Press.

Meranze, Michael. 1996. *Laboratories of virtue: Punishment, revolution, and authority in Philadelphia, 1760-1835*. Chapel Hill, NC: University of North Carolina Press.

Miller, William R. 1999. *Integrating spirituality into treatment: Resources for practitioners*. Washington, DC: American Psychological Association.

Miller, William R., and Michael P. Bogenschutz. 2007. Spirituality and addiction. *Southern Medical Journal* 100(4):433-6.

Neff, James Alan. 2006. Contrasting faith-based and traditional substance abuse treatment programs. *Journal of Substance Abuse Treatment* 30(1):49-61.

Novas, Carlos, and Nikolas Rose. 2000. Genetic risk and the birth of the somatic individual. *Economy and Society* 29(4):485-513.

Petryna, Adriana. 2002. *Life exposed: Biological citizenship after Chernobyl*. Princeton, NJ: Princeton University Press.

Rabinow, Paul. 1996. *Essays on the anthropology of reason*. Princeton, NJ: Princeton University Press.

Rabinow, Paul, and Gaymon Bennett. 2007. *A diagnostic of equipmental platforms*. Berkeley, CA: Anthropology of the Contemporary Research Collaboratory.

Rabinow, Paul, and Nikolas Rose. 2006. Biopower today. *BioSocieties* 1:195-217.

Rambo, Lewis R. 1993. *Understanding religious conversion*. New Haven, CT: Yale University Press.

Rhodes, Lorna A. 2004. *Total confinement: Madness and reason in the maximum security prison*. Berkeley: University of California Press.

Robbins, Joel. 2009. Pentecostal networks and the spirit of globalization: On the social productivity of ritual forms. *Social Analysis* 53(1):55-66.

Rodriguez, Luis J. 1993. *Always running: La vida loca: Gang days in L.A.* Willimantic, CT: Curbstone Press.

Rose, Nikolas. 2006. *The politics of life itself: Biomedicine, power, and subjectivity in the twenty-first century*. Princeton, NJ: Princeton University Press.

Scheper-Hughes, Nancy. 1996. Small wars and invisible genocides. *Social Science and Medicine* 43(5):889-900.

Simon, Jonathan. 2000. From the big house to the warehouse: Rethinking prisons and state government in the 20th century. *Punishment and Society* 2(2):213-34.

———. 2001. "Entitlement to cruelty": Neo-liberalism and the punitive mentality in the United States. In *Crime, risk and justice: The politics of crime control in liberal democracies*, ed. Kevin Stenson and Robert R. Sullivan, 125-43. Portland, OR: Willan Publishing.

Sullivan, Winnifred Fallers. 2009. *Prison religion: Faith-based reform and the Constitution*. Princeton, NJ: Princeton University Press.

Turner, Victor W. 1969. *The ritual process: Structure and anti structure*. Chicago: Aldine Publishing.

U.S. Government Accountability Office (GAO). 2006. *Faith-based and community initiative: Improvements in monitoring grantees and measuring performance could enhance accountability*. Available online from www.gao.gov/products/GAO-06-616 (last accessed March 1, 2010).

Van Gennep, Arnold. 1960 [1908]. *Rites of Passage.* Trans. M. B. Vizedom and G. L. Caffee. Chicago: University of Chicago Press.

Wacquant, Loïc. 2001. Deadly symbiosis: When ghetto and prison meet and mesh. *Punishment and Society* 3(1):95-133.

———. 2008. *Urban outcast: A comparative sociology of advanced marginality.* Cambridge, MA: Polity Press.

Chapter 12
Straight from the Devil: Contours of
"the Public" in American Public Health
William Garriott

> I do not do the good I want, but the
> evil I do not want is what I do.
> *Romans 7:19*

Introduction

There is no shortage of options for faith-based addiction treatment. A Google search of the phrase "faith based addiction treatment" generates approximately 327,000 hits, with links to numerous organizations from a variety of faiths. In 2001, The National Center on Addiction and Substance Abuse at Columbia University published a paper emphasizing the positive role faith can play in the prevention of and recovery from substance abuse and addiction (CASA 2001). Programs such as Teen Challenge, developed in the United States, have become the model for faith-based recovery programs globally (Hansen 2004).

Politically, expanding the nation's addiction treatment system by extending faith-based options was a key component of President George W. Bush's highly publicized Faith-Based and Community Initiative. During his 2003 State of the Union Address, President Bush announced the creation of Access to Recovery (ATR). ATR provided $100 million annually in competitive grants which states and tribal authorities used to create voucher systems for the provision of a range of addiction services, including those that were faith-based. By 2007, ATR had funded nearly 5,000 programs throughout the United States. Of these, over 1,000 were faith-based. Furthermore, almost one-third of all vouchers issued through ATR were redeemed for faith-based services (The White House 2008).

But there is another story to be told about the relationship between religion, addiction, and recovery in the United States. Just as faith has been touted as an aid to recovery and prevention—at times utilized by government to expand its provision of treatment and related social services through the private sphere—so, too, have religious understandings of addiction produced stigma and discouraged treatment provision in the public health sector. As Levine (1978) noted in his classic account of the development of the concept of addiction, it was through the efforts of religious leaders that the regular (and often gratuitous) consumption of alcohol was transformed from an unremarkable part of everyday life to an evil to be spurned and resisted. This moral opprobrium on the consumption of intoxicating substances inaugurated the inquiries that led to the modern concept of addiction. This same moral judgment continues to haunt efforts to medicalize the condition and turn it from a question of public propriety into one of public health (Conrad and Schneider 1992).

In this chapter I examine how religious understandings continue to be embedded in the public response to addiction in the United States. Whereas other contributions to this volume show religion's role in creating and maintaining institutions, in this chapter I show how religion manufactures their absence. That is, in the United States, the religious roots of the concept of addiction continue to prevent the creation of a robust institutional infrastructure centered on addiction as a public health problem.

The focus is on OxyContin, the synthetic painkiller that over the past decade has caused numerous problems, particularly in the rural United States, resulting in a number of lawsuits against the manufacturer. As I show, religious understandings of addiction—and personhood more generally—directly shaped how the OxyContin problem developed and was understood by the U.S. public. But as I also show, religious understandings alone did not create this situation. Rather, a variety of factors were at work, including: the marketing campaign initiated by OxyContin's manufacturer, changing conceptualizations of pain in U.S. culture, an inadequate mental health infrastructure in rural areas, the dramatic expansion of the pharmaceutical industry in the last half of the twentieth century, and the more general pharmaceuticalization of health. By locating religion in this wider social and historical milieu, I examine the process by which "publics" are made, and show how this analysis sheds light on public response to OxyContin and similar crises in health.

Addiction and the Public Sphere

In 2005, FedEx—the global shipping giant based in Memphis, Tennessee—stopped delivering packages from online pharmacies to sections of eastern Kentucky. Prescription drug abuse had become a major problem in this area, and delivery personnel were becoming scared to make deliveries. "This is just an added measure which we think provides a level of safety and security for our employees and our customers," stated Ryan Furby, a spokesman for FedEx (Alford 2005a).

Employees for another shipping giant, UPS, have had similar encounters, though they are continuing to make deliveries. "I've had reports of at least ten people gathered around a UPS truck picking up their packages," said Danny Webb, Sheriff of Letcher County. "If a driver goes up one of these hollows and comes up on six or eight people who know he has drugs on there, they may decide to take them. There's a legitimate concern there." Webb, who described the prescription drug problem in the area as "monumental," received drug-related complaints on a daily basis. The complaints often come from mail distribution centers where individuals, at times intoxicated, come to pick up or await the arrival of packages of medications from internet pharmacies, many of which are unlicensed and therefore illegal. "We don't tolerate the use of our system for illegal purposes," FedEx's spokesman stated. "We want to be the most responsible shipper in the industry. That's why we have taken on this additional measure." While Sheriff Webb understood FedEx's decision to stop making deliveries from internet pharmacies in the area, he also worried about the consequences others might face. "You've got people who get insulin and medicine that's non-narcotic. I just hope it doesn't hurt senior citizens about getting their legitimate medications" (Alford 2005a).

This is an examination of addiction. It is also an examination of how "publics" are made. By "public" I have in mind both Habermas's "public sphere" and "the public" assumed in the case of "public health."[1] The two groups are not the same. However, they share a common trait: they are both predicated on a particular understanding of human freedom. The understanding of human freedom assumed in this case revolves around the image of the "individualized, autonomous, and self-possessed political subject of right, will and agency" (Rose 1999, 1). Human collectivities with political interests—races, classes, interest groups, etc.—are imagined in similar terms. Freedom, in this instance, is defined in the negative, as the absence of coercion or domination, which allows the "essential subjective will of an individual, a group or a people" to express itself in robust terms (Rose 1999, 1).

Robust, but morally appropriate terms, of course. And this is the positive aspect of freedom, in which authoritative institutions work to "make people free" by encouraging them in the name of justice, rationality, or public health to actualize their liberty, to become wiser, healthier, or more virtuous than they would otherwise be—to become "better than well," as one author has put it (Elliott 2003).

Thus the paradox of freedom: to ensure it requires an entire administrative apparatus whose capacity to coerce and dominate often undercuts the very liberties it is there, presumably, to maintain. The subject of freedom, we might say, is thereby positioned as the limit to a certain form of power, while likewise requiring other forms of power for its production (Rose 1999, 61ff.). This paradox is captured perfectly in a statement made by Montesquieu in 1765: "Liberty consists not in doing what one wishes, but in being able to do what one ought to wish, and in not being forced to do what one ought not to wish" (quoted in Levi-Strauss 1985, 280). "But," as Claude Levi-Strauss retorts, "how can one know what one ought to wish?" (Levi-Strauss 1985, 280). It is precisely this issue, desire as a problem of governance, that the question of addiction brings into relief. As such, addiction is one of the many vanishing points where statehood and personhood interface.

Four years before FedEx made its decision to stop making deliveries in eastern Kentucky, Sam Cox of Justice, West Virginia, stood inside the New Hope Victory Center Church speaking to a reporter about overcoming his addiction to the prescription painkiller OxyContin. Mr. Cox attributed the recovery to his faith, and to the recognition that his problem was more than a simple medical condition. "I always thought I had a drug problem," he stated, "but now I know the pills are straight from the devil. The devil comes to steal your soul. That's his job every day. The drug is the demon spirit" (Borger 2001).

While Mr. Cox's recovery is atypical, his approach to recovery is not. There is a long history of treating addiction morally, as a "disease of the will," in Western culture (Valverde 1998). Here, the moral valence of what is taken elsewhere to be a strictly biological process is highlighted through the iconography of evil which adorns Mr. Cox's narrative, in which the pills are "straight from the devil" and the drug is "the demon spirit." If Mr. Cox's experience is typical (and I believe it is), then mapping the experience of addiction in its various registers—medical, legal, religious—becomes particularly important for understanding the administration of public health.

Such a mapping is the goal of this chapter. Thus, it has as a constant refrain this question of freedom. In tracing the genealogy of the concept of freedom in Western political thought, the importance of Christian conceptions of law and sin, flesh and spirit, etc., are often noted. But this influence is taken only as a moment in the overall development leading to our present administration of freedom in the context of a secular society and state. As such, this developmental approach assumes either that current notions of freedom have replaced the original Christian formation, or that the Christian form remains present but hidden, as part of freedom's genealogy. In what follows I hope to affirm both views, while also moving past them. By assuming a kind of sedimentation process in the structuring of social life (De Landa 1997), I will show how public life remains animated by religious forces even in (supposedly) secular nation-states such as the United States of America. In the "resonance" (Luhmann 1989) established between the Christian position sedimented in contemporary extra-ecclesial notions of freedom, and this position's current expression in contemporary Christian practice, the social forces shaping the experience of addiction are shown to be discordant with the concerns of public health.

OxyContin[2]

In the fall of 2003, when conservative talk show host Rush Limbaugh made a statement on his nationally syndicated radio talk show acknowledging his addiction to prescription painkillers, it was the first time many people had heard of the drug OxyContin. For others, however, it was but the most public manifestation of the "plague" sweeping certain sectors of the eastern United States. In the Appalachian region, the name "hillbilly heroin" began springing up in local papers, in which stories of illegal activities related to OxyContin use became increasingly frequent.

The rising media attention increased federal awareness. And so, in addition to Limbaugh's confession, 2003 saw the publication of a study by the General Accounting Office of the United States which addressed growing concern about the rise in crime related to the drug, as well as spikes in its divergence and unintended use. Central to this study were the conditions under which it was developed, legalized, and made available. In particular, the study found that Purdue Pharma, the company that makes the drug, was uncommonly aggressive in its marketing of OxyContin. In addition to the usual promotional and sales tactics, the study found that the company exaggerated the number of pain situations in which OxyContin could be used. But before examining the development of the OxyContin problem in more detail, it will be helpful to discuss the drug itself briefly in more detail.

OxyContin is a prescription painkiller. Its only active ingredient is the opioid oxycodone. It is similar to other opiates and opioids such as morphine, codeine, fentanyl, methadone, and heroin. It is manufactured by Purdue Pharma, a once small pharmaceutical company based in Connecticut. OxyContin came on the pharmaceutical scene in the late 1990s, billed as the cutting edge in chronic pain management. At the time it was a breakthrough because it combined a high dose of pain relief medication with a time release mechanism. This meant that one or two pills could be used to consistently manage chronic pain. It also meant that OxyContin could be used by a wider range of pain sufferers, since, it was assumed, the mechanism that would mitigate against its abuse was built into the drug itself. Thus marketing of the drug quickly moved beyond the original target population—terminal cancer patients—to those suffering more generally from pain, whether chronic or acute.

The result was a massive influx of the drug onto the healthcare scene. Doctors were misled about the drug's addictive potential. And it did not take long to discover that, by merely crushing the pill, the full dose of the medication could be experienced all at once, producing a high similar to heroin. The effect on the eastern rural United States was instantaneous, especially in the Appalachian region. From Maine down through the southern Appalachians, the drug became easily accessible and highly desired. Each of the affected regions shared a number of common features: large populations of the disabled and chronically ill; relatively bleak local economies with high rates of unemployment; a separation from urban-oriented drug trafficking; and a history of prevalent alcohol, nicotine, and prescription drug use, often at high levels.[3] Such characteristics, so it seems, provided fertile ground in which the illicit use of OxyContin could flourish.

Intimations of these developments can be found in the ethnographic record. Kathleen Stewart's *A Space on the Side of the Road* concludes with a number of ethnographic fragments from her informants in West Virginia. In these accounts, all of the above regional indices related to the outbreak of OxyContin are present. I include here the account of Sanie Walker. The richness of the account, together with its contextualization of prescription drug use, justifies quoting it in full:

> Sanie Walker says she feels bad where she has enough and other people don't. She thinks about it a lot, she really does. She has these renters who can't pay their rent. He was working on the WIN program and then he didn't get hired and they were getting checks and then they got cut off those and he started to work at Charlie's (a gas station) but he only gets thirty-five dollars a week—that's a job for a young, single man, not for a married man. And the wife cries but Sanie's not gonna do a thing about it, she'd be the last one to do a thing about it. She's got the nerves somethin' bad, she gets so out of breath after workin' for ten minutes she can't even say hello to you. She goes to bed at night and she can't sleep at all and she just screams. Screeeams. The room spins around with the dizzy and everything gets just as black as coal. She sent away some card to get some Valium in Williamson, Kentucky. She lost the prescriptions Dr. Ross gave her. Why doesn't she get another one? *Oh no*, Dr. Ross would kill her (Stewart 1996, 208-9; emphasis in original).

Stewart's account was published in 1996. OxyContin was legalized in 1995. This decision came in the wake of a general shift in the medical profession's approach to pain. Opiates and opioids, whose pain-alleviating potential has been known for centuries, were typically administered only in situations of severe chronic pain, and then only under strictly supervised conditions. Fear of the potential for addiction would allow no more. However, beginning in the 1980s a notion began to spread—based on a few clinical studies, but primarily through cultural momentum—that pain was being under-treated in the United States. The American Pain Society, for instance, recommended that pain be treated as the fifth vital sign, in addition to pulse, blood pressure, core temperature, and respiration, so that asking about pain during patient evaluations would become routine in health care settings (U.S. General Accounting Office 2003, 8). The focus was primarily the pain of cancer patients, but was soon generalized, due in large part to the collaborative efforts of patient advocacy groups and pharmaceutical companies. The result was that consumption of morphine—another opioid, like OxyContin—rose in the United States between 1990 and 1994 by 75 percent.

This period also saw the advent of direct-to-consumer advertising by the pharmaceutical industry. OxyContin was not marketed in this way to the same degree as, for instance, medication for certain allergies and STDs. However, just before its release onto the market, Purdue Pharma launched a large-scale "public education" program called "Partners Against Pain." This program used videos, journals, and electronic media to promote three basic ideas: pain is much more widespread than previously thought; it is treatable; and opioids are a viable option for treating many forms of pain.

Thus, shifts in thinking on the nature of pain, and the technologies available to manage it, were consistently developed in reference to anxieties about addiction. Indeed, it is precisely this anxiety that made the time-release mechanism a welcome development in the scientific and medical communities. But while these epistemic and technological shifts were the precondition for OxyContin's development, its deployment would depend on the wider infrastructure of the healthcare system of the United States, which remained largely unchanged despite the shifts in thinking regarding pain and pain management.

Capacities for Mental Health

OxyContin was introduced at a time when issues related to mental health were responsible for much of the illness experienced by U.S. citizens. As of 1999, depression was the leading cause of disability. Suicide was the leading preventable cause of death. And only cardiovascular disease played a bigger role than mental disorders in exacerbating disease burden. It is estimated that, at the time, one in five Americans had a mental disorder within a given year, most of these being anxiety disorders (e.g., phobias, panics, PTSD), although mood disorders (e.g., schizophrenia, nonaffective psychosis, bipolar) were also statistically significant (Levin and Hanson 2001).

Residents of the rural United States were not immune to these problems. If anything, the impact was greater, as the challenges of providing mental health care in the rural context only exacerbated the situation. The first challenge is administrative: the mental healthcare system in the United States has been developed primarily in an urban context. Thus, it faces fundamental difficulties when trying to serve rural populations. While most facilities are located in towns, the populations of these towns are never very high, with a significant portion of the population living in outlying areas. Thus services are difficult to access.

The comparative lack of up-to-date facilities adds a further complication. The facilities that do exist are often poorly staffed and poorly funded. Five years before the introduction of OxyContin, over 60 percent of rural areas in the United States were designated as federal mental health professional shortage areas. Similarly, 55 percent of rural counties did not have a single practicing mental health professional. In "frontier" counties (having fewer than 7 persons per square mile) there were only 1.3 psychiatrists for every 100,000 persons. In more densely populated counties (over 100 persons per square mile) the figure rose to only 10.5 psychiatrists for every 100,000. For physicians—who often provide mental health care in the absence of specific mental health services—the figures were similar. The most densely populated counties averaged only 180 physicians for every 100,000 persons (Levin and Hansen 2001). Likewise, the shortage of substance abuse treatment services has been labeled "severe": just two years before OxyContin was introduced, only 19 percent of rural hospitals offered substance abuse treatment services of any kind, and the services that were offered were sub-par compared to their urban equivalents (Rebhun and Hansen 2001).

The lack of convenient access to mental health services played a significant role in shaping the OxyContin problem and allowing it to fester. Obviously, the lack of mental health services in rural areas, particularly addiction treatment, meant few options for those who became addicted to the drug. However, there is more to the story than this. The relatively thin mental health infrastructure in rural areas created a fertile environment for pharmaceuticals to become a key component of general health care. Indeed, as the history shows, pharmaceuticals were incorporated into medical practice in rural areas often to counter the logistical and administrative challenges of rural health care. Thus, even before the introduction of OxyContin, pharmaceuticals had become a key technology in rural healthcare.

Psychiatric Power

To understand just how pharmaceuticals came to play such a significant role in rural healthcare, it will be helpful to examine the history of mental healthcare in the United States more generally. A major theme that emerges is the constant recalibration of the relationship between law and medicine. A watershed event in this regard came at the turn of the twentieth century when, under social pressure, the asylums of the nineteenth century were incorporated into a medical model by being redesignated as hospitals. While the intention was to provide a more humane form of care for the incarcerated and/or mentally ill, the transition resulted in a melding of the two models, in which the policies of incarceration and treatment remained little changed. What did change, however, was that the medical language of "disease," "treatment," "cure," etc., as well as the common psychiatric techniques of the time—lobotomy and electroshock therapy, for instance—were incorporated into the pre-existing apparatus of the asylum, which included such disciplining treatments as deadening routine, water cures, and straitjackets. A common language and treatment regimen developed in this milieu that deftly blended the medical and the penal in the name of the patient's welfare, resulting in what White (1988) has termed a model for "coercive custodial care."

In this model the focus continued to be on extended periods of institutionalization, especially for the "poor, uneducated, and unskilled" populations from which the asylums/hospitals took most of their patients (White 1988, 210). In the 1950s, however, studies began appearing suggesting that long-term institutionalization produced a host of negative results. The iatrogenic effects of institutionalization were argued to be debilitating for the patient, fostering a compromised sociability and creating an institutional dependency that produced its own form of psychosis.

These findings initiated another cultural shift in the 1960s, in which the focus was on finding community-based alternatives to institutionalization while simultaneously trying to find ways to reduce the large population of mental health patients. A host of clinics, halfway houses, and local hospitals emerged, designed to provide a buffer zone between the individual patient and the mental health institution, the latter refashioned as the last resort, not the only option. An emphasis on outpatient care, partial hospitalization, emergency services, diagnostics, rehabilitation services, and research programs was implemented to supplement the older model of long-term care (White 1988).

At roughly the same time, a new generation of mood-altering drugs was developed that dramatically reduced the behavioral problems exhibited by the mentally ill. These drugs complemented the new focus on deinstitutionalization and community-based care that predominated in the 1960s. By directly treating the symptoms of mental illness, these drugs made undertaking everyday activities more feasible, and institutionalization, therefore, less necessary.

This development was a boon for the psychiatric profession. The authority to prescribe powerful psychotropic medication allowed psychiatrists to bolster their position in the medical profession, while likewise differentiating themselves from psychologists, social workers, and nurses, who worked on similar issues but without the ability to prescribe medications. As a result, psychiatry came into its own, with the concomitant effect that psychotropic medications have become the primary—if not the only—psychiatric treatment for mental illness. Expansive mental health institutions became less necessary in this context, as a community-based model for care could be administered as long as there was someone to write, and someone to fill, prescriptions (White 1988, 218).

While the advent of a medication-based psychiatry allowed for treatment without long-term institutionalization, the iatrogenic effect of psychotropic drug use, both short and long-term, quickly became evident, and continues to be observable today. Physical side effects vary from medication to medication, but range from dry mouth and blurred vision to impotence and muscle spasms. Often these effects are reinterpreted within the context of the patient's illness, a move which can result in the prescription of—or at least the presumed need for—more drugs. This is especially true in rural settings, where facilities and resources are often inadequate to projected need. Moreover, as many have noted, there is a tendency in contexts where mental illness is stigmatized for mental problems to be dealt with strictly on the somatic level. The phenomenon of "nerves"—documented by researchers in Appalachia, Puerto Rico, Brazil, and elsewhere—is a case in point (Van Schaik 1988; Liebowitz et al. 1994; Scheper-Hughes 1992). The action typically desired from the doctor by the patient in this case is for the doctor to prescribe a fast-acting cure for the physical symptoms. In this context, the thin line that separates helpful treatment and administrative convenience is quickly blurred.

This "blurry" area is one in which psychotropic medications—and pharmaceuticals more generally—have come to proliferate. In her ethnographic work in eastern Kentucky, Eileen Van Schaik (1988) analyzed the life histories and "illness narratives" (Kleinman 1988) of eight women who had experienced bouts with "nerves." The symptoms expressed were numerous and diffuse, including feelings of nervousness, anger and impatience, fear, agitation and restlessness, insomnia, and crying. They also complained variously of stomach pains, weight loss, increased heart rate, elevated blood pressure, headaches, blackouts, and a form of panic attack referred to locally as "smothering" (Van Schaik 1988, 89).

The course of illness was equally diffuse and undetermined. Most cases demonstrated a chronic character, marked by alternating periods of improvement and crisis, during which time a range of symptoms was expressed in varying degrees. In turn, the recurring experience of nerves coalesced with other medical conditions. Van Schaik's informants spoke of diabetes, chronic cystitis, indigestion, "heart trouble," cancer, "ulcerated stomach," obesity, thyroid disorder, arthritis, hypertension, bronchitis, and pneumonia. And these conditions were all experienced amid the "accumulated distress" of marital discord, grief, family worries, limited economic opportunity, financial insecurity, and feelings of isolation.

It is within this context that medication enters the picture. All eight of the women interviewed by Van Schaik were taking some form of medication to combat their recurring symptoms. While shots and periods of hospitalization were common responses to nerves, the most common response was the use of "nerve pills"—a catch-all term referring most often to sedatives like Valium and phenobarbital. While two women reported using the pills regularly during the day and to aid in sleep, the majority used the pills only to combat acute experiences, likewise expressing concerns about their habit-forming nature. Evaluations of effectiveness were mixed: while most credited the pills with helping them achieve a state of calm, others complained of side effects. One woman noted her outright fear of the pills—an emotional response which tended to complicate her problems rather than provide relief. Thus, despite such ambivalence on the part of the women interviewed on the effects and effectiveness of nerve pills, there was a general consensus that such medications were the primary means through which one dealt with the effects of nerves.

There is a tendency of most studies to see "nerves" as a kind of culture-bound syndrome or colloquialism for "stress," which physicians must translate into a biomedical idiom (cf. Liebowitz et al. 1994). However, Van Schaik found that half of the women she interviewed had been told by their physician that their condition was the result of nerves. Moreover, in many of the encounters relayed by the women, the physician's use of the term indicated an awareness that conditions of nerves were deeply influenced by immediate life context—not psychosomatic but "sociosomatic" illness (Kleinman 1998). More than one of the interviewees had stories in which either they or a member of their family had requested hospitalization as a treatment for their nerves, only to be told by the physician, "No, your problems will be there when you return, piling up" (Van Schaik 1988, 95). In this instance the "blurry" space between care and convenience comes clearly into view: awareness on the part of doctors of the social context in which certain symptoms are produced is virtually irrelevant because they are incapable of addressing this context directly. Since the immediate affective life of the individual (and not the wider social, political, economic, or familial context) is the one arena in which physicians have the means to directly intervene, they are left with the ethical decision about whether medicating these symptoms/problems will do more harm or good, a decision which must usually be made on a case by case basis.

The situation is complicated for physicians when patients come in specifically requesting "something for my nerves." This, as noted earlier, comes from the common tendency to approach emotional problems somatically, and to expect doctors to provide a quick, powerful, and convenient "cure." Such an interaction is to be expected, it would seem, as the culture of biomedicine consistently encourages both patients and physicians to transform discursively affective life into "disordered biological processes," objectifiable as an object of study, available for treatment, recognizable as a disease (Kleinman 1995, 31).

But the prescription and use of pharmaceuticals—from psychotropics to sedatives—is more complicated than standard accounts of "medicalization" would suggest. Such accounts typically take biomedicine to task for applying "rational technical rules to deeply human experience" (Kleinman 1995, 34). By annexing that which is properly outside its domain, contemporary biomedicine medicalizes human experience, and so factors out the meaningful, existential—properly human—aspects of human life. All of this takes place in the name of greater bureaucratic rationality, acquiescence to market forces, and population administration through social control. With their emphasis on "medical hegemony," such analyses assume the total (and totally successful) penetration of the medical institution into the local healthcare landscape. But the proliferation of pharmaceuticals such as OxyContin has been much more ad hoc, as it is less reliant on medical infrastructure. Rather than the coercive force of formal institutions, "[i]t is more likely something as banal, if more threatening, as available technology, narrow professionalism, and a need to solve problems effectively" that has led to the proliferation of OxyContin (White 1988, 220). Of course medical hegemony works most efficiently in this realm of therapeutic pragmatics to which White alludes, as sophisticated studies of medicalization have demonstrated. However, as the above account of pharmaceutical use intimates, and as the OxyContin case makes clear, what is often key to the proliferation of pharmaceutical technologies is not the overbearing presence of an institutionalized medical bureaucracy, but its relative absence.

From Sickness to Badness

The response of state and federal agencies came quickly after a few years of negative press surrounding OxyContin's proliferation. Law enforcement, physicians, and local residents began complaining loudly about the sudden spike in cases of dealing and abuse. Newspapers throughout the country began running articles on "hillbilly heroin," the demand for which had resulted in a number of armed robberies of local pharmacies, illegal pain-clinics, dirty doctors, and even stories of Mafia involvement in the sale of fake MRIs. Meanwhile, Purdue Pharma nearly doubled in size and assets. Coming under increased scrutiny, they scaled back their marketing initiatives, suggesting a more limited scope for prescription. They also pulled the highest-dosage pills off the market and donated money to anti-abuse programs.

State and federal money was channeled quickly into programs taking a "comprehensive approach" to fighting drug abuse. One such program was the federally funded Appalachia High-Intensity Drug Trafficking Area (HIDTA) program. This program was designed to bring federal, state, and local police together in task forces to address the problems of drug proliferation. Headquartered in Kentucky, it covered sixty-eight counties throughout Kentucky, Tennessee, and West Virginia. The general focus of the program remains to reduce demand, increase law enforcement, and expand treatment for drug addicts.

Established in 1998, and endowed with an annual $6 million dollar budget, Appalachia HIDTA was originally focused on illegal drugs like marijuana. Since then, it has expanded its range to cover the sixty-eight counties mentioned, and shifted its focus from illegal drugs to prescription drug abuse, as well as the production and sale of methamphetamine. While proponents of the program consistently emphasize the importance of the "comprehensive approach," noting in particular that, "Treating people who have substance-abuse addictions is far cheaper than sending them to prison," a federal evaluation of the program in 2002 noted its failure to achieve the "key goal": to "bring federal, state, and local police together in a unified attack on drug traffickers." Thus, the emphasis is clear: in the case of addiction it is difficult to achieve medicalization apart from criminalization. And as I will show in the next section, a certain degree of "di-abolization" is influential as well, bringing both processes into a form of com-munication (Estep 2004).

"It Just Didn't Feel Like It Was Wrong"

As noted above, the genealogy of mental health care in the United States has the constant recalibration between the medical and the legal as one of its consistent themes. Communication between these two spheres has been important for de-termining the definition of disease and appropriate responses. In psychology, "addiction" has lost some of its credibility as a technical term. The Diagnostic Statistical Manual (DSM), which is published and regularly updated by the American Psychiatric Association, serves as the definitive authority on disease classification in the various fields of mental health. It does not use the term "ad-diction," but refers to such cases as "dependence." This term is then coupled with a specific substance upon which a patient can become dependent. In its most recent edition, the DSM-IV, these include a wide range of both legal and illegal substances, from caffeine and nicotine to alcohol and cocaine. Each is defined, in turn, through a description of common behavioral symptoms, inti-mating, presumably, individual neurological and psychological adaptations that have taken place.

While the medical organization of "dependence" around symptoms allows it to be more holistic, the legal implications of "addiction" are played out in more shifting and improvisational ways. Take, for example, the relationship between methadone, cocaine, and heroin. While all three are addictive from a physiologi-cal and pharmacological perspective, only the first is legal. Interestingly, when cocaine and heroin were first synthesized during the 1800s, they were hailed as cures for morphine addiction. But by the end of World War II, it was methadone that was being used to treat heroin addiction. "Ultimately," states Bourgois, "it can be argued that the most important pharmacological difference between the two drugs that might explain their diametrically opposed legal and medical sta-tuses is that one (heroin) is more pleasurable than the other (methadone)" (2000, 167).

But it is more than that, as Bourgois goes on to show, for it is because methadone has a greater success rate in making addiction functionally more manageable—and, therefore, things like working a job more feasible—that it surpasses heroin in utility, and therefore legality. Thus, methadone can be mapped on to a continuum, possibly as a limit, within the larger "soft-drug cul-ture" that has long marked Western civilization's "condition of tolerability." This culture is characterized by the daily general consumption of such "drug foods" as tea, coffee, chocolate, tobacco, and sugar, mild stimulants of colonial extraction whose consumption in Europe and America spiked around the time of early industrialization (Sahlins 1994, 439; cf. Mintz 1985).

The fungibility of these medical and legal distinctions, and the sociopolitical context in which they are made, is important to remember in the case of OxyContin. OxyContin is a legal, FDA-approved medication, whose ultimate purpose is, like methadone, to make life functionally more manageable and productive. It is, nevertheless, a substance which alters an individual's metabolism and states of consciousness, thus lending itself quite easily to addiction. But because it is legal, many have not thought of their dependence on the drug in terms of addiction. As Paula, a recovering addict from Man, West Virginia, put it, "Buying pills never seemed illegal. It just didn't feel like it was wrong" (Tough 2001, 32).

The interrelated domains of religion and family form the primary context in which such capacities for moral discernment are shaped. This work is accomplished, not by rote inculcation, but by providing an intimate infrastructure through which extralocal issues pertaining to law, technology, science, etc. can come into contact with local ethical and religious considerations. The strategies of response that develop continually articulate with nuanced feelings of "wrong" and "right." Such strategies of response, however, when deployed in the immediate context of everyday healthcare strivings, are both "open ended and stabilizing." They form "local ecologies of care" in which capacities for health are shaped in concert with "familial, economic, medical and pharmaceutical circumstances" (Biehl 2004, 476). They are shaped in such a way that these same determinant spheres are themselves recast through the processes of experimentation and testing that occur as the everyday engagement with symptoms gives way to the interplay over the longue durée of illness and health (Biehl 2004).

Religious associations in Appalachia and extended networks of kinship have long been central to these local ecologies of care. With the exception of German denominational affiliates and Scots-Irish Presbyterians, it was through the work of immigrant families during the early periods of immigration in the eighteenth century that a localized form of popular, loosely Protestant Christianity came into existence. The Second Great Awakening of the late eighteenth and early nineteenth centuries proved to be a catalyzing force in the region. It emphasized a religious ethos focused on personalism, emotionalism, the necessity of conversion, and the primacy of experience, which came to be shared by a number of independent churches and larger denominations, many of which otherwise differed widely on theological issues. In addition, a new set of religious forms rose in prominence during this period, including the camp meeting, song schools, shaped-note singing, and gospel music, which themselves came to be widely shared as they helped foster the emotionally charged and experientially rich revivalistic ethos (Humphrey 1988).

But despite the consolidating influence of the Second Great Awakening, differences remain. In his introduction to the volume *Christianity in Appalachia*,

Bill J. Leonard (1999) outlines a typology of contemporary religious expression and association for the region. He organizes it around four types: mainline churches, evangelical churches, pentecostal churches, and mountain churches. Within this typology, he locates four "theological polarities" which articulate difference and mobilize debate: the nature of authority, the idea of church, the idea of conversion, and the nature of ministry/leadership. Negotiation of these polarities in practice is the means by which the religious typology is animated. Moreover, it is through this movement that an outline of the Appalachian religious milieu takes shape.

Within the parameters of this milieu, a popular religiosity is palpable. Central to this popular religiosity is a sense that the everyday world is the stage upon which the spiritual struggle between the forces of good and evil takes place. Human beings participate in this struggle both directly and indirectly. Discerning the good and evil forces at work in the world is itself predicated on an understanding that life unfolds in two temporal dimensions simultaneously: the "here and now" and the hereafter. The "here and now" is taken typically to be the primary site of struggle between ordinary people, or the individual, and the forces of evil, or the Devil. Strength in the struggle comes directly from God (in any of the deity's Trinitarian guises), who, though the balance of power is precarious, is nevertheless assumed to be stronger than the Devil, and poised to reign triumphant in the eschaton. As such, though the hereafter is generally valued over the "here and now," the two temporalities are reciprocally related, especially for the individual whose soul wobbles precariously between the eternal destinies of salvation and damnation.

It is in these cosmological terms that practices of religious cultivation informing moral sentiment take place (cf. Hirschkind 2001). Certainty is always somewhat questionable and therefore must be continually "pursued" (James 1995). While properly disciplined bodies are the ideal precondition for moral discernment, the ideal is difficult to reach and maintain. Such bodies, whatever their moral state, are always simultaneously operative in a semiotic register. They are part of the "representational economy" (Keane 2002) through which the work of God and the work of the Devil are intimated. Thus, what Charles H. Lippy has written about religious media can be taken as indicative of the religious milieu more generally:

All proclaim a message of a God who cares for individuals and their problems. With only minor variation, all proffer a view of the world where the powers of evil are very real and intent on thwarting human happiness. In other words, all support that inchoate understanding basic to popular religiosity of a world where forces of good and evil are constantly engaged in combat for control of human life. All also present exuberant testimonies to the happiness and joy in living that comes from placing ultimate trust in the beneficent power of God, who can bring healing of illness and physical ailments as well as healing of psychological unsteadiness. . . . A simple faith becomes a panacea that brings very specific results and grants individuals a sense that they can muster the power to control their own destiny (Lippy 1999, 200).

A few more words on evil are in order. As illustrated above, mental health problems are often associated with evil forces, adding to the stigma of being "crazy" that of being a "bad person." Some scholars have suggested that this stems from representations of the demonic in the New Testament as a form of neurosis (Humphrey 1988). Take, for instance, the case of the Gerasene demoniac whose story is recounted in all three of the synoptic Gospels (Mark 5:1-20; Matthew 8:28-34; Luke 8:26-39). According to the Gospel of Mark, this man was possessed by an "unclean spirit" and lived among the tombs. "Night and day among the tombs and on the mountains he was crying out, and bruising himself with stones" (Mark 5:5). Jesus casts out the demon, Legion, sending it into a herd of 2,000 swine who rush headlong into the sea. The man, now recovered, is then said to be in his "right mind," and goes on to "proclaim how much Jesus had done for him; and all men marveled" (Mark 5:20b).

This representation of the demonic makes the mental space of the individual a place for the incursion of the Devil into human life. The image of the Devil, like sin, has been largely sublimated in mainstream middle class affairs. However, the image of the Devil has consistently been important to movements opposed to, among other things "modernism," which Marsden defines as "the adaptation of religious ideas to modern culture," rather than the reverse (Marsden 1980, 146). Alternatively, the image of the Devil has been taken up recently with great vigor in postcolonial contexts of Christian conversion. What many scholars have found is that the image of the Devil functions as a place-keeper for that which is excluded from the new cultural milieu. Thus, indigenous spirits, for instance, are maintained in the local cosmology through their association with the Christian image of the Devil. This preservation through exclusion indicates an ambivalence in the image of the Devil, and representations of evil more generally.

Birgit Meyer, in her work *Translating the Devil*, presents an overview of the Christian tradition of diabology. For theologians, diabology was a means through which to confront theodicy; for ordinary people the Devil provided a rich allegorical figure through which to understand the everyday encounter with evil forces. I will not rehearse here the narrative of the Devil that emerged from the folklore/theology dialectic (see Meyer 1999, 40-41 for a summary), but will simply note the image's allegorical associations.

Going back to the Protestant devotional literature of the seventeenth century, exemplified by John Bunyan's classic *The Pilgrim's Progress*, Meyer notes the strict dualism portrayed between God and the Devil. God consistently stands for "soberness" while the Devil stands for "the pleasures and values of this world" (Meyer 1999, 35). Antisocial behavior, illicit habits, sickness and death, bad desires of a sexual, culinary, material, or egotistical kind, were all consistently associated with the workings of the Devil in the world.

Protestant suspicion of ritualism and emphasis on individual salvation led to an increased internalization and individualization of diabolic imagery. The image of the encounter between Eve and the Devil (represented by the snake) in the Garden of Eden, in which Eve is given the choice to either obey God or give in to desire and temptation, becomes paradigmatic in this internalization of evil. "Though Satan, not the individual person as such, was considered the cause of the bad desires," Meyer states, "it was up to the individual to fight against them and allow for God's influence." She continues, "Rather than protecting themselves against these devilish attacks through rituals, Protestants had to cope with them privately, by relying on the weapon of the Word. Thus, the fight against Satan was basically a permanent inner struggle . . . Christians could never be sure of getting rid of the Devil's machinations in this life" (Meyer 1999, 45).

This is not to say, however, that understandings of the Devil went from externalized and personified to internalized and diffuse. On the contrary, such broad "mappings" of the space of evil and its various representations have always been present in the Christian tradition. What it points to, rather, is "the development of the notion that the inner state of a person was the main area of satanic action" (Meyer 1999, 45). This encouraged an increased focus on the self, especially in relation to the cultivation of moral sentiments and the governance of desire, but also provided a kind of hermeneutic through which one could approach understandings of others. The stage was thus set for the conflict between the powers of good and evil to take place at the level of the inner life. Bodies were disciplined or undisciplined; it did not ultimately matter, for either way they functioned as material signs of a spiritual struggle at work in the world.

The context of this spiritual struggle is essentially one of choice: either one chooses correctly, or one does not. The notion of a willing spirit with a flesh that is weak is resonant here. And indeed, it is precisely this willing spirit that is reproduced as the assumed subject in most of the medical, legal, and religious history surveyed here so far. It is no surprise, then, that histories of addiction and similar "diseases of the will" consistently show the failure of medicalization to take root in the public imagination, usually faltering in the face of the criminalizing, or diabolizing, impulse. As Mariana Valverde states, discussing the case of alcohol, "[D]espite many efforts to medicalize habitual drunkenness or alcoholism, the courts and the general public believed that heavy drinkers, if they really tried, could indeed flex their will and stop their destructive drinking." In the legal realm, "drunkenness, even if psychiatrically classified as rooted in a prior condition (dependence), is rarely thought to excuse crimes, although it may serve to mitigate the sentence" (Valverde 1998, 2).

Discussion: Contours of the Public

Jürgen Habermas is one of the premier political theorists of "the public." His work has sparked debate on the state and nature of "the public sphere," as well as the prospects of the notion for contemporary political life. What makes Habermas so provocative (and controversial) is his commitment to both the critical project of the Frankfurt School, with its focus on critiquing the consumer culture industry and the manipulation of the masses; and to the Enlightenment project, with its faith in reason, humanism and progress. This double commitment informs his notion of the public sphere by making it both an analytical tool and a normative category (Eley 1994, 300).

Generally speaking, what Habermas has in mind when discussing the public sphere is the sphere mediating society and state, in which private, freely associating citizens organize themselves as the bearers of public opinion. It embodies a democratic ideal of an enlightened body politic to which and through which the state can and should be held accountable and society maintained. As a concept, the public sphere emerged in the wake of the socioeconomic changes ushered in by the shift from feudalism through industrialization to capitalism. An incipient cosmopolitanism is assumed in its formulation, the character of which is of central importance in outlining the public sphere in both its critical and normative modes. Indeed, just as the rise of capitalism was a precondition for the public sphere, recent shifts in capitalist society threaten to undermine the public sphere itself. And it is with precisely this sense of danger present in the current historical moment that Habermas undertakes his project, as a means of theoretical and political intervention.

Placing religion in the public sphere as outlined by Habermas poses some interesting difficulties. The rise of the public sphere in the classic form to which Habermas is committed has as one of its preconditions the structural differentiation of the various spheres of human existence such that society, economy, politics, religion, etc. constitute separate domains. Religion, in this model, must remain within the limits of reason alone, and outside of political space. History, of course, shows that this ideal has rarely been realized in its pure form.

But stopping the inquiry here again limits discussion to the "reasonableness" of religion, and the kinds of religious discourse that may legitimately influence political legislation and debate. It thereby ignores the more common and informal means by which religion influences public life. Such is the case in an essay by Peter Beyer, in which he states: "What is required for publicly influential religion is, at a minimum, that religious leaders have control over a service which is clearly indispensable in today's world as do, for instance, health professionals, political leaders, scientific or business experts" (Beyer 1990, 374). By maintaining the ideal of differentiated spheres, the influence of religion is virtually inconceivable, except under strictly controlled conditions, such as the desecularization of the state. But, as Talal Asad has shown, acknowledging the presence of religion as a constitutive element of the public sphere "results in the creation of modern 'hybrids'" in which "the principal of structural differentiation . . . no longer holds" (Asad 2003, 182).

The critical task that emerges in this perspective involves tracing the contours of these hybrids as they come to constitute the public sphere itself. This is what I have attempted in this chapter. Emphasizing the sedimentation of different strata—medical, legal, religious—in the formation of the public sphere, I have suggested that it is in the resonance established between these sedimented strata and their contemporary expression that social life is animated. In the case of OxyContin, the understanding of human freedom peculiar to the West has proven to be particularly resonant. Animating the interactions between medical, legal, and religious discourses, past and present, this commitment to freedom has shaped the overarching response to the OxyContin epidemic. While the need for care and treatment programs consistently receives lip service, the bulk of the resources and effort allocated to addressing the problem are concentrated on stopping illegal sale and use through legal intervention. Thus, in the case of OxyContin, there is no "public" from the perspective of public health, only a bunch of poor, drug-dealing addicts who, when faced with social, economic, medical, and spiritual problems, reach for a bottle of pills rather than their proverbial bootstraps.

It is from this perspective that we should view the faith-based response to the OxyContin problem in Appalachia. In sections of eastern Kentucky, for example, church leaders have begun to view the problem as a ministry opportunity. New churches have emerged in Harlan County, as well as a ministry providing resources to the poor. In Manchester, Kentucky, churches have experienced an unprecedented feeling of unity as they responded to the needs of those affected. "I've been in ministry more than more than 40 years," said retired mission leader Larry Martin, "and I've never seen a movement of God in one community such as it is there" (Alford 2005b). In addition to these grassroots efforts, national programs such as "Celebrate Recovery"—an adaptation of the twelve-step model by Saddleback Church leader Rick Warren—have established a presence in Appalachian communities such as Harlan County. Though not direct products of programs such as Access to Recovery, they nevertheless complement the Bush administration's emphasis on providing social support services through the private sector.

The fact that these programs have emerged indicates why less has been done at the level of public health to address the spread of OxyContin addiction: from the public's perspective, OxyContin addicts are suffering from a moral affliction that is not the public's concern except insofar as it makes the subject a threat to others. Indeed, in Manchester, Kentucky, it was the rising crime rates in the community that spurred the churches' call to action as much as it was the needs of the addicts themselves (Alford 2005b). Put another way, chronic diseases to which addiction is often compared, such as type II diabetes, cancer, and cardiovascular disease, do not carry the same moral stigma, and therefore have not prompted the same kind of faith-based response, where faith is identified as a form of treatment for the condition. Thus addiction remains a moral affliction, giving shape to the particular public that emerges around crises such as Oxy-Contin.

Notes

1. "By 'the public sphere' we mean first of all a realm of our social life in which something approaching public opinion can be formed. Access is guaranteed to all citizens. A portion of the public sphere comes into being in every conversation in which private individuals assemble to form a public body. They then behave neither like business nor professional people transacting private affairs, nor like members of a constitutional order subject to the legal constraints of a state bureaucracy. Citizens behave as a public body when they confer in an unrestricted fashion—that is, with the guarantee of freedom of assembly and association and the freedom to express and publish their opinions—about matters of general interest. In a large public body this kind of communication requires specific means for transmitting information and influencing those who receive it. Today newspapers and magazines, radio and TV are the media of the public sphere. We speak of the political public sphere in contrast, for instance, to the literary one, when public discussion deals with objects connected to the activity of the state. Although state activity is so to speak the executor, it is not part of it. . . . Only when the exercise of political control is effectively subordinated to the democratic demand that information be accessible to the public, does the political public sphere win an institutionalized influence over the government through the instrument of law-making bodies" (from Jürgen Habermas, "The Public Sphere," *New German Critique* 3:49 [1974]. Quoted in Eley 1994).

2. The following account is based primarily on that given by Tough 2001.

3. Oxycodone, the active ingredient in OxyContin, was used recreationally before the advent of OxyContin. Tylox, a mild oxycodone-based painkiller, was chewed or snorted to generate a "somewhat euphoric and not very addictive" sensation. Tylox contains 5 mg of oxycodone plus 500 mg of acetaminophen. OxyContin, however, comes in 20, 40, 80, and, until April 2001, 160 mg pills. Worry over diversion and abuse caused the 160 mg pill to be pulled from the market. (see Clines and Meier 2001).

Works Cited

Alford, Roger. 2005a. Drug delivery halted in eastern Kentucky. *Lexington Herald-Leader.* February 25, B1.
————. 2005b. Rural drug addicts find relief in religion. *Lexington Herald-Leader.* May 14, B1.
Asad, Talal. 2003. *Formations of the secular: Christianity, Islam, modernity.* Stanford, CA: Stanford University Press
Beyer, Peter. 1990. Religion and global society. In *Global culture: Nationalism, globalization and modernity,* ed. Mike Featherstone, 373-96. London: Sage Publications.
Biehl, João. 2004. Life of the mind: The interface of psychopharmaceuticals, domestic economies, and social abandonment. *American Ethnologist* 31(4):475-96.
Borger, Julian. 2001. Hillbilly heroin: The painkiller abuse wrecking lives in West Virginia. *The Guardian.* June 25. www.guardian.co.uk/international/story/0,3604, 511924,00.html (last accessed September 28, 2008).
Bourgois, Philippe. 2000. Disciplining addictions: The bio-politics of methadone and heroin in the United States. *Culture, Medicine and Psychiatry* 24:165-95.
CASA (National Center on Addiction and Substance Abuse at Columbia University). 2001. So help me God: Substance abuse, religion and spirituality. www.casacolumbia.org/absolutenm/articlefiles/379So%20Help%20Me%20God.pdf (last accessed on August 11, 2009).
Clines, Francis X., with Barry Meier. 2001. Cancer painkillers pose new abuse threat. *The New York Times.* February 9, A1.
Conrad, Peter, and Joseph W. Schneider. 1992. *Deviance and medicalization: From badness to sickness.* Philadelphia: Temple University Press.
De Landa, Manuel. 1997. *A thousand years of nonlinear history.* New York: Zone Books.
Eley, Geoff. 1994. Nations, publics, and political cultures: Placing Habermas in the nineteenth century. In *Culture/power/history: A reader in social theory,* ed. Nicholas Dirks, Geoffrey Eley, and Sherry Ortner, 412-56. Princeton, NJ: Princeton University Press.
Elliott, Carl. 2003. *Better than well: American medicine meets the American dream.* New York: W. W. Norton & Co.
Estep, Bill. 2004. Appalachian project part of state anti-drug plan. *Lexington Herald-Leader.* January 22, B1.
Hansen, Helena. 2004. Faith-based treatment for addiction in Puerto Rico. *Journal of the American Medical Association* 291(23):2882.
Hirschkind, Charles. 2001. The ethics of listening: Cassette-sermon audition in contemporary Egypt. *American Ethnologist* 28(3):623-49.
Humphrey, Richard A. 1988. Religion in southern Appalachia. In *Appalachian mental health,* ed. Susan Emley Keefe, 36-50. Lexington, KY: University of Kentucky Press.
James, Wendy. 1995. *The pursuit of certainty: Religious and cultural formations.* New York: Routledge.
Keane, Webb. 2002. Sincerity, "modernity," and the Protestants. *Cultural Anthropology* 17(1):65-92.
Kleinman, Arthur. 1988. *The illness narratives: Suffering, healing and the human condition.* New York: Basic Books.

————. 1995. *Writing at the margin: Discourse between anthropology and medicine.* Berkeley and Los Angeles: University of California Press.

————. 1998. "Sociosomatics": The contributions of anthropology to psychosomatic medicine. *Psychosomatic Medicine* 60:389-93.

Leonard, Bill J. 1999. Introduction: The faith and the faiths. In *Christianity in Appalachia: Profiles in regional pluralism*, ed. Bill J. Leonard, 1-17. Knoxville, TN: University of Tennessee Press.

Levi-Strauss, Claude. 1985. *The view from afar.* Chicago: University of Chicago Press.

Levin, Bruce Lubotsky, and Ardis Hanson. 2001. Rural mental health services. In *Handbook of rural health*, ed. Sana Loue and Beth Quill, 241-76. New York: Kluwer Academic/Plenum Publishers.

Levine, Harry G. 1978. The discovery of addiction: Changing conceptions of habitual drunkenness in America. *Journal of Studies on Alcohol* 39(1):143-74.

Liebowitz, M. R., E. Salman, C. J. Jusino, R. Garfinkel, L. Street, D. L. Cardenas, J. Silvestre, A. Fyer, J. L. Carrasco, S. Davies, P. Guarnaccia, and D. F. Klein. 1994. Ataque de nervios and panic disorder. *American Journal of Psychiatry* 151:871-75.

Lippy, Charles H. 1999. Popular religiosity in central Appalachia. In *Christianity in Appalachia: Profiles in regional pluralism,* ed. Bill J. Leonard, 40-51. Knoxville, TN: University of Tennessee Press.

Luhmann, Niklas. 1989. *Ecological communication.* Chicago: University of Chicago Press.

Marsden, George M. 1980. *Fundamentalism and American culture: The shaping of twentieth-century evangelicalism 1870-1925.* New York: Oxford University Press.

Meyer, Birgit. 1999. *Translating the devil: Religion and modernity among the Ewe in Ghana.* Trenton, NJ: Africa World Press, Inc.

Mintz, Sidney. 1985. *Sweetness and power: The place of sugar in modern history.* New York: Penguin Books.

Rebhun, L. A., and Helena Hansen. 2001. Substance use. In *Handbook of rural health*, ed. Sana Loue and Beth Quill, 257-76. New York: Kluwer Academic/Plenum Publishers.

Rose, Nikolas. 1999. *Powers of freedom: Reframing political thought.* Chicago: University of Chicago Press.

Sahlins, Marshall. 1994. Cosmologies of capitalism: The trans-Pacific sector of the "world system." In *Culture/power/history: A reader in social theory*, ed. Nicholas Dirks, Geoffrey Eley, and Sherry Ortner, 412-56. Princeton, NJ: Princeton University Press.

Scheper-Hughes, Nancy. 1992. *Death without weeping: The violence of everyday life in Brazil.* Berkeley and Los Angeles: University of California Press.

Stewart, Kathleen. 1996. *A space on the side of the road: Cultural poetics in an "other" America.* Princeton, NJ: Princeton University Press.

Tough, Paul. 2001. The alchemy of OxyContin. *The New York Times.* July 29, 6/32.

U.S. General Accounting Office. 2003. *Prescription drugs: OxyContin abuse and diversion and efforts to address the problem.* GAO-04-110. Washington, D.C. December.

Valverde, Mariana. 1998. *Diseases of the will: Alcohol and the dilemmas of freedom.* Cambridge: Cambridge University Press.

Van Schaik, Eileen. 1988. The social context of "nerves" in eastern Kentucky. In *Appalachian mental health,* ed. Susan Emley Keefe, 81-100. Lexington, KY: University of Kentucky Press.

The White House. 2008. *Innovations in compassion: Faith-based and community initiative: Final report to the armies of compassion*. Washington, D.C. December.

White, John. 1988. Conscience and convenience in eastern Kentucky. In *Appalachian mental health*, ed. Susan Emley Keefe, 209-22. Lexington, KY: University of Kentucky Press.

Index

255

About the Authors

Julie Adkins is a Ph.D. candidate in cultural anthropology at Southern Methodist University, where she serves as adjunct faculty in the Department of Anthropology and the Perkins School of Theology. She has been an ordained minister in the Presbyterian Church (USA) since 1986, holding the M.Div. from Princeton Theological Seminary and the D.Min. from McCormick Theological Seminary (Chicago). Her dissertation research focused on homelessness in the city of Dallas, and, in particular, the city's response. With Tara Hefferan and Laurie Occhipinti, she has recently edited and published *Bridging the Gaps: Faith-Based Organizations, Neoliberalism, and Development in Latin America and the Caribbean* (Lexington Books, 2009). Her research interests include the United States and Latin America, poverty and homelessness, faith-based organizations, and tourism.

Janet Bauer received her Ph.D. in anthropology from Stanford University. Since 1988, she has conducted research and published widely on Muslim immigrant and refugee populations from the Middle East to the Americas and Europe. As associate professor of international studies at Trinity College, she has coordinated the collaborative student/faculty Hartford Area Refugee Research Project, investigating gender and generational differences among different refugee groups in Greater Hartford.

Janet G. Brashler is professor and curator of anthropology at Grand Valley State University in Allendale, Michigan. In addition to an active research program in Michigan archaeology, Jan also has theoretical interests in power, social justice, and human rights as they pertain to contemporary Native Americans. Her contribution to this volume looks at the work of faith-based organizations among the Sicangu Lakota on one of the most economically challenged reservations in the United States.

Wendy Cadge, Ph.D., is associate professor of sociology at Brandeis University and the author of *Heartwood: the First Generation of Theravada Buddhism in America* (University of Chicago Press, 2005). Cadge was a Robert Wood Johnson Foundation Scholar in Health Policy Research at Harvard University and a

Fellow at Radcliffe Institute for Advanced Study, where she conducted research for a book to be entitled *Paging God: Religion in the Halls of Medicine*. She has published articles about same-sex marriage, conflicts over homosexuality in mainline Protestant churches, religion and the nonprofit sector, religion and immigration, immigrant religious organizations, and other issues. Her research has been supported by the Metanexus Institute, Louisville Institute, Gill Foundation, Society for the Scientific Study of Religion, Teaching Enhancement Fund of the American Sociological Association, Younger Scholars in American Religion Program, a Fulbright IIE Fellowship, and other organizations.

Andrea Chivakos is a recent Trinity College graduate and member of Professor Janet Bauer's research team. She has also been actively engaged in the Hartford community. Her research has focused on Hartford's Spanish-speaking populations and on human rights issues.

Scott T. Fitzgerald is assistant professor of sociology at the University of North Carolina at Charlotte. His research interests coalesce around issues of social and economic inequality, religion, and social movements. His research has appeared in *Social Forces, Mobilization, Sociological Spectrum,* and *Policy Studies Journal,* and has been funded by the National Science Foundation. He recently published (with Kevin Leicht) *Postindustrial Peasants: The Illusion of Middle-Class Prosperity.*

William Garriott is assistant professor in the Department of Justice Studies at James Madison University. He is a cultural anthropologist with interests in the anthropology of law, medicine, science and technology, and religion. His current research explores the impact of the methamphetamine epidemic on rural America.

Tara Hefferan currently teaches in the Department of Sociology, Anthropology, and Social Work of Central Michigan University. A cultural anthropologist, Hefferan earned her Ph.D. from Michigan State University. Her research interests include international development, globalization, and faith-based organizations in the United States and the Caribbean. Hefferan is the author of *Twinning Faith and Development: Catholic Parish Partnering in the US and Haiti* (Kumarian Press, 2007) and coeditor with Julie Adkins and Laurie Occhipinti of *Bridging the Gaps: Faith-Based Organizations, Neoliberalism, and Development in Latin America and the Caribbean* (Lexington Books, 2009).

Lance D. Laird, Th.D., is a comparative religion and Islamic studies scholar who is an assistant professor of family medicine and pediatrics at Boston University School of Medicine. He is assistant director of the Boston Healing Landscape Project, an institute for the study of religions, medicines, cultures, and healing. Laird has authored articles on Muslims and health care in the journals *Social Science and Medicine* and *Archives of Disease in Childhood*. He is a Fellow of the Institute for Social Policy and Understanding, which supported the research on Muslim clinics and a current project on American Muslim physicians. Laird also writes and speaks about Muslim-Christian relations and religious dimensions of the Israeli-Palestinian conflict.

Katherine Lambert-Pennington is currently an assistant professor of anthropology at the University of Memphis. Her research interests include urban neighborhood development and community building, participatory action research, faith-based organizations, government-community relations, social inequality, and identity. She has conducted ethnographic research in urban Indigenous Australia and the southern United States. She received her Ph.D. in anthropology from Duke University in 2005.

Isaac Morrison is analysis coordinator for the Faith and Organizations Project at the University of Maryland and an adjunct lecturer in cultural anthropology at Montgomery College. He holds anthropology degrees from George Washington University (M.A. 2009) and the University of Maryland, College Park (B.A. 2006). His research interests include social capital among faith-based organizations, religious tourism, dual citizenship, and transnational technology and culture networks between the United States and the Middle East.

Leah Mundell is community-based research associate in the Program in Community, Culture, and Environment at Northern Arizona University, where she works closely with local faith-based and other organizations working to increase democratic participation in the Flagstaff area. She has taught in the anthropology department at the University of Arizona and in the urban studies department at the University of Pennsylvania. She received her Ph.D. in anthropology from the University of California, Santa Cruz, in 2004.

Laurie Occhipinti is currently an associate professor of anthropology at Clarion University of Pennsylvania. Her research interests include economic development, faith based organizations, indigenous peoples, and religion in Latin America. She is the author of *Acting on Faith*, which focuses on the role of Catholic NGOs in economic development in indigenous communities in northwestern Argentina. With Tara Hefferan and Julie Adkins, she recently edited *Bridging the Gaps: Faith-Based Organizations, Neoliberalism, and Development in Latin America and the Caribbean*. Occhipinti obtained her Ph.D. and M.A. in anthropology at McGill University in Montreal, Canada.

Julie Pfromm received her M.A. in applied anthropology at the University of Memphis, where she worked on the South Memphis Revitalization Action Plan. Her research interests include community building and empowerment within a nonprofit framework.

Laura Polk completed her B.A. in psychology at Eastern Mennonite University and her M.A. in applied anthropology at the University of Maryland. She is currently working as a staff aide at the Prince George's County Council in Maryland.

Timoteo Rodriguez is a Chancellor's Fellow and doctoral candidate in the Department of Anthropology at the University of California, Berkeley. He is also a Graduate Fellow in the Center for the Study of Law and Society at Berkeley Law, University of California. Concurrently, Rodriguez is the National Institute of Mental Health (NIMH) Pre-doctoral Diversity Supplement Fellow, and the project anthropologist on the RELATE Project (HIV Risk Among Male Parolees and Their Female Partners) at the Center for AIDS Prevention Studies (CAPS), University of California, San Francisco. His dissertation research focuses on urban faith-based drug recovery programs in California, studying at-risk-behavior and substance abuse among formerly incarcerated Latino men who are recovering from long-term heroin addiction through faith healing.

Jo Anne Schneider is currently a research associate at the Schaefer Center for Public Policy at the University of Baltimore and associate research professor in anthropology at the University of Maryland, College Park. She has served as director of the Faith and Organizations Project since its commencement. Recent publications include *Social Capital and Welfare Reform: Organizations, Congregations and Communities* (Columbia University Press, 2006), lead editor for the *American Anthropologist* special issue on welfare reform (September 2001); and special issue editor and author of article on multi-methods ethnography for "Research to Practice: An Interdisciplinary Conversation on Research Methods for Non-profits," Special Issue, *Nonprofit Management and Leadership* (July 2006).

Ethan P. Sharp received his Ph.D. from Indiana University in 2004, and is assistant professor of Latin American studies at the University of Texas–Pan American in Edinburg, Texas. He is the author of "Testimonies and the Expansion of Women's Roles in a Transnational Mexican Parish" in *Language and Religious Identity: Women in Discourse*, edited by Allyson Jule (Palgrave Macmillan, 2007) and *No Longer Strangers: Mexican Immigrants, Catholic Ministries and the Promise of Citizenship* (Indiana University Press, forthcoming). His current research addresses the roles of faith and spirituality in Mexico's "war on drugs."